CRITICAL PERSPECTIVES ON NIGERIAN POLITICAL ECONOMY AND MANAGEMENT

A Book of Readings and Cases in Social and Political Environment of Business

CRITICAL PERSPECTIVES ON NIGERIAN POLITICAL ECONOMY AND MANAGEMENT

A Book of Readings and Cases in Social and Political Environment of Business

Pat Utomi

Spectrum Books Limited
Ibadan
◆Abuja ◆Benin City ◆Kaduna ◆Lagos ◆Owerri

Published by
Spectrum Books Limited
Spectrum House
Ring Road
P. M. B. 5612
Ibadan, Nigeria

in association with
Safari Books (Export) Limited
1st Floor
17 Bond Street
St. Helier
Jersey JE2 3NP
Channel Islands, UK

Europe and USA Distributor
African Books Collective Ltd.
The Jam Factory
27 Park End Street
Oxford OX1 1HU, UK.

First published 2000

ISBN: 978-029-192-X

Printed by Meg-Comm Network, 7

Dedicated to my late father,
Golden Anthony Iwegbuna Utomi

Contents

Preface

The pioneer has his joys and his pains. As a pioneer in teaching a subject titled "Social and Political Economy Environment of Business" I have no doubt had my fair share. This adjunct of business policy was designed to explore the interface between business policy and public policy in the Nigerian environment, where the impact of government policy and social norms in transition, on businesses, is very significant. As a pioneer I had very little ready material to draw on for my teaching in the MBA and executive programmes at the Lagos Business School. I had, therefore, to hurriedly prepare technical notes and cases. I was also able to get more out because of pressure to discuss a variety of issues related to the environment of business on the public speaking circuit where I had more than my fair share of invitations.

Since most groups that want a speaker at a major public event are not fastidious about the subject so long as it is a particular speaker, I have managed to select topics on which I wanted to develop notes for my SPEB sessions. That way I have been able to generate a list of readings for SPEB.

This book is a collection some of some of those readings and cases. Few of them have already appeared in journals and others have been published in part in newspapers. Given the sense of urgency with which I have approached this task I have no doubt that I have sacrificed some quality in favour of getting it out there. I have chosen to live with that opportunity cost. This book is designed to be a companion to my business policy text, *Managing Uncertainty: Competition and Strategy in Emerging Economies,* which was also written in a hurry but surprised me by winning the Bashorun M.K.O. Abiola prize as the best academic book published in Nigeria in 1998.

That award and the very generous words in which that book has been commented on by people like Dick Kramer, erstwhile managing partner of Arthur Andersen in Nigeria, and Chief Ernest Sonekan, former Nigerian head of government and head of state, and the flattering reviews of it by the likes of George Thorpe, erstwhile CEO of Sterling Health and managing partner of Tequila, gave me the courage to rush through this volume.

Kramer's description of the book as a *MUST READ* for executives has encouraged me to write more Nigerian case studies– a few of which appear in this volume.

In addition to the cases which make up the rear section, the readings have been grouped around issues such as strategy and competitiveness, macro-economic environment, finance and banking, budgets and budgeting, and values and the environment of business.

Making this volume available with the speed it has been put together leaves me much indebted to so many. My colleague Chantal Epie who as general editor always manages to bring more sense out of many carelessly written sentences of mine, Oscar Nkanta who provided secretarial support and Emeka Iwelumor who carried out interviews and contributed drafts of the case studies.

Much gratitude also goes to my late father who was the original workaholic and whose memory still pumps my adrenalin. Golden Anthony Iwegbuna Utomi would have approved of the commitment that made this volume possible. This book, as my 1982 doctoral dissertation, is dedicated to his memory.

Pat Utomi
September 1999
Lagos.

x

SECTION I

STRATEGY AND THE NIGERIAN ENVIRONMENT

1

Business Strategy Beyond the Year 2000 in Nigeria*

I have been asked to share my thoughts on business strategy in the year 2000 and beyond. I have also been urged to spend some time looking at how this affects the small and medium enterprises sector, while I am at it. It is indeed a tall order, if we are to do justice to so important a topic. For your sins in making such a request I am likely to subject you to one of the longest reflection I have put an audience through.

As I contemplate the subject I am reminded of one of the more troublesome remarks about the African condition that I have ever heard. It is the statement credited to the great French leader Charles De Gaulle. General De Gaulle is quoted as having said of this century that it is not Africa's century. Perhaps this is why members of the chamber have chosen to turn to the next century in the exercise of hope. The classic De Gaulle arrogance in that statement was to prove prophetic as the spurt of growth and development that marked the first development decade of the 1960s was replaced by an era generally described as the age of Afropessimism.

If we aim to truly understand what must be done to achieve progress in this new century at whose threshold we stand it is imperative we recognize that the decline of Africa and the pessimism this generated was aided and abetted by African leaders and African businessmen. From the predatory state, marked by military adventurism to businessmen who were mere commission agents, the blame for Africa's decline was quite obvious. As we blame the politicians, in mufti or in uniform, and the businessmen, we do not exonerate the teachers who romanticized the problems rather than dwell on the prescription of practical solutions, hence the unproductive dalliance with left wing ideologies that ignored the moral truths of the nature of man in society. The denial of man's basic freedoms, ostensibly

---

*Address to the Nigeria-British Chamber of Commerce on 6-2-98

in the interest of the collective, proved not to be for the common good and invariably became the Achilles' heel of those ideologies.

Interestingly, afropessimism is on the wane even if this new hope is tinged with the paradox that Africa's most populous and potentially most wealthy country is perceived as pursing a contrary trend. The world has never been more pessimistic about Nigeria's future as it is today. As an individual, however, I am quite optimistic about the future. The brave new future I foresee is dependent on how all of us here and our compatriots elsewhere commit ourselves to the Nigerian reconstruction. The issues I raise in this essay regarding business strategy in the years beyond *A.D.* 2000 are anchored on this optimism.

In discussing business strategy in the new century I expect to dwell at some length on the subject of national strategy which business strategy needs to be aligned with, and some trends in the environment of business. Among these trends are the impact of the convergence of telecommunications, broadcasting and computing, the coming of the age of the knowledge worker, corporate globalization, and the effect of regional blocks on the next round of beggar-thy-neighbour policies. Other trends include the imperative of product quality and the shift of power from the producers of products and services to consumers. Critical to how we are able to respond to all these is the way institutions which facilitate economic intercourse evolve, and the health of an indigenous private sector.

The strategy that businesses develop to compete in a world of reduced boundaries in the next millennium will depend on these factors and the competence that give distinctive advantage to those businesses. They are matters we should all be gravely concerned about because the nature of these strategies will determine how wealth is created in our country and the quality of life of all of us citizens. But they are matters we should not discuss outside of context. Too often matters of business and governance are discussed 'objectively' outside of a view of man in society that is moral, ethical or based on a clear value orientation. The results of 'objective' neutrality are often short-lived.

Unless and until a clear set of principles result in leaders of business and government deeply driven by respect for other human beings and the noble search for a place in history, it will be fruitless to pursue the kind of analysis outlined below in the hope that the outcome, a more profitable social order, could emerge. With this in mind let us truly now begin by asking: what is business strategy?

1. What is Business Strategy?

A useful understanding of business strategy has to begin with the reason for which business enterprises exist People tend to go into business because they have seen the possibility of creating value that can meet the needs of a group of people. The challenge of venturing is therefore to create use value that attracts enough customers for the entrepreneur to extract rewards that justify his profit motive or whatever other motive that drives his desire to do business.

If a business venture is not to be a meteor, a one-season wonder, then the preoccupation of the businessman is to recognize that the environment is constantly changing and that a long term success is a function of continually adapting the strengths of the firm to changing opportunities and threats in the environment while managing its weaknesses to keep it from becoming vulnerable in competitive terrain. The art of building sustainable competitive advantage over rivals such that the firm remains successful in the long term is the soul of business strategy. It involves a skilful analysis of the environment of business, projection of trends in that environment, the development of assets and capabilities, the so-called competencies, within the firm that allows it to out-perform its rivals relative to evolving customer groupings in this world of continuously shifting perception of needs by customers which results in businesses often redefining the attribute-bundles that determine a market segment.

To consider strategies that could produce firms that will enjoy prolonged success in the next century and, through such success at wealth creation, take Nigeria out of poverty, we have to consider how some of the competitive forces we have identified shape strategy of firms. In my work, I have developed a model for analyzing how competitive forces shape the strategy of firms in emerging economies fraught with acute levels of uncertainty for decision makers. This model, the 3E framework (Emerging Economies Environment framework) has already appeared in published papers and gets full elaboration in *Managing Uncertainty: Competition and Strategy in Emerging Economies*. We shall draw from this framework in this discussion but we will avoid following it in a fastidious manner because we will begin to sound academic.

As much as we want to keep from becoming academic I think it worthwhile to lay out the key elements of the framework of competitive forces that drive strategy. Building from the Porter model that was for years the dominant paradigm in strategy literature, I offer a platform more sensitive to the poor country environment. To Porter's five forces we have added what I call megafactors typically salient in emerging economies but hardly of issue in mature economies. These are the predatory acts of government officials and the lopsided effect of government's action; weak institutions which do not increase certainty and thus heighten transaction costs; and the role of business associations in modulating government action. Another megafactor drawn from a competing paradigm on strategy is the core competence of the firm. Add these to threats of substitute products, entry barriers, power of buyers, power of suppliers and intensity of existing rivalry from the Porter model and strategy emerges.

In recognition of the need to be very practical we will lead off by looking at the fact that business strategy is likely to be more successful if it is aligned to national strategy, especially where national strategy is sensitive to global trends such as corporate globalization, and the emergence of new rules of international trade under the World Trade Organization which followed the Uruguay round of GATT (General Agreement on Trade and Tariffs).

2. National Strategy

What is Nigeria's national strategy? Conventional wisdom will suggest that this should be discernable from the perspective plan that Dr Kalu Idika Kalu and his staff struggled with during his years as a cabinet minister, and the rolling plans that supposedly have been rolling off that perspective periscope. Since I do not want you to become too anxious too early in this presentation I will not encourage any attempts to compare our rolling plans with the ambitions of the perspective plan. What we know is that there is not much in our current spending pattern that resembles the perspective plan. While the agencies of government were doing their planning a gradual movement was beginning in the private sector, in terms of patterns of collaboration with other sectors, to fashion a modus vivendi in Nigeria. This movement accounts for what would later be the most proximate to Nigeria's national strategy.

My recollections give credit for this movement to a series of activities stimulated by the Nairobi conference on an enabling environment for private sector participation in development that was sponsored by the

Aga Khan Foundation in 1986. The tripartite 'talking together' involved the private sector, private development agencies (non-governmental organizations, NGOs) and the public sector. This processes metamorphosed into the Enabling Environment Forum which, in my opinion, sowed the seeds of the Nigerian Economic Summit and ultimately the NES fostered the Vision 2010 project. In the report of the Vision 2010 we hope to find some articulations of Nigeria's national strategy. Or do we?

If in Budget '98 we find that steel is not just still alive but can access foreign exchange at 22 to one dollar where education cannot, then you must ask if Vision 2010 is being implemented in a way that it can be truly construed the definitive statement of Nigeria's national strategy.

If the same budget of 1998, which is seen as a benchmark pointer to commitment to following the path of Vision 2010, leaves the impression that national strategy is limited to purely economic prescriptions then there is yet cause to wonder if it is the document of national strategy. This is because economic progress is so intimately tied to social and political factors in this information age when everybody's troubles are available as staple diet on global television and on the internet. Clearly the Vision 2010 prescription went beyond economic dictates. Just to illustrate how myopic it could be to consider national strategy without issue of political and law and order strategies, let me draw from a few experiences I had just last week. I visited several places in Europe and North America during the cause of last week. In my zeal at encouraging foreign investment in Nigeria I took advantage of every dinner, meeting or conference to sell the future of Nigeria.

I came away wondering if those who run Nigeria truly ever get an accurate impression of what the world thinks of extant Nigerian reality. My fear is that too many of them have been isolated for too long to recognize how hard it is to convey how badly we have sunk. Even in this period of African revival and the waning of Afropessimism the news on Nigeria is so bad that economic progress that definitely needs the external sector is unlikely to be forthcoming without major reforms. I was still smarting from the pains of the feedback I got in Europe from old Nigerian friends in the media and business circles when I arrived in New York to a CBS programme on the morning of 29th January on what else, 419 victims in America.

Two things stood out from all of this that must be addressed as imperatives of national policy: the end of military rule and the reconstruction of Nigerian institutions.

2a. Ending Military Rule and Rebuilding Institutions

Unfortunately for us the matter of military rule is hardly ever discussed objectively. The military has been unable to deliver on progress not because they lack intelligent or well-educated officers. They have those in abundance, the problem is simply that the command structure of military hierarchy is inappropriate for a political culture that is ideally regional federalism in nature, and an economy that is for reasons of the foregoing, better as a market economy in which the spirit of enterprise is given full bloom.

Attempts to cite Pinochet and Suharto, by apologists for the extant order, falls in the face of the march of history. There is a time for every strategy. The mood, thinking and level of understanding of development process effectiveness in the 1960s created room for bureaucratic-authoritarian coalitions to be given the benefit of appropriate vehicles for change. This thinking of that era was no doubt conditioned by ideological conflicts of a bipolar world. They also did not have the benefits of the 1997 South East Asia financial meltdown which proved that a heavy cost that is debilitative of smooth development is associated with the lack of transparency that strong-man regimes always tend to be known for. So that even with a developmental orientation and rapid growth there comes a time to pay for absence of integrity in a system. After 1997 the window of acceptability for a form of government other than democracy and representative bureaucracy as platform for accountability in public choice remains quite slim. Without acceptance in a situation where the external sector is so critical progress will be very limited.

Indeed Gen. Ibrahim Babangida, after the Gowon era, was the strong man that could have moved Nigeria forward under the assumptions of a modernizing dictator of the type of Kemal Ataturk or Suharto. His failure to claim the opportunity thrust before him by history makes him perhaps the most tragic figure of modern times. He lost that big chance in 1991 when he squandered the gains of SAP instead of consolidating on them with the windfall of the Gulf War. The terrible events of 1993 were only a seal to what had become failure writ large. Indeed the most potent of the lessons of that experience is that unless leadership is driven by a vision of how history will judge them we would continue to have leaders who under-perform their potential.

To move forward we need not only reform institutions of government but also of markets. Capital markets, venture capital institutions, enterprise incubator schemes and industry extension services need to be revisited so they can be fashioned to enhance development.

Returning to our national strategy, it should now not only be clear that our national strategy will not only have to evolve along lines of open transparent and accountable democracy supported by institutions that reduce uncertainty in gauging human conduct but it should also be a strategy that aims at rebuilding a middle class severely damaged by the bad policies of the last few years. This is critical if we are to salvage the capacity crisis that makes policy implementation a nightmare as the competent middle class has been streaming out into any country willing to give them the basics of a decent existence.

2b. Middle Class Reconstruction

The profound crisis of purchasing power which has hurt the growth possibilities of the consumer sectors of the economy has been predicated partly on the fact that the middle class has been literally wiped out by an unjustified fear of wage-price inflation. In addition to the failure to pay public servants a living wage unending policies have resulted in a process of de-industrialization which has seen many managers lose their jobs. Many cannot find alternative employment and are unable to sustain old consumption patterns thus adding to capacity utilization challenges. Not only is the potential for growth stultified by this phenomenon which leaves warehouses full of inventory, the effect of falling quality of life has driven many middle class professional types abroad. The result has been an acute lack of capacity to execute most of the policies required to move the development process forward.

The kind of desperate call for increased effort at manpower development made in the 1998 budget is a direct consequence of the policy measures that have during the last fourteen years systematically pronounced the middle class irrelevant. A national strategy is incomplete without addressing this issue, yet I see no effort at reviewing policies that have led us down the path of a Gini index that shows a dramatic widening between the highest and lowest income segments of the society. The nature of the challenge in the Gini co-efficient is made more complex by the fact that most of those at the top of the income scale have made their money not from anything productive but from extracting rents out of the access they have or the abuse of positions of public trust. This often means that their money seeks the safety of foreign banks, contributing to the hemorrhage of the circular flows of income. The consequences are devastating. This pattern is creating a new enclave economy in which sophisticated shopping malls comparable to others in Europe and North America have been springing up in Victoria Island to service expatriates and a narrow local elite with consumption profiles totally unrelated to the production of local industry. This further heightens the problems of an economy with pockets isolated from each other such that heightened activity in one sector has no knock-on effect on the other. We already have the oil sector so oriented, to allow other sectors to emerge standing in isolation is to make the economy harder still to manage.

To be sure, the question of national strategy is much more encompassing than the matter of the state of the middle class and military. We shall however limit the questions we raise on this aspect of the environment of business for business-strategy making to these two and the nature of elite attitude to government-business relations. We are taking it for granted that public pronouncements and Vision 2010 already indicate that the intent of national strategy is private sector led free enterprises oriented mixed economy. The ideal of a just and egalitarian society has been a refrain for too long to warrant restating.

3. Government Business Relations

A recent invitation I received from abroad to speak on the state of government-business relations in Nigeria had the provocative title of "Business – Target or Partner." A clear national strategy should include an appropriate response to this question. I think it is easy to glean from how political economy structures have evolved in post-independence Nigeria an attitude towards business by the public sector. The nature of this attitude is of great consequence in shaping business strategy and for the pace of economic development.

We see in the early days a mixed economy approach shaped by the ideas of Fabian socialism in the United Kingdom of Great Britain from which we had recently become independent. This prompted initiatives to develop industrial estates, such as the Ikeja Industrial Estate, to which multinationals were invited to invest in industrial production. The multinationals accepting the invitation implored the participation of the regional government so as to increase their comfort levels. The regional federalism of the time which triggered a somewhat healthy form of competitive communalism resulted in a competitive response from other regions once one region initiated this form of partnership with investing multinationals. The effect was steady economic growth up until military rule and the civil war.

In the oil boom-driven unitary command economy under military rule the nature of government-business relations was for a long time marked by suspicion and command to business. This relationship, ameliorated somewhat by the NES and Vision 2010 experiences, have resulted in de-industrialization and stunted economic development.

In the foregoing we have tried to understand what Nigeria's national strategy is, recognizing that it is cardinal to evolving a business strategy that is effective within Nigeria. All we have done is raise a few areas with cause for anxiety. It is safe, however, to assume that the vision 2010 document is as close to our national strategy as we can get especially as it has been adopted without corruption by Abuja.

Since I have not seen the document I am not sure how much this document focussed on the importance of the SME sector which we desire to emphasize a bit in this presentation. Clearly our national 'strategy' in this area, if we can call what we have seen so far a strategy, is a disjointed potpourri of whatever seems to have worked elsewhere. More troubling, of course, is that we have had no heart in the business of implementing these programmes. Our response to the crises of the SME sector has been to accept the conventional wisdom that the problem is a problem of funding and appropriate capitalization for new ventures. A number of development finance institutions have been sponsored in response to the challenges. Almost all have been monumental failures, from the microfinance level of Peoples Bank to the development banks like the Nigerian Bank for Commerce and Industry (NBCI) and the National Economic Recovery Fund (NERFUND). Yet there are studies from the

World Bank and elsewhere which show that moral hazard problems which have badly affected these institutions can hardly be found in traditional or informal banking institutions.

My current research effort which dwells on comparative evolution of the role of institutional frameworks in fostering and nurturing entrepreneurship, essentially, is a search for the reason entrepreneurship flounders so badly in a country of such enterprising peoples as we have in Nigeria. *Enterprise in Ascent: Institutions and the Evolution of Enterpreneurship* builds on earlier work I have done on competition and strategy in poor countries published in *Managing Uncertainty: Competition and Strategy in Emerging Economies* explains how institutional weaknesses have constrained venturing in Nigeria in a way different from the experiences of several other countries. Why government agencies like the Ministry of International Trade and Industries in Japan stimulated manufacturing activity in Japan and the chaebols emerged in South Korea while several government initiatives in Nigeria fail so miserably is explained in the latter volume on entrepreneurship in ascent, in terms of how institutions help reduce uncertainty even in the face of infrastructure deficiencies. Surely the SME manufacturing sector is vulnerable in an environment where electric power is hardly available and the diesel power alternative sources scarce, but this individual problem could be solved by industry clusters in which inputs are shared, a situation of 'coopetition' (competition and cooperation). To understand why the creative option of clusters are not pursued and venturers choose instead to stay with trading, one has to understand the forces that have resulted in the collapse of civil society and the weakness of horizontal linkages among Nigerians. Surely a national strategy worth the paper it is printed on would have to seek the roots of these fundamental problems. How else can we explain that the UNDP began an effort to start business incubator centres in Nigeria the same time it began in China and Brazil. Even communist China accepted a private focus and now has more than 500 incubator centres whereas Nigeria has remained bogged down by the fact of government effort at control. The only centre that got started seems mired in disputations of all kinds.

Elements of the Environment of Business

In aligning strengths and weaknesses of the firm to the opportunities and threats in the environment which are constantly changing, firms of the twenty-first century will have to astutely 'read the leaves' on some of the trends in the environment that we identified earlier on.

a) Convergence of Telecommunications and Computing

As an undergraduate shortly after the Nigerian civil war, I was privileged to read the writings of Ben Bagdikian and others on the coming electronic revolution and the global village it would create. I used to be slightly amused by what seemed like a quasi-science fiction intellectual effort. Today, twenty five years removed, the laugh is on me. This has happened essentially because two streams of technology, telephonic communications and computing have converged. As a result I can from the comfort of my bedroom run a global business at the cost of less than local telephone calls. Information asymmetries which added to the cost of business have literally been wiped out. With broadcasting converging with telecommunications and computing, Information and Communication Technology (ICT) is sure to affect how every business is run. New competencies will emerge from how people adapt to this technology and will confer competitive advantage on some while making some enterprises dinosaurs. If you add to this the lowering of trade barriers following the Uruguay round of GATT and the establishment of the World Trade Organization we see that the luxury of developing a business outside of a highly competitive environment is gone. The luxury of high tariff wells are gone.

b) Regional Trading Blocks

These trends will shape strategy but we have to be careful with how we assess the permanence of openness that technology and trade laws seem to force on us. The history of international trade is characterized by periods of openness in which trading nations enjoy the benefits of free trade and then periods of over-reaction to the downside of business cycles which result in beggar-thy-neighbour policies that fuel economic depression. My suspicion is that the next round of such reactions will probably be around regional blocks. If we look at fortress Europe (EU), ASEAN talk about an Asian Monetary Fund during the onset of the 1997 financial meltdown and thoughts in North America about marching South with NAFTA and we see the brave new future. In that future the persisting failure of regional integration in Africa will be a critical factor as others will be in blocs that are effectively customs unions assuring a considerable market in the event of a return to beggar-thy-neighbour policies.

c) The Age of the Knowledge Worker

There is much talk about capacity building in Nigeria. This happens perhaps because policy makers recognize the need to respond to the global buzz of "the age of the knowledge worker." From statistics available the only category of workers who have suffered a substantive real decline in wages in the United States since the 1950s have been those with less than high school education. Brawn is not enough anymore. Even the Detroit factory worker has to be able to work with robots and computers. No firm can compete in the next century without workers who are knowledgeable enough to increase productivity in their interaction with technology. Knowledge can, in fact, be said to be the currency of the new age and ICT the vehicle of the currency; this is a factor anyone formulating a company's strategy has to bear in mind.

With all this in mind it seems right to ask how we develop human capital in Nigeria. The truth is that real policy is in direct contradiction with public pronouncements. To read the newspapers for the period I was out of the country last week was like watching the media at war against decisions they seem convinced were designed to harm manpower development in Nigeria. For a firm to have a winning strategy it would have to find a creative way of building its human capital stock in the face of a country inadvertently hostile to the idea of developing quality human capital.

It is interesting to note the mismatch between engineering skills available in Nigerian universities and the direction of productive engineering. Today's engineer needs skills in microprocessing if he is to be relevant. Our system lags behind in this shift. This is typical of how we respond to the cry for capacity building when we are not preventing willing private sector agents to provide education and let the market decide if there is value in the quality of instructions from various schools.

Maybe I should at this point share a personal experience that indicates how the love of this country can exhaust a person and push the faint heart to the verge of despair. Two years ago I was on sabbatical in the United States and became acutely sensitive to the diminishing relevance of our engineering education in terms of Nigeria's global competitiveness. I then tried to fire up a group of Nigerian professors of engineering and computer science beginning with those next door to me at MIT. They were quite willing to set up a network of their kind and to give of their talent and knowledge, for free, to a programme, for re-educating bright young Nigerian engineers right here in Nigeria. On my part I was to create a network of entrepreneurship and management teachers to impart management skills to these young engineers. To complete the picture we wanted genesis grants of three to five million naira to go to teams of the pupil engineers whose projects win in competition for commercializable ideas. These grants could only be cashed in as a start-up for a company to commercialize the project idea. With this seed money as confidence booster a network of venture capital companies, to be encouraged, could then back the young entrepreneurs. It has been one year since I returned. I have tried to share this idea with some in policy positions or in agencies throwing money around in the name of moving the country forward. All that was required was institutional support, facilities and the genesis grants. My services and those of these Nigerian professors would come for free except for flying them in and accommodating them. They were even willing to teach via satellite. No one has gone further than a polite "that's a good idea" on this. By now the Nigerian professors I fired up with the patriotic fervor have given up. For them it is one more reinforcement of the notion that the country they left in frustration is still to become serious.

d)   Quality as Given

In the next millennium the shift of power from the producer, whose goods an emerging consumer class scrambled for at the beginning of this century, to the consumer, whose bargaining power was enhanced with the addition of more and more installed capacity, will be complete. The reason for being in business which is to give use-value to the customer will then have no mitigating circumstances. Quality of goods and services will have come to be taken for granted. In this era anyone still discussing things like TQM would be yesterday's story. This is why I would say that even the smallest of small businesses will have to incorporate best practice into its original conceptualization.

e) *Institutions*

If we are still dealing with the uncertainties we have to respond to today in the next century, the transaction costs will be far too high to be competitive. It is institutions that set the limits of acceptable conduct, increasing, as a result, the volume of economic activity. But who builds these institutions. Our typical wisdom in Nigeria suggests that governments create institutions. A careful reading of the school of Institutional Economics will show that this local wisdom is perhaps the reason our institutions fare so badly. Douglas North, for example, argues convincingly that institutions evolve and oftentimes do so from the interest of those participating in the enterprise to protect their subsequent transactions even if they could "profit" temporarily from defecting in transaction behaviour as things stand. The recognition of future lost opportunities motivate them to building institutions that limit themselves to the confines of certain norms. Unfortunately our private sector people fail to act in this way and big brother government moves in to act, setting up institutions that sometimes act contrary to the real needs of business with the consequences of a legitimacy crisis and a failure to attain conduct that becomes habitual compliance as in the 1937 definition of Gerald Coarse.

The private sector has therefore to develop a long term perspective on things and to move proactively to set boundaries of conduct that its members see value in, thereby complying.

f) *Purchasing Power*

No economy can truly grow unless most of its people can have the capacity to purchase what is produced. The direction of the Nigerian economy in 1997 is a classic example. The kinds of business strategy that will be pursued will depend on what purchasing power is available. Income distribution trends also have significance for the kinds of business you choose to be in and what positioning to take within the industry. High margin premium brands in small niches make more sense in the short to medium term than a mass merchandising.

g) *Domestic Enterprise Class*

The shape of the environment of business in the next century will be affected by the state of local enterprises. The domestic enterprise class is no doubt weak. This weakness limits the strategies generally pursued to global orientations of multinationals. I am much supportive of an open economy and foreign participation but I recognize that unless incentives exist to stimulate domestic enterprises the economy will continue to be a patchwork of enclave economies. This has consequences for strategies that follow from competitive response to other players in the economy. A close look at the 'miracle' growth of North East and South East Asia will show that the evolution of local enterprise was critical. Even countries like Malaysia which had more direct active foreign multinational venturing has had to have either state or local private venture activity. In the age of globalization in which multinationals are quick to move in response to trends, only indigenous enterprise will weather great storms. They are at the core of development but Nigeria has underdeveloped this sector.

Conclusion

We could go on but that would be to overstretch the punishment of keeping your attention for so long. In summarizing therefore let me suggest that the next century is a minefield of threats to business and a harvest of opportunities. How successful companies can become will depend on national strategy and some of the competitive forces we have discussed. Firms, especially small and medium enterprises, have to learn to build their strategies around national strategy, developing competencies that help circumnavigate difficulties rooted in the national pathos. The visionary firms that have built up the right competencies will succeed and when Nigeria outgrows its current nightmare, which it will, if it continues to survive, that firm could have the strength of a world beater. My optimism arises from the fact that Uganda which was the laughing stock of the world in the early 1980s is more favourably considered than Nigeria today. It also comes from the great story of the lives and times of such Japanese entrepreneurs as Akio Morita and Maseru Ibuka who, when they were discharged from the Japanese Navy after World War II, had hardly any capital but mustered enough imagination to start SONY and built it into one of the world's great corporations within their lifetime. We must not despair.

2

The New Nigerian Order: Creating an Oasis of Commitment and Progress*

It would be easy to assume that my biggest challenge is to address you only a few hours after touching down here in Washington from a journey of several thousand miles. I must admit that I had another source of anxiety. This was how to make the Nigerian reality come alive in my presentation in a way that could make you see for yourselves a rewarding role in the Nigerian reconstruction and restoration. How to do this without exciting people on the two extremes of the often noisy debate of the Nigerian political logjam called for reflection.

A Caveat on Extremism

The trepidation I have, if one can call it that, stems from my experience during the period I spent with you here in the United States last year and early this year. The anxiety comes from occasions during which I shared the podium with people at opposite ends of this imagined divide in Nigeria. One such occasion was at the Carnegie Endowment for International Peace here in Washington D.C. in December 1996. At a point I had to publicly rebuke both some of the delegation from Nigeria and those of the opposition here in Washington. There was a benefit to the experience and it is one I believe should guide us here and in the future. Those observations at the Carnegie conference on Nigeria led me to observe more closely what happened in Bosnia, what is happening in Northern Ireland, Rwanda, Burundi and elsewhere.

From these observations I have arrived at what I call the Iron Law of Extremism. This encapsulates the tendency for people who take extreme positions in contentious issues in public discussion to seek to polarize discussion, hounding the timid and those anxious to keep their peace out

---

*Address to the inaugural meeting of the national umbrella body of Anioma Association, U.S.A. on 24-5-97

18

of the middle ground. The major outcome of this phenomenon, which I believe derives from mental laziness in not wanting to subject one's ideas to test from the point of view of all the parties involved, is debilitative of social discourse. Bosnia and Rwanda epitomize this in recent experience.

In observing the phenomenon of extremists sucking people away from the middle ground I am in no way suggesting that the exact middle of every argument is where the truth lies. That is even more slothful than opting for the extreme where extremes are embraced so we can stay consistent with our prejudices. The middle ground for me is found in staying consistent with some principles you believe in and considering how every issue affects the anxieties of all the parties involved. These principles could be biases, but at least they are founded on certain fundamental views about human nature that are reasoned, generally fair; the principles apply equally to all people in all situations, and this keeps us from the myopia of the fact of the day. Among the principles I have allowed, or struggled to allow, to guide my position on issues is the principle of discomfort with the idea of military rule. My position on this flows from my understanding of the nature of markets and hierarchies. Military rule as the ultimate hierarchical command reduces the scope of input into the public choice process. I have remained consistent since 1984 in my opposition to the military rule option and have found no reason to hold different views to date. Similar to the reason I reject military rule is the basis of my preference for market economies. I am grateful that some of the impassioned debates between me and some of my friends in academia who favoured command socialistic principles have been settled in my favour by the course of history. My preference for free enterprise-led growth with redistribution that would build a consumer class and social balance has been vindicated by the Malaysian experience. That model is obviously preferred by the current Vision 2010 effort.

Then there is my view of ethnicity. I was in shame each time I encountered these shouting matches between Nigerians and saw them reduced to ethnic cursing. It should not be a surprise that another principle I have pursued is the rejection of generalizations about issues from an ethnicity base.

What is important in this long preamble is not my principles holding up well with time but the fact that principles are a better determinant of, or compass to, the middle ground away from the polarization that has done so much damage elsewhere.

I hope that the following presentation on the changing Nigerian order, based on the foregoing and other principles too numerous to outline in a caveat set out upfront here, will give you enough of a feel for the way forward in Nigeria. Hopefully this will stimulate or annoy you so that all of you as a group or as individuals will seek out roles in the building of a new Nigeria.

It should be obvious that part of the role you can play is to be worthy ambassadors of Nigeria. A proper brief on extant reality in Nigeria should help in this assignment.

You live everyday with obtuse media images of Nigeria. Some are deserved, some come from the incompetence of those responsible for articulating a national image for Nigeria as government officials, and some come from unfair stereotyping of Nigeria for things nowhere nearly as bad as can be found in the American backyard. If in your conduct you are model residents and guests and you also make efforts to challenge that done unfairly, these images which affect your own individual self worth will begin to change. I know one or two of you were aware of my response to a Mike Wallace casual but unfair reference to Nigeria in his Farrakhan interview on *60 Minutes* last year. My insisting his portrayal of Nigeria fell short of the standards of good journalism but made for good theatre caused Mr Wallace to call me and discuss Nigeria. I think most of you are in a position to do more if you want to and are properly briefed.

Extant Reality and the Challenge of Existence

Economy: Let us begin with the economy because the paramount objective of the human being is to meet certain needs which are made possible by his economic endeavours. The story of the Nigerian economy is riddled with many sad wounds inflicted by policy choices over the years. From steady, albeit not extraordinary, growth of 3.2 per cent of the GDP between 1956 and 1966 Nigeria has stagnated from 1973 to date at growth levels of 0.017 per cent. If you consider population growth rates in excess of 3.0 per cent the nature of the stagnation comes into sharp relief. It is noteworthy that 1973 is the year oil prices were quadrupled. As we were unable to manage the Dutch disease that followed the collapse of oil prices, the plight of the Nigerian has indeed become pathetic because many have a quality of life today that is far below that which they had in 1960 when we became an independent country.

The daunting problem of poverty has sadly become the biggest challenge facing the Nigerian people. This challenge is compounded by the increasing unevenness of the distribution of income in the country. The 1996 Nigeria Poverty Assessment report of the World Bank shows how the Gini index – the measure of income distribution in the economy – has been getting progressively worse. As those who have are having more, and those who have not are having less, there is a visible decline of purchasing power which has left warehouses full. With full warehouses there is hardly much new investment. It is nearly June and the first quarter budgeted allocations have not been released to government agencies. In an economy in which the government is the biggest spender the consequence of that for depressed economic activity is obvious. These expenditure management tactics lower the prospects of growth. The rich who earn more keep their money abroad and spend most of it abroad. With our rich there is very little trickling down. Besides the consumption pattern which is external, the questionable nature of the source of their income makes them keep and spend it abroad.

It has not been all negative. In 1995 and 1996 there was some progress in the area of some of the badly flawed macro-economic fundamentals. One such area is inflation. It dropped significantly in 1996 to about 23 per cent at year's end. The exchange rate stayed stable through most of last year and the stock market performance was one of the most attractive of the emerging markets. There was also the promise of privatization which would release us from the abduction we find ourselves in, under the yoke of some of the most incompetent and corrupt state-owned utilities anywhere. Some of the promises remain promises; the challenge is how to make government deliver on these promises made here in Washington by Finance Minister Anthony Ani.

The real pity is we can actually do much better if we want. Some of the politics of the moment add to the hurting. Nobody should tell us who our friends should be but there is in my opinion something wrong with what seems to be a deliberate strategy of cultivating the world's pariah states. The more we isolate ourselves the worse off our economy will be.

Politics: With politics, things are even more confusing for simple-minded people like me. The transition programme is making progress in form but in content it must rival the *Titanic* for ways to spell disaster. We have had local government elections and there is talk of postponing the gubernatorial elections. My own real worry is that most of the time is spent debating whether Abacha will run. In the meantime none of the candidates are seriously addressing issues that affect people's lives which are in dire need of well thought-out options.

As for whether or not General Abacha will run I do not care. He is a Nigerian and can do whatever he wants to do. What I know is that if he runs I will most probably not vote for him. I will not vote for him for a very simple reason. I am convinced that if we are to make progress at all, those who were active during the build up of the state of national discord that remains so potent should not play high profile roles so that wounds may heal more easily. Whether or not my vote makes a difference does not matter; the key is that I will have followed my conscience. With this as the dominant issue and all the accusations of rigging and sponsorship of preferred parties by government, the transition programme seems all dressed with nowhere to go. This is truly sad. But the situation is not hopeless. If the people in Abuja can see things less from a point of consolidating personal power and more from the point of their place in history we could see progress. I do believe this is possible, in fact probable, even if it might surprise many. In a sense this is an article of faith for me, but is based on my reading of Nigerian history.

Vision 2010: The journey into the future has been receiving attention not so much from the politicians in mufti and in uniform but from a movement that came out of the business community and was adopted by the current regime – the Vision 2010 project. The problem with the project remains that we failed to follow the brief of the Malaysians on how to share values. National reconciliation is the key. The Malaysians have told us what they learnt from Lyndon B. Johnson, which is that it is better to be inside the tent pissing out than outside the tent pissing in. Surely the tent will smell foul if we piss into it. Our tent does smell foul with many of our finest intellectuals abroad and embittered with the neglect and humiliation inflicted on them in the universities. Also urinating in are many of the politicians in exile abroad. I am convinced that getting true value from Vision 2010 will involve letting Sultan Dasuki, Chief M.K.O. Abiola, Gen. Olusegun Obasanjo, Gen. Shehu Yar'a dua, Chief Olu Falae and others return to society, especially given the questionable basis on which most of them have been detained or jailed.

Foreign Policy: The visioning process is considering Nigeria's strengths in the international arena. It is hoped these strengths will translate into key success factors. Unfortunately, Nigeria's foreign policy has been so badly degraded in the last few years by those charged with formulating and implementing policy. In what seems to me an excessive urge to shout long live the king, the king's men are doing damage that will take more than one generation to correct.

A few factors are responsible for the misguided approach to foreign policy as we pursue it today. The first is an exaggerated notion of Nigeria's importance in the scheme of things in today's world. I believe that you can say 'I am somebody.' To assume, in a megalomanic sense, that a world focussing on so many drivers of prosperity, in an age in which human freedoms attract premium value, will care much for one of the poorer countries of the world with a questionable track record in the human rights arena is clearly a failure of the process of critical self examination.

Deliberate bellicosity in policy pronouncement may have its apparent immediate short term benefit of wearing out the perceived adversary. The cost, in terms of how people condition themselves to deal with us, can linger for a long time. The truth is that bellicosity is symptomatic of a crisis of reason and serves as a substitute for thinking. The consequence is the growing sense of isolation and pariah status. Certainly, nobody should pick our friends for us. That is our prerogative as a sovereign nation. But what nation chooses friends that are more likely to bring them grief than opportunity? Obviously, someone is getting the wrong advice. I remember two examples that show we used to have thinking people running Nigerian foreign policy in years gone by. During the civil war, France was extremely soft on Biafra, and Lagos was clever enough not to break diplomatic relations with Paris. This paid dividends later. Ditto for the expulsion of some Nigerians from Ghana in those civil war days. Lagos nearly responded. As my research reveals, government enquiries led to the decision that it was better not to retaliate. Compare to the British Airways saga, relations with Canada and a number of issues, and you see that it is not only the quality of life that has deteriorated in our country: the quality of thinking also has.

Institutions in the Challenge of Change

As things change many institutions are under pressure to adapt. I regret to confirm that there has been a major depreciation of many of our institutions. If we understand institutions for what they are – rules that have become habit and set outer limits for behaviour – we see them as guarantors of predictable conduct and therefore of increased economic and social intercourse. The judiciary is one of the most important of our institutions. Those who have studied the role of property rights and judicial rulings on them in the United States will tell you it was the root of the rapid economic takeoff of your host country. The economic upsurge here in the 19th century had much to do with the evolution of property rights. Unfortunately for us, enforcement of commercial contacts are as threatened as human freedoms with the rule of law having suffered so much under the military. The recent confrontations between the NDLEA Chairman, Gen. Bamayi, and a judge illustrate this point just as well as the disputations between Gen. Jerry Useni and NECON over the election of local government officials in Abuja.

It is not only the judiciary that has changed. The media is changing too. I used to complain about the polarization of the media along lines of the acerbic anti-government and government mouth organ media. But there were elements in the media that took on a middle position. They held critical but responsible establishment positions. Many complain today that this segment has lost the will to be critical. I have been away for too long to speak authoritatively on that. If it is true, it would seem that we are left with the rabid licentious muckrakers and praise singers. Other institutions such as the police, public service and school systems are in worse shape. Our biggest need for aid will have to come in the area of rebuilding our institutions. Truly you can see the effect on how people behave on the streets. If you see a film of Lagos traffic you will get a feeling for the dehumanization of the Nigerian. Interestingly, most of us who live with it every day are unable to recognize the damage to our psyche caused by institutional failure.

The Nigerian Restoration

If my reflections on the present situation frighten you, take heart. I am actually quite optimistic about Nigeria's future. Most times when I proclaim myself an optimist about the future, people ask me what the source of my optimism is. Do I know something they do not know? The answer is Yes and No. It is No in the sense that a particular set of policies that will arrest the rot has not been secretly revealed to me. It is Yes, however, in a few senses. First, I have had the privilege of being a close observer of the top policy machinery in Nigeria since I was 21 years old. Both in observing closely and sometimes in actually offering advice to those who make policy in Nigeria, I have been able to 'feel it' close enough to conclude that the problems are only skin deep. I shudder often when I hear Nigerian leaders described as monsters so pathologically greedy that the damage resulting from how they rule means so little to them. From my experience, the truth is that these so-called leaders are sometimes driven by some of our distrust of other groups within the country or that they use this distrust to acquire power. In reality what leads to the damage they do is not a vicious mix of greed and wickedness, as some people suggest. Rather it is really a bit of ignorance and perhaps some incompetence with a lack of humility which makes learning difficult. Yes, there is some greed – but there is a bit of that in all humans – yet greedy Asians make much progress. As I know that even some of the worst dictators mean well deep inside, I am encouraged that the right events will move them forward. The other reason I am optimistic is that a country with the human resources Nigeria has can allow the world to leave it so far behind for only so long. People like all these bright Nigerians from the North, West and East living in a global village with CNN bringing the progress of others into their living rooms will one day say "No more!!" The road to Zaire is far too long with Nigeria's kind of human beings. Even if in the vexation of the moment some of us have talked about the Zaireanization of Nigeria, I doubt that we will fall that far. Yet we should not take anything for granted. Who would have believed 20 years ago that we could become a banana republic? But we have, if the truth be told.

Finally, I am optimistic because in these last few years I have been active in groups building broad national alliances committed to what I call the Nigerian restoration. In these professionals I meet with I find a love for Nigeria, for peaceful co-existence and for progress that cannot but be a source of hope.

Non-Resident Nigerians and the Restoration

Since India began to open up in 1991 there has been a surge of new investments in that country. Coming right after the United States as source of new investments in India is a category called NRI (Non-Resident Indians). The same phenomenon of Chinese abroad leading China's resurgence can also be observed. I expect that non-resident Nigerians will be critical in the Nigerian reconstruction. How are you getting ready for this role?

There are many ways NRN can help with the Nigerian Restoration. One way is in how they conduct themselves in their host society. The image of Nigeria abroad is so bad it takes a punitive toll on the country. This image is not deserved. We draw the attention of the world on human rights. If you look closely you see that we are not a paradise but we are much better on that score than many countries that are hardly vilified on this subject. It must be our desire to help rid our society of all abuses but it should be important in our interactions with people– politicians, the media and businessmen here in the United States– that our personal conduct casts doubt on this unfair image.

Then there is the area of investments. As I mentioned, the performance of listed companies make the NSE one of the most attractive emerging markets. There is no doubt you will get higher returns from Nigerian investments than you will find here. The issue that affected investors confidence in the past was country risk. As Nigerians you can tell better on those things. Since the abrogation of the Foreign Exchange Act of 1962 and the NEPD statutes, the Nigerian market has been easy to enter and exit. If the biggest source of new investments in Nigeria were from Nigerians abroad, think of the clout it would give you to influence policy and the general direction of governance.

I have been in the middle of trying to influence some American and Nigerian Capital Market operators to set up a Nigerian venture capital fund. Such a fund would certainly be a growth fund that would do well for both the investors and accelerated growth of the Nigerian economy. If such comes along I urge you all to trust it with your investments. Recent reforms at the Nigerian Stock Exchange, especially the introduction of an automated clearing system and the internationalization of the NSE, will lower transaction cost and make investment easy. I expect, however, that you will not be satisfied with portfolio investments. Set up factories in Anioma area or any part of Nigeria for that matter. I am convinced however that the Niger basin is destined to become Nigeria's industrial heartland. So whatever investments you make there will benefit from industry clustering in the manner that Michael Porter shows vividly in his book *The Competitive Advantage of Nations.*

The Restoration Group

I speak so confidently about what I believe Nigeria must become because I have invested quite a bit of my life collaborating with others to develop small oases of values and strategic alliances that can make it happen. In the wake of the crises of 1993 I was part of the founding of the Concerned Professionals, a grouping of professionals that was perhaps the most strident and active group of non-politicians demanding that the right things be done in those trying moments. When I discovered that some were typecasting the group as one of the South-West (Yoruba) groups, even though the initiators were mainly not from the South-West, I encouraged a broader group which included formal groups of professionals from the North, the East and some minority areas. I call that group THE RESTORATION GROUP. I was proud to host meetings of this group and to share the initiative of starting it with a friend of mine, Waziri Mohammed. The idea was to restore Nigeria's lost values that could carry a united, open and development-conscious society into the future. I am also encouraged by my experience at the Lagos Business School. When I quit my position in Industry to return to academia, of my own volition, many thought I was crazy. Today LBS is perhaps one of the most respected institutions in Nigeria. The South Africans in fact consider it the only competition on the continent by the testimony of the director of South Africa's leading business school. If we can do this in four years, think of Nigeria's true potential.

Leadership and the Future we Deserve

Leadership is at the core of issues of the Nigerian restoration. There is little or no doubt in my mind that current history, the history of what many rightly refer to as the Nigerian tragedy, is the direct result of the failure of leadership. I must admit that sometimes I wake up hoping that God will pinch me and startle me out of a horrifying nightmare. Again and again, I rediscover that I am not sleepwalking, I am living the sad experience of a Nigeria taken hostage and damaged, unwittingly, by its own children who claim to lead it, be they military or civilian.

I have, in exasperation, been known to suggest some curious solutions to the problems in the past. Perhaps we should visit two or three of them. As the strongman of Ibadan politics, Alhaji Adedibu has suggested, Nigeria has failed because of the greed and the pursuit of excessive personal gain by the politicians (which should include their counterparts in military uniforms). In the past I have suggested, in a deliberate display of rascality, that all the proceeds from oil sales be given to the soldiers to get together with their friends in *agbada* and share. Nigeria should then be left alone to be governed by the real people. It was not meant seriously. If all the research evidence available is anything to go by, and the record of 3.2 per cent annual growth for Nigeria between 1956 and 1966 compared to 0.017 per cent, average GDP growth rate since the oil boom began in 1973 counts, the Nigeria that gives a windfall of loot to its generals will be a much better off country. A second suggestion in frustration as Nigerians are put to cruel and unkind punishment by NEPA, NITEL and other public monopolies is a simple one. Since our leaders know how much misery these parastatals bring to us and retard economic growth but they will not privatize them because this is where they make their fortune and do favours to friends, why don't we allow competing private utilities to give good service and still keep the parastatals to give subsidized service to the military, government agencies and anybody who prefers "cheaper" service? That way the parastatals can still be available for our leaders to do as they please and the suffering people can get relief from the private competitors. Wealth created by enterprises starting because of the new infrastructure certainly can then employ more people and reduce poverty.

In these situations of deep pain I have always wished current and future Nigerian leaders could sit through one of my classes discussing the case of Singapore, if only they could come out of these discussions wondering if it is not the same God that created them who worked on Lee Kwan Yew. They do not have to be as good as Lee. But must the gap between them and Lee be so much?

I am convinced that we should pray fervently for those who lead us, that God may give them the grace to be humble enough to recognize their ignorance and the real extent of the damage that their pursuit of power, rather than purpose, has done and continues to do. It is hard to put a value on the damage that bad leadership has done. Take the example of the restructuring of the United Nations Security Council. The world is clearly in a quandary about what to do about Africa. Nigeria would seem a natural choice for a permanent seat for Africa. Even as much as I love my country, I am not so stupid not to recognize that Nigeria's history, especially the last five years, does not give it the dignity a permanent member should have. Other African states do not see Nigeria as a good role model and the world outside of Nigeria is even more negatively disposed towards what Nigeria has been made by its leaders. So, these days we hear of considerations of South Africa and others. But truly these countries are less than appropriate choices for the role. Yet we are hard to accept because our response to world issues continues to wear out both our friends and our people. The joy is that it will take very little to overcome the problem.

Truly, the Nigerian tragedy is about a severely poor country with much potential which its leaders have systematically squandered, out of greed or just to stay in power. It is a country that has declined so much it is hardly of much consequence in the world. In spite of its potential its economy is so marginal that if it was excised from the world economy hardly a blip would be noticeable on the computer. Yet its elite and leaders imagine it of such consequence that the world should stop at their holler. This tunnel vision of both the educated and the misinformed is why Nigeria is unlikely to change unless there is a reawakening or a new leadership able to truly appreciate Nigeria's real position rising from the ashes of the extant order. It is the self deceit in the way we think of Nigeria's importance that has held us back from striving to realize the potential that exists. This is even more reason to pray for humility to recognize what we truly are.

Conclusion

Groups like the Restoration Group, the Lagos Business School whose alumni have made the creation of an oasis of sanity in Nigeria, and others I cannot mention or do not know of, represent oases of commitment to progress. It will feel good to see Non-Resident Nigerians (NRN) become a big oasis of Nigerian progress. From the time I have spent in Boston and Washington DC during the last year I believe that is quite possible. It is about committing to progress and not giving up when things veer off the trajectory a little. If you all think of how many jobs you hold down here in the United States just to be able to send a few hundred dollars home every other month to support poverty-afflicted relatives, you will recognize that the more you can do towards contributing to the creation of economic opportunity the better off you are, and fortunately the better off will Nigeria also be.

3

Expectations of Nigerians in the New Millenium: Economic Prospects and Fears*

Let me begin by acknowledging that I am pleased to spend this time in the company of the future. To you who have the twenty first century as your full heritage, the subject you have requested me to lead in discussing is no doubt a matter of paramount importance. I hope I can say enough about it, to make you insert yourselves in a very personal way into the process of creating this modern competitive economy that provides the greatest good to the greatest number of our people, while responding to global forces that are changing the drivers of effective economic performance faster than many of us are able to adapt. Before we get into the subject proper, let me respond to another somewhat extraneous matter.

Your invitation to me indicates that this is a two-part event. One part involves your bestowing a certain honour on me. I must admit that, even as I cherish your generosity of heart in coming to the decision regarding the honour I have to say in good conscience that it is undeserved and would be inappropriate for me to accept. I think it is stretching things a bit to suggest that I am the 'Economic Guru of Our Time.' I know that on the occasion of my 40th birthday, some three years ago, I 'complained' about the burden of being referred to in those terms by the former World Bank resident representative and the Indian High Commissioner. I must say that in the case of the honour you propose, I am unable to see this as a fair description of the reality, given many seasoned and hardworking economists working quietly at the challenges facing this economy.

I think that my circumstance is really more of a concerned citizen who had the privilege of liberal American education which created room to apply himself almost equally to the policy sciences, political science, economics and management during years of graduate study. Applying

---

*Address to the community of Yaba College of Technology, Lagos, on 13-7-99

this background to everyday concerns and expressing myself frequently on them could qualify me for honour as a concerned citizen, but not the 'Economic Guru Of Our Time.' Forgive me therefore if I pass on the award.

Now back to our subject matter proper.

Expectations of Nigerians

What expectations do Nigerians have of the new millennium and what are the economic management imperatives of these anticipations? Let me say that the most marked phenomenon of this age – information and communications technology (ICT) – has had the effect of progressively universalizing expectations. In this global village in which satellite television brings the quality of life of distant peoples, their joys and their anguish, into our living rooms, as they are happening and being experienced, culture tends to have a global flavour. For the most part, what the Nigerian people will have in the next millennium will be what the Americans and the aborigines of Australia want.

In the main, those things they want which will more and more be part of a charter of rights that citizens are entitled to include higher quality of life, greater freedom to do what they prefer within the bounds of the society's norms, the elimination of poverty, easier access to adequate health care delivery, and the opening up of a brave new world in which there are no barriers, outside of individual capacity for education and self development.

Can These Expectations be Met?

I see myself quite fortunate to be able to witness the tentative first steps taken by the recently elected federal government. I have preached for years now that tackling corruption head-on, rebuilding institutions and re-inventing the public service were prerequisites for growth and development. As I see President Obasanjo proceed in the manner of a man who has given much thought to these matters, I am tempted to call up friends who were upset that I endorsed his candidacy and who called me naïve for insisting that he would shock them by being his own man in office. The good news from Abuja notwithstanding, we are still a long way from moving in the right direction. The actions of President Obasanjo are necessary but not sufficient conditions for the Nigerian restoration.

There are several issues, in my opinion, which have to be satisfactorily addressed for the expectations to be met. Some of them I have spoken elaborately about elsewhere and should therefore not dwell on here. Others that will bear recapping and increased emphasis, I shall treat as such. I may also raise the matter of one or two phenomena I have not talked on as such in my previous comments on the challenge of development. From skipping through the issues I will turn again to the challenge of policy implementation. In all of these I shall be encouraging you all, as young people and true heirs of the new millennium, to think not what is being done with and about the future, but to think how you can affect that future and shape it to assume the pattern of your dream in this gestalt flowing from your collective consciousness.

Policy Framework

At a broad level, the battle for the soul of the Nigerian economy has been fought over the dominance of either controls or markets. Our country has always considered itself a mixed economy. Since oil became a dominant factor in the economy, the mix has largely been skewed in favour of government ownership. Time would show the ease with which goal displacement emerges with the weak corporate governance capabilities of the public sector. The result has been massive retrenchment of the economy following decline in oil prices from the peak of $40 a barrel during the 1979 Iranian revolution following the first price quadrupling at the onset of the Arab-Israeli war of 1973. Stagnation was soon consequent upon failure to diversify the base of the economy. Stagnation also became manifest because government dominance, reflected in a regime of controls, stifled opportunity to create value. Economic decisions for the private sector were even further complicated by a high level of uncertainty enveloping many areas of private sector activity. These created high transaction costs and low commitment to engaging in economic intercourse, further deepening the recession.

An inevitable adjustment programme in the mid-1980s focused attention on a greater role for the private sector as a way of reducing the inefficiencies of the economy. The first wave of privatisation and the deregulation of the foreign exchange markets sent a signal that emboldened private sector operators to engage government in dialogue to move the economy down the path of private sector-led development.

The economic summits and the vision 2010 programme that followed in their wake do not seem to have brought the debate to a conclusion because there is a degree of negative reaction to vision 2010 that may be a function not of what is in the book but what is on the cover. The fact that it happened in Abacha's time has troubled quite a few people.

A second problem flows from the patriotic fervor of incumbents in Aso Rock. Every country can use a good dose of patriotism in its leaders. Like everything in life, however, there is the law of diminishing returns. An overdose of patriotic fervor could get us on the other side of the bell-shaped curve and policy choices will not have optimal outcomes. A newspaper editor recently described the core of the central leadership as caught in the mode of super patriots. We have to be careful that super patriotism does not lead us to fighting a third millennium war with twentieth century weapons. We saw patriotism lead Milosovic of Yugoslavia to use tanks against NATO air power. We have to resist the temptation of patriotism leading us down the path of implementing in the new millennium policies that apparently worked in the 1970s. In the post-Uruguay round world in which the WTO holds sway and ICT makes corporate globalization a driver of investments and trade, we may be in error to reject markets which will put us in a position to develop country competitiveness in favour of massive state intervention in response to a patriotic stimulus and the idea that governments exist to solve problems, be they social or economic.

I am in no doubt, given the unfolding scenario, that the context of the policy framework debate will pitch the 'patriotic' neo-interventionists against those who argue for the efficiency of markets. I continue to favour markets, even though I recognize that markets may not be perfect, which is why I place a premium on facilitating the evolution of institutions and some guidance by the state in terms of focusing the citizenry's attention on certain preferred sectors in which value can be created in a way that results in a concerted effort at growth.

Let me mention here that I am in early stages of developing my research agenda, a strategic alliance with a globally renowned country competitiveness consulting firm to study the competitiveness of our economy. I expect to find the outcome of the collaboration with the Boston firm revealing.

Critical Phenomena

To achieve fiscal viability and high growth, it is my opinion that we have to pay particular attention to certain phenomena and processes. For me these include financial deepening, building venture capital industry, building institutions that enhance a payments system and reduce transaction costs in banking. Also critical are policies directed at the SME sector, agriculture and infrastructure development. Given the dawn of the age of the knowledge worker, human capital development policies will also move to the fore.

Financial Deepening

I have discussed this subject extensively elsewhere. Let it suffice here that policies designed to lower entry barriers into banking were intended to result in higher efficiency, reduced transaction costs and a higher willingness of money to stay in the banks. This should result in higher savings rates and opportunities for capital to be moved to deficit areas from areas of surplus. In this process of intermediation that results in more investments, we are likely to see increased productivity and competitiveness and, inevitably, economic growth.

The financial system is much burdened by weak payment systems and procedures which make the cost of the use of banking high for many Nigerians who opt instead to keep their money elsewhere. This perception of transaction costs of banking leads people to bear the risks of unsafe custody of money such that each market fire usually results in millions of naira going up in smoke. As a result of this banking habit, or lack of it, only a small fraction of money in circulation enters the banking system. This tends to render money supply contraction policies impotent or to stifle any growth possibilities: only a very deep cut to have any effect since it can impact on only a small fraction of money in circulation. The stabilization securities of the past and the special Treasury Bills of the present are apt illustrations.

To my mind a clear-minded attack of this problem is necessary. It may require a collaboration between the CBN and NDIC to put some systems and rules in place that reduce the risks of banking transactions, make payment systems easy, reliable and quick and provide incentives for the banks to lower transaction costs for profit benefits to themselves. After such policies are in place I will encourage a change in the colour of the currencies again to force all monies to pass through the banks. Just as First Bank dramatically increased its deposit base by aggressively selling savings schemes to recipients of Western Union money transfers, I trust that banks can market their way into keeping more money in the banking system. With that achieved, the challenge of financial deepening will be on the way to getting tackled.

Related to this challenge is the need to stimulate savings through making the insurance sector more effective. It is not meaningful to talk so much of foreign investment without facing the issue of domestic savings. There is by now more than ample evidence that growth is more dependent on domestic savings than on foreign investment which is no doubt valuable. Insurance sector companies elsewhere have proved a big sponsors of venture capital because they are better able to mobilize long term funds. Here they seem to be perpetually locked in squabbles.

3I and P4

Most of the other critical variables except human capital development are summarized under the banner of the 3I and the paradox of purchasing power parity (P4 in my shorthand pattern). In the 3I I have discussed the importance of investment derived from local savings and foreign direct investment. As we have shown citing a 1998 IFC study of financial institutions, high growth developing economies have derived those rates of growth from investments supported by domestic savings.

In a country where transaction costs are very high because the judiciary cannot be relied upon for dispute arbitration and the crooks can abuse *ex parte* motions to tar innocent parties in a dispute, the rebuilding of institutions such as the judiciary, police and regulatory agencies such as the Central Bank and the NDIC are imperatives for reducing uncertainty in the environment, thus stimulating economic intercourse.

The third is for industriousness used here as patterns of encouraging entrepreneurial activity. I am aware that members of the indigenous quoted group of the Nigerian Stock Exchange point out that the biggest deficiency of Vision 2010 is that it does not dwell adequately on how to stimulate and support value creating venturing of their like and creating an environment that allows such indigenous entrepreneurs to grow and become competitive. I am convinced that growth will depend on deliberate effort through transparent institutional action by the state to support accelerating indigenous entrepreneurship without creating a playing field so uneven as to be a disincentive to other investors. I must reaffirm here the imperative of building local value-adding businesses, not glorified agents and brokers.

Programmes in this frame should be of interest to most of you. When you graduate from here, there will be very few jobs available for you. Coming from a school of technology there should be skill available to you which, with some entrepreneurship inclination and determination, can lead to ventures blossoming and providing job opportunities for others. To make a success of venturing, we all must forget the old ways of economic rent seeking where to be a businessman is to have contacts that provide opportunities for inflated contracts and supply jobs. If we can identify urgent needs of people and we work with integrity to create use-value that fulfills these needs, we could be tomorrow's empire builders. This is what the moment calls for. I do indeed look forward to great stories some day that capture the triumph of the human spirit in detailing how some of you took a dream and transformed nothing into something unbelievably useful and profitable. That is nation building. Regarding P4, it allows me to deal with how infrastructure problems turn the logic of the law of one price on which the purchase power parity concept is based. I have spoken much elsewhere about this and will avoid boring you with details.

Micro-Credit and Poverty Alleviation

One of the areas for which I favour government intervention against the current passion in the Bretton Woods Institutions is micro-credit delivery to the rural and urban poor. I will modify the typical government intervention mode by suggesting the use of NGOs as vehicles for implementation with PTA-type monitoring and implementation management. I have shown elsewhere studies by British finance and development scholars which refute the empirical basis of the so-called Ohio School that is the basis of new orthodoxy at the World Bank on this matter. I not only favour intervention, I have a preference for one that is highly focused on moving the micro sector to integrate with East Asia type industrial policy at the top of a hierarchy that has incubator chains for the SME sector.

Credit Support Home Ownership and New Growth

Just as we pay attention to savings and investment, consumption cannot but be dealt with as a necessary condition for production growth. We are aware of the crisis of purchasing power in the last few years as Ani's inflation-fighting policies constrained purchasing power and resulted in full warehouses. Manufacturers had to restructure as a result with the effect of job losses.

To build purchasing power and consumption, there is the need to create institutions that democratize access to credit for consumption while reducing the risk for the credit granting agencies. In this category will be mortgage institutions and the democratization of home ownership. The time has come when housing starts will be a standard measure of economic activity.

In proposing here a credit system to boost consumption, am I suggesting a counterpoint to the savings challenge? Not really, in the sense that I hope consumer credit will be grown, designed to begin with locally manufactured products with potential for becoming internationally competitive.

The Nobility of Spirit

Resulting from the foregoing is the question of what needs to be done to ensure faithful implementation of the ideas that will help Nigerian resume growth and attain the double digit GDP growth rates advocated in Vision 2010. I have heard many young people say with much aggravation and with doubt that the appointed officials around the president do not seem capable of moving the country down the path of such an ambitious trajectory. To many who have spoken so passionately on the matter I have often counseled a noble spirit. In my conscience I think what matters is outcome, not what in the prisms of our mind we think of those people. If they fail to perform then we can complain. To write off people either because of their ages or elements of their antecedents seems to me to be lacking in charity. Let us give them a chance and cooperate with them in the great task of national reconstruction. Whenever people's antecedents are raised in evidence as to their irredeemability for an assignment, my mind goes to Brazil.

In the late 1970s when I pursued postgraduate study in the area of International Political Economy, there was a celebrated scholar advocating selective delinking from international capitalism. He would become prominent in later Brazilian history. That scholar who was one of the 'dependistas' of the dependency theory school in international political economy happens to be Enrique Cardoso, current President of Brazil. I am sure he does not argue for selective delinking any more. People can adjust to reality. This is also why I persist in reminding Aso Rock not to return to economic policies that seemed to have worked in 1977. The conditions have changed. We do not have the resources today as we had then and the economics of that era do not fit the age of corporate globalization. Tanks will not do in this war. We need air power. Even if we have a more patriotic team in place, the return to fertilizer subsidies may not be the best way to transfer support to farmers who need real help to save that critical sector of the economy. Besides it sends a signal that might be unwholesome.

What this should do for us is to enable our spirit to seek to criticize in a way that helps move things forward rather than bellyache over what we think or do not think of the quality of the cabinet. For you who are very young, I understand some of the impatience with a cabinet with an average age close to 60 running a country of people mostly under 30. But I do not see much gain in polarizing our country on age lines. Yes, there may be problems with the fact that many of them do not understand what the Internet is and that they may seem anachronisms in the age of e-commerce; but if enough ideas are made available in the market place of ideas they could still govern aright from the ideas the markets throw up. Let us not forget that most of America's great corporate leaders are themselves not computer literate because they came from a certain age.

This generation debate is not new. Let me go back a few years to illustrate. Chief Chris Ogunbanjo had on one occasion pooled leading lights of Nigeria from politics, business and academia and pulled them to his centre in Erunwon to discuss the future of Nigeria. I was fortunate to get invited. I arrived a little late because I had a class to teach. When I came into the hall, one of the first people I saw was Professor Akin Mabogunje. Thank God you are here, Professor Mabogunje said to me. As he was leaving his home that morning, he told me, his son had asked how come a collection of people who were about to die were gathering to discuss the future of the younger ones. My appearance meant to him that his son was not fully accurate in his assessment of the meeting. I thought for one quick second and shouted above the rain pounding the aluminum roof that older people with a noble spirit would want to get it right so that their children do not suffer the same indignities the older generations endured for not doing the right thing. Indeed it turned out that perhaps only Fola Adeola and I were under 50 years of age in this gathering of up to 100 Nigerian men, most of whom had made a mark in their chosen spheres. The quality of discussion took nothing away from a future that could have been constructed on their ideas, their age range notwithstanding. What it takes to make progress is that noble spirit.

Conclusion

Clearly, the century which closes in a few months concludes an age which cannot by any stretch of imagination be considered the African millennium, even if there remains evidence of great learning in universities at Timbuktu hundreds of years ago and vast empires on the continent. As we move from Pax Britanica to the American century, it is time to ask whether the continent that was a victim of devastating slave raids is ready to claim its own century. If our new leadership in Nigeria manages to get it right and lays the platform for liberating the people from pernicious poverty, then there will be a basis for beginning to consider the possibilities that the vast human and natural resources of this land can be better mobilised and utilized to make Africa more relevant in the next century. In that endeavour none can afford to sit on the back benches. We must all obtain our tickets for the front row and as we do so, let our consciousness be filled with images of that Kennedy refrain: think not what your country can do for you but what you can do for your country. But you cannot think this way if your mind is focused on gang wars and violent despicable uncivilized conduct in which you intimidate and kill your teachers, staff and one another in the name of secret cults. The private tragedies of parents who send off their wards for an education to enrich them, but are called to claim their corpses cannot continue. These tragedies caused by impotent students who want to scare lecturers, feel powerful and bully others belong to the retrogressive. The future that I talk about belongs to those who want to work and apply their intellect to creating value.

The challenge of your participation in rebuilding Nigeria in the new millennium is the challenge of raising a generation with higher order values. My charge to you and my prayer for you all is that you endeavour to be the salt of the Earth.

4

Business and Civil Society in Africa*

Increased concerns about civil society, voluntarism and associational platforms of social action autonomous of the state, in Africa, has come largely from efforts to explain the performance of the state in post-colonial Africa. Fuelled mainly by donor agency frustration with leakages that have resulted in goal displacement that see foreign loans and aid enrich individuals in authority while the development challenge they aimed to eliminate persist, the conceptions of civil society have attracted much attention in the literature. In spite of the attention, conceptual clarity regarding its very thrust remains problematic. The objective in this essay is to try and evaluate the role of the business community in Africa and to analyze linkages of phenomena that can add to our understanding of how civil society can enhance governance and yield superior performance outcomes for both the state and private enterprises in Africa.

The Civil Society Perspective

There is not much doubt that the dissatisfaction felt about the state in Africa after much expectation had been invested in it, by both development and modernization theorists as well as citizens, aid agencies and multilateral development institutions, encouraged the search for surrogate agents of social transformation. These states which gave rise to many dictatorships had been tolerated in their autocratic forms, in the hope they would deliver on development. Some autocratic regimes even 'thrived.' They provided superpowers the opportunity for managing client states in the competition for influence in a bipolar world. But they failed to deliver on development goals. The obsession of regimes with self-preservation and a base of legitimacy resulted in attempts at incorporating potential opposition groups. The making of the corporatist state was also the undoing of traditions of civil action which allowed free rein to ineffective policies driven by narrow interest.

---

*Address at a Conference at Ohio Central University

After a while malgovernance began to produce a coalition of academics and bureaucrats, opposition politicians and 'new entrepreneurs' of voluntary association. As repression increased and employment opportunities declined, personal troubles of the ordinary people exploded. This led to venturing into voluntarism to mushroom into a major growth industry. While many of the bureaucrats of voluntarism reflect enterprise creativity in response to donor agencies' loss of confidence in the state, some voluntary groups were to foster traditional group interest. These other groups like business associations wanted to see policies that favoured business as the main source of wealth creation.

In a sense, the emergence of a civil society perspective in the study of African development is driven by the quest for discovering how the state can be more effective in delivering higher quality of life to the people. Efforts to extrapolate from the experience of societies where the state is thought to have delivered thus result in 'fishing' for phenomena in these cultures that may have explanatory power regarding the African condition. The place of civil action in many of the countries emerged as a phenomenon of interest as a result of this quest for explanation.

Since many African countries were unable to sustain multiparty universal adult suffrage-based democracy after independence, it is tempting to offer hypotheses that explain the deficiencies of economic development in terms of the failure of democracy learnt from the colonial regimes, even if colonial administration was far from democratic in nature. The failure of learning or imitation of the conventions of the home governments of the colonial governors, some suggested, could be the reason for the absence of economic advance. Elements of democratic culture are thus offered as possible explanations within the civil society perspective. Not surprisingly, there has been a plethora of views on how civil society facilitates the democratic ethos (Diamond, 1996; Nelson, 1996; Bayart, 1986; Foley and Edwards, 1996). This tendency to reduce the idea of civil society to a bulwark against fundamental freedoms and the democratic norm is not without its critics (Osagie, 1997; Allen, 1997; Bratton, 1992). In the main, the tendency has been to treat civil society as the sharing of the public domain with the state by voluntary associations and organizations capable of socializing and mobilizing elements of a broader society. This is largely to ensure that the welfare of the citizen takes a central place in the conduct of the state.

Here we offer a view of civil society as the construction of horizontal linkages between individuals and groups who contest for space within the public domain with the state and other groups for the purpose of social accounting and of civil, non-violent, canvassing of perspectives on social action that promotes the common good.

This definition includes the idea of horizontal linkages which denote the cutting across of parochial basis of aggregation and evolving of a locus of the common interest that unites peoples against possible excesses of state power with regard to that common interest. This immediately leads to questions about associational forms grouping members of a society with the same ethnic background. Indeed not cutting across parochial boundaries means that it is easy for the state to question the motives of the association and to play some elements of society against others. This pattern is discernable in the actions of the embattled Nigerian state in 1993 and 1994 when it employed every propaganda asset at its disposal to create the impression that some of the groups contending for public space and contesting the annulment of the results of the presidential election were groupings of people from the Yoruba-speaking southwest of the country. Even the "Concerned Professionals,"[1] whose primary initiator was non-Yoruba and two of the three formal conveners were not Yorubas, was dressed in the 'southwest' garb by the regime.

The proposition of what constitutes civil society also suggests that these individuals and groups who come together aim to contest for space within the public domain. This nature of civil society is particularly important because the post-colonial state in Africa has used the deficiencies of 'low capital accumulation' among entrepreneurs to assume the commanding heights of the economy (Ayida, 1989; Asiodu, 1993; Okigbo, 1987), the threat of ethnicity to national integration (Nelson and Wolpe, 1971; Joseph, 1994) and the mobilisational needs of the challenge of development and naked descent into praetorianism among others (Diamond, 1995), to so completely dominate the arena of the public domain. With corporatist state incorporating union leaders and other possible sources of alternative ideas, competing views drowned, became muffled or were muzzled out. At the same time as these ideas shut off the public domain, structures of public choice either because of

---

[1] The idea of the Concerned Professionals was articulated first in OPED articles by Pat Adam who along with Atedo Peterside and Sam Oni concerned the CP. Of the threee, only Oni has Yoruba antecedents.

military rule, or one-party state or extreme polarization of political parties (with the idea of loyal opposition considered anathema), became more restrictive. Society became unable to attract competing ideas on public choices issues such that optimum outcome could result from the public choice process. With a more narrow base, the tradition of "Complex Redundancy" (Wildavsky 1979) which built in a certain robustness into decision making, providing for the public domain to be shared in the belief that outcomes would be more effective, was lost. All these made it imperative that power for contestation of the public domain be sought in the collective strength of voluntarism and association life. It is power unavailable to the individual where there is inadequate development of institutions that protect individual rights.

Another phenomenon captured in the set of linkages that establish civil society as has been proposed here is social accounting. Part of the purpose of contesting for space in the public domain is to be able to use the weight of associational life to require agents of the state to give account of their stewardship to society. In this sense the relationship between civil society and the state should in a manner akin to corporate governance be both adversarial and cooperative. The adversarial element will of necessity be higher in civil society state interface as different from board-management relationship because the board has formal authority whereas civil society derives power from the quality of its organization and its people mobilization competence.

There has been a tendency in the literature to emphasize the adversarial nature of the relationship between the state and civil society (Bayart, 1986, Bratton, 1994;) but if the civil society is to be effective in the governance aspect of this relationship, it must be able to establish a level of mutual respect and identification of shared goals in which case a corporative component, even if grudgingly offered, will, of necessity, underlie this relationship.

Beyond social accounting, the definition of civil society offered here also portrays it as existing to canvas social action in the interest of the common good. What is the common good? The common good here refers to universal concepts of fairness and justice associated with conscience and the norm of governing as effort to improve the quality of life of citizens and enhancing their dignity.

Of significant value to conceptual clarity is how autonomy from the state applies to civil society. Indeed civil society cannot be dependent on the state if it is to play well the governance role. Civil society should therefore be autonomous from the state to the extent that the leadership depends not on the state but on its membership for legitimacy and that its funding comes from sources other than the agents of the state. It is however not autonomous in the sense of deep cleavages between state and civil society in which the reconstruction of the state is a permanent goal of civil society. State and civil society indeed should cooperate whenever activity autonomously arrived at by both as being for the common good is identified. This has been traditionally the case with the role cf business associations epitomized lately in Nigeria by their leadership in developing a national modus vivendi (Vision 2010) in Nigeria. The nature of the autonomy of civil society from the state should indeed be like the autonomy of the 'loyal' opposition from the ruling party in British-style parliamentary politics. Business associations became the surviving part of civil society under the onslaught of the military, perhaps because they were not so advanced or because the first generations of African businessmen were creations of the states to which they were beholden so that they avoided conflict with governments.

Based on the foregoing understanding of what is meant by civil society, the following review and analysis focus more on business and civil society, identifying why business associations have not been as threatening to the state as human rights groups; for example, if it needs, for its own reproduction and sustenance, to be an active part of civil society in Africa. Even though this review draws from examples of the West African Enterprise Network and experiences elsewhere in Africa, a case study approach, using Nigeria as reference frame, has been opted for so that deeper insights may be established.

Civil Society and the Corporatist State

The place of business in contesting the public domain has been much affected by the evolution of state structure that sought to incorporate elements of evolving civil society. The corporatist state was on the ascendancy through much of Africa in the 1970s. In Senegal, for example, associational life in the business community evolved from a monopoly of French commercial interest which literally set trade policy for the government until the political crisis of 1968-70 when foreign domination of commerce became a thorny political issue. During this period two nascent business groupings of native Senegalese came together as UNIGES *(Union des Groupements Economiques du Senegal)*. This new organization of small-scale business persons championed the cause of an indigenous enterprise class that felt locked out of trade and industry opportunities (Diop 1972).

The vigour with which UNIGES articulated its discontent shocked President Senghor who had considered this class a core part of his political base. Senghor moved quickly to pacify and ultimately to co-opt UNIGES. By 1971, a new government-sponsored business association, *Groupements du Senegal* (GES), had been founded with UNIGES leaders appropriately rewarded with positions of significance. GES pledged to work within the framework of options set by the government (*Jeune Afrique,* 23 June, 1970). Senghor had learnt his lesson and the corporatist State was in ascent.

In the same manner as the Corporatist state took hold in Senegal so did it in the classic divide-and-rule patron-client culture of Arap Moi's Kenya and Ibrahim Babangida's Nigeria.

The Place of Business in Civil Society

Should business play a role in civil society in Africa? Many executives of multinational corporations pressed to take an interest in matters of human rights and good government in countries where they operate tend to shy away from the subject. Frustrated activists sometimes turn to calling them names for this. To such abuse, executives coolly reply that their business is to ensure a decent return to shareholders and tangling with autocrative regimes could be costly to their primary objective. While various possible responses can suggest that business takes a short term view and that not collaborating with corrupt regimes could create a better playing field to the profit of those same shareholders, it is hard to fault the logic of the executives. In the long term most of them could already be dead. The risk averse nature of the typical manager prescribed the instinct of wishing for good government but doing little that is business-goal-threatening to achieve it. It would seem therefore that the place of business in civil society has to be directly congruent with the immediate goals of business.

What are these immediate goals of business? The essence of enterprise in any environment of competitive rivalry is to deliver sustainable superior performance over rivals (Porter, 1985). The strategy that helps firms deliver superior performance is shaped by competitive forces. Michael Porter identifies five of these forces which shape strategy; these include: intensity of existing rivalry; barriers to entry into the business; threat of substitute products or services; power of suppliers and power of buyers relative to the firm. The nature of these competitive forces determines whether or not firms will compete away their profits and therefore whether the industry is attractive. If the industry is attractive, those forces then help determine the positioning within the industry as different positionings attract different kinds of returns on the investment (Porter 1990).

The Porter hypothesis has great explanatory power in mature market economies but tends to come up short in developing countries. In pursuit of a more robust framework that explains the behaviour of business enterprises in transition economies, I have proposed a new framework (Utomi, 1996). This framework, the Emerging Economies Environment Framework (or 3E Framework), essentially identifies some variables that do not get the attention they deserve in the Porter model. It shows that some of these variables are in fact megafactors with overarching influence on the five competitive forces Porter has isolated. These variables which I call megafactors are: Government Action and the Predatory Acts of Government Officials; Institutions; and Business Associations (Utomi, 1998). In addition to these megafactors, the competence portfolio of the firm which shapes its capacity for competitive innovation helps round off the terrain of Strategic Choice behaviour.

For our purposes here we will dwell only on the first three megafactors. The factor of government action and the predatory action of government officials essentially deals with the tendency of government officials to affect the playing field such that it is not level. The idea is to favour cronies and the self but it distorts the environment of business. Part of the consequence is very severe levels of uncertainty that usually result in limited momentum of economic intercourse. As Douglas North shows vividly in his work, institutions have been primarily responsible for reducing uncertainty and engendering economic activity and the rapid growth and advancement that follow these activities (North, 1990). As institutions evolve, they act as a source of constraint on what governments can get away with and on the predatory behaviour of officials of government. The evolution of property rights in 19th century United

States, for example, is given credit for the rapid development of the country in that century. So institutions and how they evolve become of high value if we are to understand what drives the strategy of firms and the performance outcomes for competing enterprises. Here again North's thesis is helpful.

North makes the point that institutions which ultimately levelled the playing field were sometimes the outcome of the selfish intentions of powerful economic actors. In that sense a business association like the Lagos Chamber of Commerce and Industry can propose a tariff policy to benefit its members who are importers of consumer goods, then one or two integrate into manufacturing. This creates a problem that is ultimately resolved in favour of tariff policy that is even or neutral to the expectations of specific interests. In that sense we considered business associations a megafactor primarily because of the role they can play in the evolution of institutions.

What are business associations but key elements of civil society that contest the public domain with the state to advance the interest of businesses? The associations invariably seek to influence the process of institution formation that acts to constrain the conduct of the state which could negatively affect the process of wealth creation. This would be a matter that is for the common good. Let us therefore consider the history of business associations in Africa to evaluate their impact on the state of civil society.

Business Association in Africa

Military Rule and Civil Society in Africa

The emergence of business associations in Africa as a subject worthy of study is fairly recent. This flows partly from a tendency in the immediate post-independence era to treat them dismissively as they are assumed to have been malformed by dependence (Lucas, 1997). The decline of government authority and disappointment with development performance in the state-led development paradigm seems to have earned these business associations some reprieve and even caused donor agencies to stimulate the formation of a new genre of these associations such as the West African Enterprise Network.

Lucas offers some reasons for the resurgence of business associations in countries such as Africa. First, business support for the interventionist state had begun to wane by the late 1970s as an indigenous enterprise class began to emerge. Then the failures of the interventionist state began to be manifested in economic crisis and threats to property rights. Also at play was the erosion of the corporatist mechanisms by which the state had previously subordinated business. Finally, globalization has been alternating the bargaining relationship between government and the private sector.

The effect of this trend of emerging business associations has been more widely felt in the more prosperous countries of Africa such as Nigeria, Kenya, Senegal, Cote d'Ivoire and Zimbabwe (Ibid p. 86). The business associations in these countries canvassed policies that helped bring about indigenisation programmes which profit members of their groups in Nigeria (1972/73 and 1977), Senegal (1969) and Kenya (1967).

The effectiveness of these business associations in holding up alternative views to those of government varies from country to country. The experience of the West African Enterprise Network is that the francophones tend to be much less strident than the anglophones even though some of the Senegalese hold their own quite well. With socialism being abandoned in countries like Tanzania, and South Africa emerging from apartheid, there will be a greater tendency to see more business associations autonomous of the state and contesting the public domain with the state.

How have business associations fared relative to other elements of civil society? To understand that is to understand military rule and the effect it has had on civil society in Africa. Military rule has been a continent-wide phenomenon (Pecalo, 1976; Bienen, 1978; Oyeleye, 1979; Utomi, 1985). We will however focus on the Nigerian case for a more in-depth analysis of how civil society has managed under military rule.

On January 1, 1984, Nigeria recorded its fourth coup since independence as soldiers swept President Shehu Shagari out of office. Ever since, the military has been in power. It is usual to discount the very short-lived Interim National Government of Chief Ernest Shonekan before his subsequent removal by the present military regime of General Sani Abacha on November 17, 1993. During the years of military rule institutional reforms, arbitrary use of power and predatory acts of the regime have ensured that civil society defined by Edward Shills as *"the part of society that conducts a particular set of relationships between itself and the state, possesses mechanisms that safeguard the separation of state and civil society and maintains ties between them"* has been severely strained by the pressure to dominate society by these military regimes.

One of the major victims of the assault on civil society by the military has been the Nigeria Bar Association. Strong and strident in times past the NBA fought for the independence of the society. This, of course had consequences for confidence of potential investors in gauging the resolubility of contract disputes. Repeated efforts to fictionalize the NBA, install lawyers sympathetic to the regime etc. eventually resulted in their becoming crises-ridden.

The biggest victim of the assault on institutions by the military has been the judiciary. Retroactive laws have rendered judges impotent as was the case with the sentence of two journalists from the Guardian Newspapers in 1984. Their offence was that they published a story on the choice of ambassadors before formal announcements were made. This was not a matter that was against any law at the time of this report.

A more recent experience occurred in 1996 under the present administration when the Federal High Court presided over by Justice Babatunde Belgore ordered the Chairman of the National Drug Law Enforcement Agency (NDLEA), Major General Musa Bamaiyi, to re-open the business premises of two auto dealers which had been shut since 1995. The order was ignored repeatedly despite pleas by the Attorney General of the Federation that he should comply. Instead Bamaiyi chose to write a letter 'lecturing' the judge on the jurisdiction of the courts.

In stifling the judiciary, the military went for the jugular of the Nigeria Bar Association (NBA), the umbrella body of lawyers respected by the role it played in ensuring healthy checks and balances. It seemed at a point that it was the high regard the military had for any view held by the association that informed their decision to court the body by appointing its President as the Attorney General of the Federation and Minister for Justice. In 1985, Babangida appointed the then NBA President, Prince Bola Ajibola, as the A.G. This was followed by Clement Akpamgbo, starting what seemed like a tradition for a NBA President to transform into the country's Chief Legal Officer. However, when it dawned on government that this tradition was not a guarantee that the body would support every one of its policies with the emergence of Priscilla Kuye, efforts were made to affect the association differently. The regime tried to influence who emerged as President of the Association.

In 1992, the NBA could not hold its annual general conference to elect national officers due to sponsored intrigues which led to a stalemate of the convention of the association. The election which had been billed to climax the one-week-long conference held at the Port Harcourt civic centre was turned into a free-for-all fight as members of the legal profession descended on one another with fisticuffs and weapons. Three candidates were vying for the presidency, namely Alhaji Bashir Dalhatu, Chief (Mrs) Priscilla Kuye and late Kanmi Ishola-Osobu. The government was strongly opposed to Kuye's re-election because of her radical stance against the Babangida administration when it detained Gani Fawehinmi and other members, and instead supported Dalhatu with necessary resources to ensure his victory. A crisis ensued leading to court litigations and several injuctions and for six years, the NBA could not speak with one voice. The promulgation of the Legal Practitioners (Amendment) Decree 21 of 1994 by the Abacha administration which ceded authority of the management of the body to the Body of Benchers only served to exacerbate the problem and further weakened the NBA.

Labour was not spared. Military incursion into the affairs of labour started in 1977 when the government of then Olusegun Obasanjo aborted the inaugural conference of labour unions and set in motion processes which led to the restructuring of over 1000 house unions into 42 industrial unions. This led to the emergence of a government imposed Nigeria Labour Congress (NLC). However, events since 1978 have not helped the achievements of the expectations of sustained labour unity. In 1988, the administration of Gen. Ibrahim Babangida was to intervene again in the affairs of the NLC with the dissolution of the National Executive Union (NEC) of the body and the appointment of Michael Ogunkoya of John Holt Plc. as Sole Administrator. This intervention came as a result of division in the trade unions by way of the emergence of two tendencies – the democrats led by Tarka/Shamang of the Electricity and Gas Workers Union and the progressives represented by Alli Ciroma. The sanctity of the 1978 decree which provided for only one central organization in the

NLC was broken and the Babangida administration acted in such a manner as to perpetuate this division in order to weaken workers' resistance to its structural adjustment policies.

This systematic emasculation of labour continued with the Abacha regime with the 1994 dissolution of the apex workers union and since then labour has been in chains. The place of labour in civil society was, however, recently highlighted at a tripartite Vision 2010 committee meeting, involving representatives of government, labour and the Nigerian Employers Consultative Association (NECA), on how to sustain industrial harmony and social partnership in industry. NECA lamented that vices, such as moral decadence, indiscipline, bribery and corruption, fraud and get-rich quick syndrome which flourished under military rule have made it continually difficult for Nigeria to achieve socio-economic breakthrough. Prisca Egede writing on the annual May Day celebrations on 1st May, 1998 noted that *"the prevailing impasse within the country's labour movement occasioned by government's continued clampdown on the central labour organization in the last four years between 1994-98 eroded any reason or causes workers may have to celebrate."* Corroborating this, the Deputy General Secretary of the National Union of Petroleum and Gas Workers (NUPENG), Elijah Okoro, stated that *"the central labour organization had not survived after two decades as the NLC and the country's entire labour movement are under chains and in distress."* It is interesting to know that Frank Ovie Kokori, the National Secretary of NUPENG, and Dabiri, the President, who have been in detention since 1994 for choosing to defend the assault on civil society by the military, were only recently released.

The Press was equally gagged. The Buhari regime enacted Decree No. 4 in 1984 which convicted Messrs Tunde Thompson and Nduka Irabor who were imprisoned for the earlier cited offence. Babangida returned with a chain of decrees all aimed at muzzling the press and distracting it from the function of serving as the watch dog. First it was the offensive Publications (Proscription) Decree 35 of 1995, and then the Newspaper Decree 43 of 1993 which proscribed about 10 publications, established the Newspapers Registration Board (NRB) and stipulated stringent registration requirements for newspapers and magazines. It also initiated a policy of disbursement of huge amounts of money to the NUJ as part of the 'settlement' culture. This practice was to reach extreme magnitude during the tenure of Mallam Sanni Zorro when it was alleged that NUJ operated as a department of government. Abacha was to continue this policy. In July 1995, the Newspapers Registration Board resurrected in the new garb of constitutional Decree 107 which empowered the Federal Military Government to make laws for the federation or any part thereof with respect to the registration of newspapers and magazines published or printed in Nigeria. The total yearly registration fee of ₦350,000 and penalties ranging from ₦50,000 to ₦200,000 and prison terms of two to ten years were also invoked in the decree. Unable to pay, many print media have been compelled to shut down, journalists thrown out of job and the few media houses which managed to pay increased their production costs which were ultimately passed to the public. This does not guarantee cheap, free flow of information and the civil society which ought to be continually informed is the worse for it. There were more journalists in detention under the Abacha administration than at any other time in the history of Nigeria.

The Nigerian Medical Association, vocal and sometimes radical, has been active in defense of civil liberties and people's right to decent health care in Nigeria up until the 1980s. Its strong place as a bulwark of civil society earned it much trouble when a member of the association, Dr Emmanuel Nsan, Minister for Health, was used by the Buhari regime to humiliate the association. Its strike action to attract attention to the poor state of facilities in hospitals resulted in mass sacking of doctors, threat of eviction from their official residences and proscription of the NMA.

In 1992 Gen. I. B. Babangida donated the sum of ₦20 million to enable the association construct a secretariat for itself and the Confederation of African Medical Association and Societies (CAMAS) at Abuja. Many considered this part of his way of buying the loyalty of possible opposition groups. The money which was allegedly mismanaged by the Boniface Oyediran-led executive led to a split in the association which the regime exploited. The present administration continued in this resolve to weaken the ranks of the doctors with the last NMA elections. According to one of the contestants for the post of President, Dr Kitchener, the outgoing President sponsored a certain Dr Okpagu to succeed him and then went ahead to employ methods considered unethical by some colleagues towards realising this ambition. Figures seemed manipulated. Due processes were said to have been subverted in the elections, leading to the emergence of two factions – Lagos and Abuja. The Abacha government in utter disregard for the sanctity of the constitutional requirements of the NMA went ahead to recognize the Abuja faction. It was in the light of this that the Lagos faction petitioned that the recent discord in the NMA was a calculated ploy by the government to decapitate their body.

In the educational sector, ASSU, the Association for Senior Staff of Universities, has been proscribed several times from the Babangida era to the Abacha regime. Dissident groups have been sponsored on campuses to break the rank and file of the university lecturers and, only recently, in 1997, the National Universities Commission (NUC) on the orders of the military government directed vice-chancellors to enforce the no work, no pay system for striking lecturers.

As this denigration of civil society has persisted so has the socio-economic fortunes of the country dipped. The level of uncertainty that is associated with weakened civil society has affected the competitive terrain with obvious consequences.

This history of military suppression of civil society in Nigeria is a consequence of the military's quest for legitimizing attributes. Without the legitimacy that flows from convention, for a monarchy or the ballot box, the military often use surrogates such as support by traditional rulers (an art abused and perfected during the Abacha years) and appointment of well-known politicians to the cabinet (Gowon in the crises of 1966). They also depend on 'negative legitimacy,' that is to say, legitimacy that flows from how much you can show what is unacceptable in the group you forced out; and on keeping alternative perspectives out of the terrain of the public domain. This constant pursuit of a basic need for all governments' legitimacy, in the absence of following established convention, means pressure for the state to dominate and exclude from public space.

The Evolution of Business in Nigeria's Civil Society Under Military Rule

The business associations in Nigeria have never managed, even in their own very narrow self-interest, to be as strident as the Nigerian Medical Association or the Trade Unions. Several reasons can be adduced for the character of the organized private sector which makes it less threatening to the military. First, the private sector has been largely dominated by multinational companies and alien entrepreneurs who have limited commitment to the long term interests of the country. In addition, the indigenous private sector is characterized by weak levels of capital accumulation which leads to a tendency to be much dependent on government support through policies. Also a factor is the fact that government is such a dominant actor in the economy that most of the private sector, local and foreign, relies heavily on government contracts. The fear of the loss of these opportunities tends to make business associations much less aggressive (Utomi, 1994).

To a large extent, therefore, the public domain as it concerns business and economic activity remained largely uncontested with the state until the middle 1980s. A conference on an enabling environment for private sector participation in national development which took place in Nairobi under the aegis of the Aga Khan foundation promoted the idea of a tripatite approach to development in which government, the private sector and private development agencies (NGOs) cooperated to make room for private sector facilitation of development and gave venue to the new initiative. Those returning from the conference, including the Nigerian-born Chief Executive of a multinational company, a cabinet minister, and NGO chiefs convened an enabling environment conference. The Summits of the Enabling Environment Forum (EEF), as it came to be known, provided the momentum to politely engage the state in this arena (Utomi, 1998). This movement in a sense, spawned the Nigerian Economic Summit Group which was birthed when co-chairman of the EEF, Chief Ernest Shonekan, became the head of the transitional government of Nigeria in 1993 and convened a Nigerian Economic Summit. The Nigerian Economic Summit was different from the EEF Summits only in the sense that the public sector profile increased because the convener was the head of government. After a second NES the frame was set for what became the Vision 2010 project.

The Vision 2010 project was to bring a broad group from the society, government and foreign business and diplomatic interest together in a year-long effort to construct a *modus vivendi* for Nigeria, borrowing from the visioning efforts of East Asian countries like Malaysia which has its Vision 2020 project.

Conclusion

In the foregoing effort we have tried to put the increasing attention being received by civil society in Africa in context so as to explain the role the business community has played in the contest for public space in African countries. An analysis of the state of voluntarism and contestation of the public domain with the state in post-colonial Africa led us to conclude that in some countries business associations are becoming more active in the public domain because it is in their strategic interest to do so. This increased quest for part of the public space has been generally less antagonistic towards the state than that of other voluntary associations such as human rights groups. This is largely because of the nature of the private sector and what they stand to lose should government develop a hostile attitude towards them. In some cases these new business associations have become sub-regional, strengthening the capacity of the private sector to act both in terms of learning from colleagues from more liberal environment and from the fact of a stronger support base. The West African Enterprise Network, including a new generation of entrepreneurs and not incorporating the multinationals, is an example of this new model. This trend should lead to a pattern of evolution of institutions that will eventually reduce uncertainty and produce an enabling environment for growth in economic activity.

References

Asiodu, Phillip. "Civil Servants as Economic Managers" in *Essays on Nigerian Political Economy* (Lagos, Sankore Publishers, 1993) p. 404.

Ayida, Allison. "The Federal Civil Service and Nation Building" reproduced in *Reflection on Nigerian Development* (London, Malthouse Press, 1987) p. 38.

Aryectectey, Ernest, Hemamala Hettige, Machiko Nissanke and William Steel. "Financial Market Fragmentation and Reforms in Ghana, Malawi, Nigeria and Tanzania" in *The World Bank Economic Review*, Vol 11, No. 2 (May, 1977).

Azarya, V. "Civil Society and Disengagement in Africa" in (J.W. Harbeson et al, eds) *Civil Society and the State in Africa* (Boulder and London, Rienner, 1994).

Barkan, J.D. "Resurrecting Modernization Theory and the Emergence of Civil Society in Kenya and Nigeria" in (D.E Apter and G. Rosberg, eds) *Political Development and the New Realism in Sub-Saharan Africa.*

Barnes, S.T. "Voluntary Associations in a Metropolis: The Case of Lagos, Nigeria" in *African Studies Review* (18: 2: 1975).

Bayat, A. "Uncivil Society in Africa: The Politics of the Informal People" in

Third World Quarterly, Vol. 18, No. 1, 1997.

Bayat, J.F. "Civil Society in Africa" in (Chabal, ed) *Political Domination in Africa* (New York, Cambridge University Press, 1986).

Bratton, M. "Beyond the State: Civil Society and Associational Life in Africa" in *World Politics* (41:3:1989).

Dia, Mamadou. *Africa's Management in the 1990's and Beyond: Reconciling Indigenous and Transplanted Institutions* (Washington D.C., The World Bank, 1996).

Diamond, Larry. "Nigeria: The Uncivic Society and the Descent into Pretorianism" in (Larry Diamond, Juan J. Linz and Seymour Martin Lipset (eds.) second edition) *Politics in Developing Countries: Comparing Experiences with Democracy.* (Boulder, Lynne Reinne Publishers, 1995) pp. 460-461.

Fatton, R., Jnr. "African in the Age of Democratization: The Civic Limitations of Civil Society" in *African Studies Review* (38: 2 1995).

Forrest, Tom. *The Advance of African Capital* (Charlottesville, University Press of Virginia, 1994).

Illife, John. *The Emergence of African Capitalism* (Great Britain, The University of Minnesota Press, 1983).

Israel, Arturo. *Institutional Development: Incentives to Performance, A World Bank Publication* (Baltimore, The John Hopkins University Press, 1987) pp. 24&26.

Jeune Afrique "Les Affaires au Senegal: les Senegalais s'absentent" No. 494 (23 June 1970: 50).

Knack, Stephen and Philip Keefer. "Institutions and Economic Performance: Cross Country Tests Using Alternative Institutional Measures" in *Economics and Politics* (November, 1995).

Miles, W.F. "Decolonization as Disintegration: The Disestablishment of the State in Chad" in *Journal of Asian and Africa Studies* (30: 1 1995).

Ndegwa, S.N. *The Two Faces of Civil Society: NGO's and the Politics in Africa* (West Watford, Kumarian Press, 1996).

Nelson, Robert and Howard Wolpe. *Nigeria: Modernisation and the Politics of Communalism* (East Lansing; Michigan State University Press, 1971) p. 127.

North, Douglas. *Institutions, Institutional Change and Economic Performance* (New York, Cambridge University Press, 1990) p. 54.

Okigbo, Pius. "Management of the Nigerian Economy 1960-1980" in *Essay in the Public Philosophy of Development* (Enugu, Fourth Dimension Publishers, 1991) p. 127.

Osaghae, E. "The Role of Civil Society in Consolidating Democracy: An African Comparative Perspective" in *Africa Insight.* (27: 1 1997).

Siddiqui, R. (ed) *Sub-Saharan Africa in the 1990s: Challenges to Democracy and Development* (Westport, Conn., Praeger, 1997).

UNIGES "Rapport General du Premier Congres," Dakar (1 June, 1968).

Utomi, Patrick. *Managing Uncertainty: Competition and Strategy in Emerging Economies* (Ibadan, Spectrum Books, 1998).

Utomi, Patrick. "Institutions and the Evolution of Competition in the Nigerian Banking Industry" in *LBS Management Review,* Vol. 1, No. 2, July – December 1996.

Wildavsky, A. *Politics of the Budgetary Process* (Boston, Little, Brown & Co., 1979).

5

The Future of Manufacturing in Nigeria*

I am quite pleased to be with you all at your AGM. I have been asked to share some of my thoughts on the future of manufacturing in Nigeria at this meeting.

I will try to discuss the subject first by looking at how the Nigerian economy has evolved in the last four decades and the place manufacturing has had in this turbulent history. Next I will look at the biggest challenges manufacturing has faced so far in Nigeria. After this we will explore some strategies for coping with these challenges in Nigeria. In exploring coping with the challenges of manufacturing in the experience of industrialization, we should draw from experience in our host city, Nnewi. We will then turn to the impact of globalization on Nigerian manufacturing. Finally, we will draw on the consequence of changing corporate scope to hazard a guess on the future of manufacturing in Nigeria.

Manufacturing in the History of the Nigerian Political Economy

I will present it as briefly as possible. We all know that until the early part of this century our economies in what became Nigeria were peasant subsistence agriculture economies. Colonial trade needs of the British led us to cash crops and then by the late 1950s, as self government came, the development needs of the country began to be defined by the regional governments in terms of location of manufacturing activity. The Ikeja industrial estate was to become the symbolic pioneer of this thrust of public policy.

Even as industry was attracting the attention of governments, the regional governments through the marketing boards continued to pursue agricultural commodity exports. All of this effort added up to a steady 3.2 percent growth in the Gross Domestic Product between 1956 and 1966 before the civil war.

After the civil war, oil was in ascendancy. Production increased dramatically as did oil prices. By 1973 the Arab-Israeli Yom Kippur War

---

*Address to the AGM Manufacturers' Association of Nigeria (Anambra State Branch) on 9/5/97

produced the oil embargo and resulted in the quadrupling of oil prices.

Nigeria was in the oil boom age. These boom proceeds were translated into consumption power for the citizens through schemes like the Udoji Awards. This retroactive increase of salaries and the huge arrears paid to workers meant consumer items would move quickly off the shelves. At this same time, government also channelled some of its windfall into an import substitution industrialization strategy by setting up State Owned Enterprises (SOE) or joint ventures in manufacturing to assemble some of the hitherto imported items.

When oil prices crashed, Structural Adjustment became inevitable. A consequence of SAP has been that many ISI manufacturing enterprises proved not to be competitive. The struggle between protecting industry to give it room to grow and liberalizing to make the country more attractive for more appropriate investments in manufacturing and elsewhere have gripped policy makers and various interested parties.

Challenges Facing Manufacturers in Nigeria

Among the often cited problems facing manufacturers in Nigeria are inconsistency of government policy, confused taxation philosophy, poor state of infrastructure and collapsing purchasing power in the economy. Not often mentioned but equally critical is the competence level of manufacturers and how they develop the capacity for managing around their environment and build up ladders of opportunity that will enable them beat some odds that seem stacked up against them.

The matter of inconsistency of government policy comes at us from tariff policy to the problems of planning based on what will or will not happen to the exchange rate and sometimes what is lawful to produce or not, if you recall the experience of the pharmaceutical industry in trying to cope with the sudden appearance of the Essential Drugs List (EDL). What we can do on that score is try to expand the scope of dialogue between the private sector and government. Clearly the Vision 2010 project and the Nigerian Economic Summit Group along with the Enabling Environment Forum have been helping to improve things in this area.

On confusion in tax policy, I know you all have had to struggle with either billboard taxes that are applied at the whims of the official involved or with sales vans being requested to pay billboard taxes in several local governments they drive through. Failure to coordinate tax policy has no doubt frustrated manufacturers. When I served in the National Council of MAN, we spent much time on this issue with Alhaji Hassan Adamu always promising to get better feedback from the Vice President, Admiral Augustus Aikhomu.

Infrastructure deficiencies are immense in Nigeria. A World Bank study that compares infrastructure deficiencies in Nigeria with those of Indonesia and Thailand show that 92 percent of Nigerian firms had their own generator, compared with 6 percent in Thailand and 66 percent in Indonesia.

This situation adds to the On-Cost of manufacturing and makes Nigeria less attractive to manufacture in. Given declining purchasing power in the population, it means that goods made in Thailand will clearly be more competitively priced than those in Nigeria even if the local managers are equally competent.

This brings us to the challenge of growing poverty. I have noticed with mixed feelings the new spate of talk about poverty. A year or two ago, I complained very much about the fact that poverty was mushrooming into a major growth industry in Nigeria and policy-makers carried on as if there was nothing happening. I am happy in returning from having been away for a while and finding discussion programmes on television about poverty. With Vision 2010 officials also pointing to the issue of poverty, I should be thrilled that my shouts of fire have caught on but I am also worried that there is a glamorization of the subject because I can see little relationships between the new concern for poverty and the policy choices being made by government. A true concern for poverty, it would be seen to me, would have meant a quick implementation of a programme of settling debts to local contractors by government. This would put more money in the pockets of many ordinary people who can spend in ways that will move inventories currently rising up to the ceiling in many warehouses of manufacturers. I also notice that the spending patterns of the big source of flow of cash from government into the economy, the PTF, has still been narrow in channelling resources. My feeling about narrowly channelled money is that a few get what has been saved off most of us. The recirculation that is lost affects the momentum of the economy. This is worse if such beneficiaries have businesses that tend to hit the Fx markets and the money exits the economy.

The challenge that is hardly ever talked about is that of the managerial capacity: our own limitations as managers and the passion for sustaining effort in the face of adversity in an environment with so many different sources of social pressures. Simply put, the environment manages many of us instead of the other way round.

Strategies for Coping with the Challenges

One of the big challenges we have identified is the poor state of infrastructure in Nigeria. How do we as manufacturers overcome infrastructure difficulties? Different coping strategies exist around the world. Of particular interest should be cooperative production of infrastructure where the private sector in effect substitutes for the state. My friend Deborah Braughtigham who has studied industrialization in Nnewi suggests that there is quite a bit of that going on here. Experience from Asia also indicates that a resource like electrical power can be generated and production in excess of need sold to neighbours. Under current Nigerian law this is not allowed. Manufacturers can, however, pursue dialogue for a variant of this to be accepted.

I have for long advocated that we pursue industrial development along the lines of economic zones of development with industry clusters tied around the comparative advantage of five or six zones of development allowing for focussed investment in infrastructure. This could be done in partnership between the private sector and government, using Build Operate and Transfer (BOT) schemes to fund optimum levels of infrastructure to service the industry clusters in these zones of development.

Manufacturers can cope better by increasing the level of cooperation in non-competitive areas. Presently, it is easy for a government that is too short-sighted to recognize the need for partnership with the private sector to divide and rule the so-called organized private sector. The benefit to maintaining a united front in dealing with government can be immense.

Let me also address the business of coping with the frustration with industry linkages. I know the difficulty some automobile parts producers faced in trying to supply local assembly plants. Let me dare say we can better cope if we know the KRA of the other party.

Globalization and Nigerian Manufacturing

We live in a rapidly changing and rapidly shrinking world. The powers of telecommunications and computing have meant that business competition is defined in global terms. This has had its effect already in the de-industrialization of some sectors of the Nigerian economy. The idea of globalization may sound like highfalutin academic and new frontiers business idea. I dare to say this at this forum only because I know that many of you have had your learning on manufacturing shaped in global industries. The man who began to import spare parts from France, found a cheaper source in Taiwan, then learnt to make it from the Taiwanese and now produces the parts for customers across West Africa is initiated into globalization. The only thing I want to point attention to is that matters of production quality, what to produce and the plant size that is appropriate will have to be conceptualized beyond national boundary terms if we are to be efficient and to produce quality that will allow us a decent share of the market.

Is There a Future for Manufacturing in Nigeria?

Many anxious and frustrated manufacturers are asking this question. But allow me to use the experience of the UAC group in textiles and the subject of corporate scope and policy shocks to illustrate. The UAC group once had nearly a third of its profits coming from textiles but had no investment in manufacturing textiles. As adjustment came and the manufacturers began to commit more heavily through backward integration those who were in more flexible arrangements like UACN began to lose market share. It should also be a useful lesson that the Churchgate group which is arguably the fastest growing conglomerate in Nigeria is heavily into manufacturing. I suspect that we will find that their fortunes have held up better than similar enterprises that are more trading focussed.

There is no question that trading is a good entry point and good quick cash source if you have the competence for it. In the final analysis, failure to migrate upward into manufacturing will cost you dearly. So let me assure those of you in manufacturing that you have chosen well. Nothing good comes easy. This is why you must commit more time and energy to developing a clear vision of what you want to be in manufacturing and then assiduously develop the knowledge that will help you build the strategy to take you to the point of your manufacturing dream. Your passion for getting there should translate into how you motivate those you are leading in the firm, without them you cannot reach this promised land.

I am sure you can do it. You must be determined to circumnavigate all the obstacles that will no doubt come your way. The relish of the success at the end of the road should keep you going. My sincere good wishes go with you as you rise to the challenges.

6

Nigeria's Agenda in the Age of Globalization

Globalization is the buzz word of the times. Few are those who avoid it these days. But many are they who really do not understand it. Understand it or not, globalization will impact on the quality of life we achieve, the peace and stability of our environment and our sense of relevance in a new millennium that is but a breath away.

In its simplest form globalization is about a process of integration of economies of the world. The process is driven by an information and communication revolution that first seems like cultural dominance as Hollywood entered and set the values agenda of most of the people of the planet. The convergence of three streams of technology – computing, telecommunications and broadcasting – was to ensure that the once farfetched, almost science fiction, global village had become reality. The dramatic drop in the cost of transportation, extraordinary productivity gains brought on by technology and the collapse of the great ideology wall or iron curtain when Mikail Gorbachev began a process that developed its own momentum and consumed the Soviet Union were to ensure the inevitability of globalization.

In the main the globalization debate has raged between those who see in it opportunities for economic growth and more efficient markets and those who see a distinct disadvantage for the late starters such as African countries. More subtle but lurking somewhere in the debate is the recognition that corporate globalization will result in the erosion of state powers, a scenario in which the presidents of powerful nations will have little power in relation to Chief Executive Officers of the super corporations of the world whose quotations on Stock Exchanges in several continents mean that they have no national loyalties as such.

Such are things that it is harder and harder to imagine any country objectively opting out of global economic integration – what with China, one of those with endowments that make autarky more imaginable, now systematically entering the world market. Our challenge should be to draw up an agenda which Nigeria must focus on if it is not to be a big loser from globalization. An agenda for approaching the age of globalization should of necessity include the following priorities: creating an information and communications technology penetration strategy; managing economic fundamentals right, especially with regard to the impact of public sector spending; building up institutions to ensure a level playing field for businesses and transparency in government conduct; reforming the educational system; developing the capacity for investment promotion; developing the ability to match capital flows with economic fundamentals to avoid the kind of crisis South East Asia fell into; building a disposition towards global thinking in indigenous entrepreneurs; promoting national reputation professionally; and facilitating regional economic integration.

These items are too numerous and all deserving a more detailed exploration than the limited space for this discussion allows. I will therefore expand on only a few. An appropriate beginning is the state of Information and Communication Technology in Nigeria(ICT). Low purchasing power caused by years of bad economic choices by governments and failure to implement a policy that truly acknowledges the dependence of the new age on computers has, sadly, made the availability of computers in Nigeria sparse. The development of Information and Communication Technology is further hampered by the failure to fully deregulate communications, making NITEL more of a blockage to Nigeria's entry into the information age than a facilitator of it. When I have attended global knowledge conferences abroad, it has always been a matter of embarrassment that Nigeria lags far behind poorer African countries in ICT penetration. It is now time to take a strategic view of ICT at the national policy making level. The consequence would be that at department levels such as NITEL, ministry of education or of science and technology, we can align policy to ensure computer literacy, availability of personal computers to most people and training in micro-processing for our engineers. I have made several proposals in this regard to people who could influence policy. So far, I have seen nothing encouraging.

One of the consequences of easy information flow and cheap transportation costs is that companies locate where production is most efficiently carried on. With the Uruguay round of GATT and the World Trade Organization, the barriers that could keep them from shipping those products into less efficient countries have tumbled. This is unlike the 1960s when you located more or less where there was a market. This generally means the availability of infrastructure, knowledge workers, political stability etc, and shipping from there to anywhere in the world. The already obvious effect on us is the process of de-industrialization that has set in in several sectors. To stem this trend and make integration positive, we have to deal with our infrastructure shortcomings and keep our economic fundamentals aligned to global trends.

Nigerian entrepreneurs are in short supply. In the private enterprise-driven global order, we need to encourage entrepreneurs, seek them out, support them and celebrate their successes. Here I mean hard-working risk-takers, not rent-seeking people driven more by a desire for money to burn and egos to massage than by a vision of empires they could build. If we build an indigenous entrepreneurial class, we have to educate them that the Nigerian market is not their entire universe. They need a global mentality and the Internet can dramatically reduce the cost of their going global.

On the financial front, it is important to note that the speed with which capital flows can take place today constitutes both an advantage and a disadvantage. To be able to manage that process and also to fund and encourage a certain balance between foreign direct investment and portfolio investment is critical to making a success of integration. We can identify in the example of the crisis in South East Asia some problems deriving from capital flows. Once the good news is out on an economy, capital inflow can build up to a surge. If the financial system is not adequately developed you could suddenly have a lot of easy lending to real estate development, for example, until you reach a point where supply cannot be justified by demand and commitments cannot be quickly amortized as in Thailand. This can also lead to a situation where managers of the economy take their eyes off the current account situation as they slide into deficit. This can happen because of the flow portfolio money that can make a quick exit. This is what happened in Malaysia resulting in the plunging of the Ringgit.

The pace of activities in information economies is such that bureaucratic responses make countries uncompetitive. To be competitive in a global economy means that civil service reform, privatization of the holdings of the state in areas that could be better managed by private enterprises, should move forward quickly. It is certainly a peculiar irony that at this stage bureaucrats anxious for power are holding back education by inventing all kinds of administrative laws to control things. Here power is a substitute for purpose.

To conclude this summary review of agenda items for Nigeria as we contemplate the inevitability of globalization, it is useful to make a point about reputation management. Nigeria has for many years had a reputation which has hurt its prospects for growth and development. Sometimes the reputation is deserved. Most times it is unearned. The challenge of those who lead Nigeria is not only to strive to eliminate the sources of that bad reputation such as coups, civil disturbances, 419 or advance fee fraud, corruption, security etc., but also to manage what is said about Nigeria. Poor management of how we are perceived has been the biggest source of damage to Nigeria's reputation. This is the reason any perceptive person cannot but praise enough the recent travels of General Abdulsalami Abubakar and his openness and availability as he travelled. It is only a starting point up a long hard road.

7

Thriving in Nigeria's Chaos*

That the business environment in Nigeria has been unstable and somewhat chaotic for many years has by now become a cliché. The manifestations range from high inflation and other macroeconomic dysfunctions to frequent unpredictable changes in tariff and tax policy, and a general reward system that tends to encourage sharp practices. So deep in the character of the Nigerian economy in the 1980s and 1990s have these manifestations become that reform-minded pressure groups have blossomed into a major growth industry with the Nigerian Economic Summit (NES) group and the Enabling Environment Forum (EEF) being among the better focussed enablers. Yet quite a number of enterprises across sectors of the economy continue to sustain a tradition of superior competitive performance, earning enviable return on investment even as some environment-wearied multinationals divest.

This essay drawing from our on-going research essentially strives to identify the basis of success of these superior performers, suggesting that success in a scenario of continuing crisis, or thriving in chaos, is to a large extent a function of learning systems that allow entrepreneurial and empowered managers to consistently spot opportunities and extract value in a short period of time without losing the focus of long term strategy. We are also concerned here with how rapid change is managed by these firms who thrive in chaos and the possibility of identifying the best practice in their managerial approaches. We should perhaps begin by setting the context of the uncertainty environment.

The Current Business Climate

We can group the external issues that dominate business decision-making in Nigeria today around macroeconomic issues, political issues, policy process issues and consumer confidence issues.

---

*Part of a course in Social and Political Environment Business, Lagos Business School

Perhaps the highlight of macroeconomic management in Nigeria in 1995 was a significant improvement in the management of inflation through tight monetary policy and the stepping down of deficit spending even if the effect of the policy approach on some government obligations and stimulating the economy has been questioned. This one step forward follows in the history of many two steps backward and a few one step forward in economic management. A decade earlier, price control was in place as a means of fighting inflation. True to tradition, the policy only managed to transfer profits to middle men and politically connected brokers who earned substantial rent while producers suffered losses and struggled, often without success, to convince price control authorities of a preferred fair price.

The inflationary trend that Nigeria faced in the middle 1980s was directly related to the Dutch disease, the phenomenon in which a country's rapidly rising earnings from a mineral commodity lead to budgetary expansion and then the price of the commodity collapses, forcing contraction. When oil prices collapsed, the marked characteristic of Nigeria's response was artificially maintaining a high exchange rate, ostensibly to protect the living standard of the middle class (Utomi, 1995). This opened up such a gap between the exchange rate and the country's purchasing power parity that it was clear it could not sustain import demand. Failure of the Central Bank of Nigeria to honour due trade debt led to frozen credit lines from correspondent banks of Nigeria banks. Import licensing which was used to ration scarce foreign exchange became a celebrated path to the extraction of Ricardian rent by the well connected.[1] So deeply rooted were these habits that a significant feature of economic life in Nigeria today is the intellectual energy invested in seeking opportunity for rent in most policy issues.

Austerity measures soon followed the 1980s oil price collapse as did a major effort at countertrade, especially with Brazil. Countertrade proved inefficient and ridden with anomalies that resulted in a panel of inquiry that probed the programme. Inevitably a Structural Adjustment Programme (SAP) came in 1986. By 1989 the yield of SAP was single

---

[1] Annual reports of companies from 1984 and 1985 are replete with frustration at the import licence process that was corruption-ridden.

digit inflation, nominal GDP per capita growth rate in excess of 5 percent per annum and a process of privatization and deregulation that unleashed entrepreneurial energies, turning quiet residential streets in Lagos into high streets such as Awolowo Road in Ikoyi, Allen Avenue in Ikeja, and Adeniran Ogunsanya Street in Surulere. In the name of giving SAP a human face, policy had by 1990/91 turned to profligacy with huge budget deficits in spite of the windfall from oil sales during the Gulf War in 1991. The twin challenges of inflation and recession returned with inflation exceeding 100 percent in 1994.

The stagflation of the 1990s has been made worse by the difficulty of reading the sincerity of the military whose transition programmes have produced one annulled presidential election, a leadership vacuum, political violence and much instability. On the other hand, the human rights record of the military has earned Nigeria the status of a global pariah.

At the same time as the business community has had to deal with problems arising from a seemingly endless political logjam, it has had to cope with erratic policy decisions by ministers whose short and unpredictable tenures leave business struggling to recover from one policy choice when another follows. In the wake of policy process reforms of the 1980s, cabinet ministers empowered as accounting officers of their ministries often made major policy decisions with marginal input from the bureaucracy as one of our case studies of the pharmaceutical industry, and the essential drug list (EDL) cited below, illustrates. The effect of military rule on the public choice process was the absence of rigour in the policy process and the loss of the benefits of complex redundancy which democratic regimes provide for public choice (Wildavsky, 1979). These days policy process uncertainty is so pervasive that nobody can tell when the annual budget of the federal government on which most private sector planning is based will be made public.

The climate of business is also characterized by issues of consumer confidence. Bank failures and general instability of the financial system,[2]

---

[2] Bank distress between 1994 and 1996 had such severe consequences that a draconian decree to "sanitize" the industry has resulted in one of the biggest abuses of human rights in recent memory.

and consumer confidence in the prospects of the economy, combine with weak confidence by many executives in the economy to create a soft platform for strong business performance.[3]

Odds Beaters

Unalluring as the business climate described above seems, there are companies that have consistently beaten the odds, returning an above average return on investment consistently. We have picked a sample of some of these companies from different sectors to illustrate the best practices that allow them to thrive in the chaotic environment of uncertainty from which some of their rivals have been divesting in frustration. Among these companies are Nigerian Breweries Plc which for some years has been the ultimate blue chip in the Nigerian stock market, from a sector that has shrunk from 1983 position of 22 brewing companies with 34 breweries and 46 brands of lager to one in which there are basically two majors and less than ten regional and marginal players. From banking we have chosen the Investment Banking and Trust Company (IBTC), Guaranty Trust Bank, Owena Bank, Citizens International Bank and Nigeria International Bank (the Citibank affiliate in which Citibank is currently seeking full control) and from pharmaceuticals, Glaxo, Pfizer and Sterling Health (recently acquired by Smithkline Beecham in the global restructuring of the industry). From agrochemicals we have chosen a very entrepreneurial mid-size company, Candel.

The strong banking sector representation in this sample essentially underlines the reality of the biggest growth in the economy in recent times coming from the expansion of active players in banking following SAP - inspired deregulation of the banking sector which reduced a major barrier to entry– licensing of new banks. The inclusion of Owena Bank, emerging as a dramatic case of organizational transformation, provides deep insights into how management practice affects performance.

[3.] A survey of chief executives attending the 1995 Chie Executives Programme at the Lagos Business School (CEP IV) indicates little confidence in economic prospects. One respondent to the question on potential growh areas in the economy suggested Crime Management and Religion as very high prospects.

Examples from pharmaceuticals have also been selected because few sectors so visibly portray the trend of divestment from Nigeria as the pharmaceutical sector. That Pfizer and Glaxo have brought in new investments from abroad in recent years marked them out as sources of practices that enable them flow against the current. These companies are part of a larger pool we have been tracking in an on-going research at LBS that is trying to identify the impact of public policy on competing and changing industry structure in five trade sectoral groups in the Nigerian economy.

Lessons From Thrivers

The many lessons that we can learn from the management practices in these 'thriver' firms that overcome challenges of extreme uncertainty have been grouped under the following headings: unceasing environment scan; tracking shifting dissatisfaction gap; unlearning, and learning investment and uncertainty; values, strategy and short term opportunities; obsessive questing across the value chain; human resources and strategy fit; flexible organization structure; and, generally, more open internal communication philosophy, and the leadership style that focus on the long term and values while capturing short term opportunity.

Unceasing Environment Scan

The axiomatic proposition that an organization is bound for extinction if the rate of learning in the organization is not equal to or greater than the rate of change in the environment (Garrat, 1990) is perhaps most apt for an environment where the place of idiosyncrasies in policy formulation is extremely high, and the tenure of policy makers marked by unusually quick turnover,[4] and changes of feeling by incumbents, as illustrated by the following story. While explaining the 1995 budget the finance minister who had just announced the lifting of the ban on importation of rice got a note slipped to him before a huge audience of businessmen and television cameras and very matter-of-factly told his

---

[4] Most Nigerian ministries have had an average of one minister a year since independence. Departing World Bank Resident Representative in 1995, Mr Gerald Flood, remarked at his farewell reception that he had had the privilege of working with six finance ministers in three years.

audience that the presidential villa had just informed him of a change of mind regarding rice importation. Firms that are unable to quickly identify emerging policy shift in this kind of setting, through a strong capacity for environment scanning and interpretation of policy process dynamics, miss opportunities and sometimes make commitments that result in their death. The pharmaceutical industry paid a high price for a weak capacity to scan the environment when erstwhile health minister, Professor Olikoye Ransome-Kuti's attraction to socialized medicine resulted in an Essential Drug List (EDL) decree in 1989 that limited to a list of mainly generic products the drugs that pharmaceutical firms could distribute. One chief executive in the industry found out about the forthcoming decree when, on a casual visit to the Ministry of Health, a director there said there was this decree that seemed to be somewhere in the pipeline. It was soon law and many of the pharmaceutical companies found themselves with stock that had become illegal. The industry suffered a loss of 300 million as a result of being unprepared. The effect of the EDL was to accelerate the industry's restructuring which has been marked by the exit of several key players.

The pharmaceutical industry has since improved its capacity for scanning the environment with key players like Pfizer and Glaxo/Evans committing more executive time to this objective. It is not surprising that when a new minister of health, Dr D. Tafida, tried to return to the EDL as a maximum list concept which had been formally abandoned in 1993 after it had done severe damage to many pharmaceutical companies, the industry made a preemptive move, threatening even to go to court. The minister backed off.

Tracking Shifting Dissatisfaction Gap

In venturing, a clear source of entrepreneurial opportunity is in the gap between the desired level of satisfaction of customers and the service offered by the lead performers among existing competitors in that market area. In an environment of frequently shifting policies that affect markets rather significantly, sometimes dramatically, the dissatisfaction gap is shifting all the time. Superior performers have to be able to track the shift and redefine the essence of competition by offering products and services that close the gap for customers.

Banking provides a good illustration. In 1987 lending and savings rates were deregulated. By 1991 the growth in lending rates had resulted in regulation of lending and deposit rates, which were deregulated again in 1992. Interest caps meant that companies that needed to borrow to buy foreign exchange went from developing skills for off-the-book negotiation of interest rates under interest cap regimes to assessing market response to prices in a time of astronomical growth of interest rates following interest rate deregulation. Some banks like the Nigerian Intercontinental Merchant Bank (NIMB), taking advantage of its flexible organization structure, sought quick feedback that tracked shifting customer-needs and quickly offered new products to satisfy the new need.

In the early days of deregulation, some banks such as IMB quickly responded to the shifting dissatisfaction gap by offering customized products including futures deals. As IMB was weakened by internal management problems following Ebitimi Banigo's departure from the CEO position, this responsiveness was more notably a feature of the Intercontinental Merchant Bank where flexible structures were deliberately aimed at quickly capturing opportunities.

In the airline business, the long monopoly of Nigeria Airways was marked by the uncertainty of passengers as to whether they would arrive at their destination the day they had planned to. The dissatisfaction gap stood out clearly when entry barriers were lowered with deregulation of the industry. Okada moved quickly to fill this gap, building a reputation in the late 1980s and early 90s for gutsy flying in testy weather conditions, while weather was the perennial excuse for operational delays by Nigeria Airways. Okada established advantage by just "getting people there," even though the aircraft in the fleet were old and the cabins very shabby. The dissatisfaction shifted to shabby cabins and discomfort with the safety of the aging fleet once people got used to getting there nearly on time. ADC responded to this gap with cleaner cabins, better on-time arrivals and departures and more reliable reservation systems. Even with Bellview striving to raise standards, ADC has continued to migrate down the value chain, filling gaps like transportation from city points to the airport and back for their passengers in cities where the airports are not adequately or are too exorbitantly serviced by ground transportation providers.

Unlearning, Learning Investment and Uncertainty

Past success can be a major hindrance to creativity and organizational innovation. In very few circumstances is this as critical as when uncertainty underlines the nature of the environment. Let us draw illustrations from the banking industry. During the season of *laissez-faire* in Nigerian banking which peaked in the 1940s and 1950s, up to 20 indigenous banks were established and all but one failed within two years of opening their doors for business. The 1952 Banking Ordinance began to restore order. This process was consolidated by the CBN Act of 1958 and the 1969 Banking Act. These marked the beginning of supervisory and regulatory effort that provided a stable oligopolistic industry cordoned off by the high entry barriers of licensing.

When deregulation came in 1986 new banks introduced practices of service excellence that resulted in a flight of deposits from the big banks to the new ones. Significant in this 'flight to quality' was pace of learning in the new banks and the problems of unlearning in the old banks. Guaranty Trust Bank, one of the 'thrivers,' was clearly committed to activating new knowledge and socializing this knowledge into the culture of the firm. This is evident from the fact that Guaranty Trust Bank was at the top of the list of companies committing resources for developing their staff at the Lagos Business School, and in the fact that the chief executive and other executives rotated through work at the counters of the banking hall. In so doing they reinforced learnt behaviour, showing how to pursue service excellence and reinforcing the value of the dignity of every job.

This learning in the focussed new banks, which resulted in new products and process flow improvements for enhanced service delivery, was met in the big old banks with resistance to new ways by people who recalled the ways of old that did not fail the bank where they worked. A focus panel of past and incumbent executives in banking noted that many of the traditional managers would not empower subordinates or accept new technology or other process improvements because they believed the strength of the bank was in their own personal direct contact with

---

[5] A focus group of banking industry executives including past and incumbent CEOs and Central Bank Deputy Governors brainstormed this subject on 7th December 1995 at LBS.

the customer.[5] Most of these contact issues were of minor value but constituted process blockages that resulted in very slow service. Sometimes the managers were reluctant to change because of the perception of loss of power over the customer. The challenge therefore was as much to get the staff of the old banks to climb the forgetting curve (Prahalad, 1995) as getting them to learn new ways. In some cases, refusing to forget resulted in their keeping regular files as 'back up' after they had learnt about computers and how to computerize their operations.

These issues were resulting in a strong shift in competitive advantage to the new banks. The outcome could have been the demise of the old banks, but they have managed to survive the competitive onslaught only because weak supervision by the apex authorities led to failure of some of the badly managed new banks with the generalization of distress in the system. This caused anxious customers to embark on a 'flight to safety': the return of badly needed deposits from the new banks into the big banks.

Values, Strategy and Short Term Opportunity

One of the challenges before Nigerian managers is the formulation of long term strategy and the development of a set of values that can sustain the passion for winning along the lines of set strategy, that is, strategic intent (Hamel and Prahalad, 1989). Many feel incapacitated in the conceptualization of a strategy; much less can they build values that sustain strategic intent. The reason given by executives is that it is hard enough to imagine what the next week could look like and therefore, it is foolhardy to imagine the distant future. On the contrary, Segun Agbetuyi, who is leading a dramatic restructuring at Owena Bank, talks confidently of inventing a future in a heady move to take what was once part of Nigerian banking's five basket case banks to one of the leading commercial banks through service quality and speedy processes. Already some Owena Bank branches are implementing a programme of shining the shoes of any customer who is in the branch for longer than a few target minutes. The flagship 21st century banking hall in its Victoria Island head office branch is already returning profits in excess of ₦3 million a month. Few could have imagined the Owena of four years ago playing in the terrain of wholesale commercial banking up market in

NIB territory within a few metres of NIB head office.

The challenge of effectiveness in strategy implementation for Nigerian managers lies in the values that orient managers' response to short term opportunities. Those unable to build the right values find that they are derailed from their strategy by every short term advantage they see, or by any challenge posed to the focus of their strategy by ever-changing public policy. It is, in fact, as a result of this that many do not bother with strategy, and then lose focus of the business, investing in areas where they lack the core competencies to sustain competitive advantage (Prahalad and Hamel, 1990).

There is however the example of Candel, a young indigenous agrochemical company which in three years has surpassed most of the dominant multinationals in the pesticides market. Part of its strategy is to dominate certain market niches, building on a range of generic products in those price sensitive segments of the market. But the value frame it adopts is to operate with high ethical standards. In response to the value frame it generally avoids exposing its staff to the possible corrupting influence of the Agricultural Development Projects (ADPs). As such it generally avoids doing business with ADPs. Where an irresistible opportunity to oil cash flow with ADP business becomes available they use a variety of options to minimize contacts.

The true challenge for Candel will be its response to a policy that suddenly prohibits generics that are not so environment friendly. Such a policy would immediately provide the multinationals, those that market more environment-friendly molecules from the range of their licences, with an opportunity that could threaten Candel strategy. So far Candel has continued to consolidate its strategy by package sizes that are small enough to address the cash flow problems of small-holder farmers. Interestingly, one of the big players that had begun a process of surrender in its agrochemicals area is now working on introducing such smaller packaging.

Some of the best practices as far as thriving in chaos with strategy that is sustained with values can be found in one of the Nigerian Stock Exchange top performers, Nigerian Breweries Plc.

Compared with its closest rival, Guinness Nigeria Plc., Nigerian Breweries has shown a strong capacity to absorb environmental shocks and improve performance in the process. The strategy of Nigerian

Breweries has been to grow the beer habit through a basic brand, *Star* beer, and move up market where it can extract more value, while defending traditional markets from penetration. In pursuing this strategy Nigerian Breweries has found the need to adjust to short-term opportunity and to challenge entrants into the beverages market in a way that prevents rivals from becoming strong enough in niche markets to challenge Nigerian Breweries' leadership. Nigerian Breweries' entry into the malt drinks market with *Maltina*, and defence of that market at the low calorie end with *Amstel Malta*, illustrates the point. At the same time Guinness has allowed the market leadership of *Harp* lager beer to collapse and the challenge of its traditional monopoly, the stout business, by NB Plc with *Legend,* whose current repositioning is not unlike the early experimentations with *Gulder* to attract less than a consuming impassioned defence.

What is perhaps most instructive about how Nigerian Breweries deals with uncertainty and frequent change in the environment of business is how it manages to retain focus, driven by its strategy, its invented future state, even as it adjusts to new demands of the environment.

During the Nigerian civil war (1967-1970) the beer market was growing by about 30 percent per annum. Given the loss of capacity in the eastern parts of the country, which was the theatre of war, all the breweries operated at full capacity. When the quadrupling of oil prices in 1973 followed shortly after the civil war ended, the market became characterized by increased purchasing power in the economy and inadequate capacity to meet demand of consumers. The outcome was that from less than half a dozen players in the beer market before the war, the market exploded to include 28 brewing companies with 34 breweries and 46 brands of lager.

The supply demand scenario allowed brewers to ignore issues of customer satisfaction and effective marketing practices. Literally everything that could be produced had willing sellers at the gate, pleading for allocation. Many of the new brewers did not even bother with developing proper channels of distribution for their products. This scenario was magnified by the price control which was introduced. This increased the view of marketing as allocation in the industry, causing some players to abandon strategy.

While Nigerian Breweries kept on adding capacity it did not retreat from oiling the machinery of distribution and emphasizing customer service. A leadership driven by values that sanctioned unethical conduct severely kept the company from reclining into the comfort of the moment that capacity provided.

Soon market volumes began to shrink as buying power slipped downwards in the face of the impact of Dutch disease on the Nigerian economy. The coming of a Structural Adjustment Programme loosened controls, and competitive forces were unleashed to chase after a bigger share of the declining market. Nigerian Breweries, with a team described by industry peers as among the most disciplined in the industry, kept its focus on customer satisfaction and upstairs migration to premium brands. Remarkably, *Gulder*, the premium brand, has since overtaken *Star* as the volume leader. The effect has been to establish commanding leadership position in the beer market. Even as fortunes have dipped, resulting in investment cutbacks and shutdown in the industry, NB Plc has continued reinventing in equipment and upgrading the quality of its manpower. The commitment to manpower development was symbolized by international exposure for its managers and leadership in participation in LBS training programmes in 1993. These investments have allowed it a level of Good Manufacturing Practice that gives it a competitive edge, but the strategy that sustains the pattern of reinvesting, it would seem, leaves NB Plc a cash mountain attractive to corporate raiders on leveraged buoyant. So far, the underdeveloped nature of the Nigerian Stock Market has been a shield, if not it should be attractive to use NB Plc cash flow to amortize commitments from a leveraged assault on the company.

Obsessive Questing Across the Value Chain

Prime among the catalogue of paradoxes in the environment of uncertainty is the paradox of flexibility of asset profile versus extracting value across the value chain. Whereas it is easier to respond to new changes, if commitment to a current order of things in terms of assets holds one hostage, questing across the value chain can deepen the gradient of the value, price and cost vectors, resulting in enhanced performance for the firm. If we take the traditional view of a venture as making something happen where nothing existed, the value that is perceived by a customer can result in sales only when the value vector is longer than the price vector. The customer is essentially buying the difference between the price and the value he sees in the product. The whole transaction can result in profit only when the relationship between the cost vector and the price vector is a reasonable gradient. Venturing across the value chain can result in opportunity for making the gradient across the vectors steeper; in other words, resulting in the extraction of higher value or more profit by the firm.

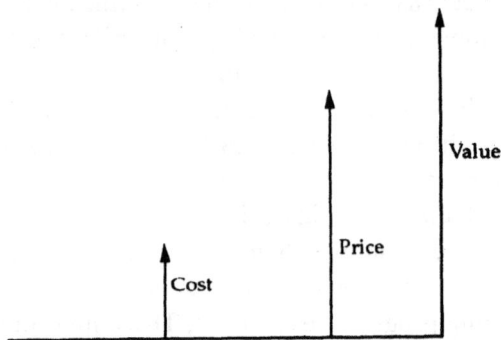

Good environment scan capabilities can produce a cost price, perceived value relationship that can lead to a windfall in terms of value extracted by the firm. Often, it is not sustainable and when the firm loses focus of its strategy because of such opportunities it jeopardises sustainable competitive performance.

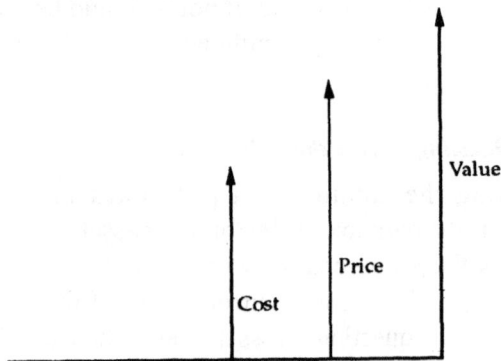

In most cases, the cost price value relationship is balanced. The efficient company strives for a steeper gradient on the cost-price slope and the marketing-driven firm seeks to drive up the value vector as perceived by the customer to get a better price.

ADC airlines again provides best practice illustration of constructing a steeper gradient through deploying assets to capture opportunity lurking at points in the value chain. In many cities served by ADC airlines where the airport is a considerable distance from the city, ADC provides a shuttle bus service ferrying its passengers into town for a fee considerably lower than taxi rates. In Abuja for example the difference between ₦900 taxi fare and the ₦150 charged by ADC to passengers, who feel safer in the ADC bus than in the taxis, increases significantly the value perceived by passengers in flying ADC.

If ADC were now to embark on a major bus service, building up fleets of buses and tying itself down in the bus business where the core competencies could vary significantly, unless a learning process has left a broad transportation competence in the company, it could mortgage the flexibility to respond to changes arising in this environment of uncertainty. But that is not what ADC is doing. Essentially ADC is utilizing an asset required to move its staff around but which could otherwise be idle most of the time, not only to earn a higher return on its assets but to deepen customer perception of value which creates room for higher price possibilities and enhanced performance.

The valuable tool to use here to prevent a passion for questing across the value chain from resulting in being locked in by the asset holding of the firm is a critical Economic Value Added (EVA) analysis of firm activity. The EVA, a veritable tool for measuring economic value added by an enterprise, is increasingly used for evaluating corporate performance (*Fortune Magazine, 1993*).

Human Resources and Strategy Fit

Part of the reason ADC is able to venture across the chain from catering services to airport shuttle services is the quality of its human resources compared to the more laggard performers in that industry. Beyond training of employees being a strong competitive advantage factor, it is evident that the best practice companies are more likely to align the human resources they hire to the firm's strategy. For Investment Banking and Trust Company (IBTC) committed to playing in a non-labour intensive niche market of financial engineering, the pedigree of all potential employees is so important that the traditional reference is given little value. Until someone known to the company puts his reputation behind an application the rest of the c.v. gets little attention. While this has created perception in the minds of some industry watchers that old school ties make the difference, a charge not novel in any way as the old Banigo-led IMB was similarly perceived, it has nonetheless affected performance positively as with the old IMB.

Regulatory agency (CBN) officials see in this the root of the practical absence of fraud at IBTC, a fact not negligible in a strategy that has confidentiality as a major attribute. This is particularly instructive because for many executives in the industry strategy is an esoteric matter and hiring is a practical matter. It was therefore not inappropriate to respond to pressures from friends and the powerful in making hiring decisions.

Clear indicators emerge in best practice companies in our sample that leadership perceived as committed, and leading by examples that reinforce the values that are preached, attract employee loyalty and sense of ownership of the challenge of overcoming environmental obstacles. In each of the cases we have studied, not only were the CEOs identified closely with the values shared in the firm but they were hands-on managers who had more than ample opportunity to live what they preached. Citizens International Bank, in a second year of a corporate renewal programme in which Larry Osa-Afiana has committed totally to 'winning values,' shows the impact of leadership. In Nigerian Breweries, Guaranty Trust Bank, ADC Airlines and IBTC leading has been from the front and has been sustained by a passion for a certain set of values. There is unanimous acknowledgement in brewing and stock market circles that the personal discipline and leadership traits of Felix Ohiwerei has contributed much to the NB Plc difference.

Conclusions and Generalizations

In closely observing processes in companies whose results mark them out as market leaders and who have been identified by peers as organizational leaders, we can conclude that effectiveness over the long term involves a tendency towards being highly focussed. The focus is sustained in spite of the distractions of so many environment-induced challenges and opportunities, by values that keep stakeholders focussed on the winning qualities of the strategy or central vision of the organization. The evidence suggests indeed that firms that get pulled astray by short-lived opportunity spurred by environment changes, like

ADP business in agrochemicals, tend not to be long-term winners.

The less focussed firms in this chaotic environment of pervasive uncertainty tend not to defend their markets robustly in the face of opportunity that may not be sustainable. This can quickly degenerate into a process of corporate surrender clearly visible in agrochemicals where major players who are diversified product groups retreat from agrochemicals into products that seem to give them good enough return without significant competitive threats. Soon they find they are retreating from all directions.

We have sought also to show that firms with higher capacity for scanning the environment tend to quickly extract value from short-term opportunity and contain the damage or potential damage of policy choices outside their domain, one area in which the pharmaceutical industry has learnt well at a high cost.

It is also a worthwhile conclusion from available evidence that beyond downsizing, organizational flexibility, such as the 'olympic rings' structure of the interlocking teams that make up IBTC, lead to more proactive behaviour and more rapid response to threats or opportunities in the environment.

In the end, it is clear that the key success factors in thriving in chaos and pervasive uncertainty include the capacity to manage change and construct the firm on the architecture of an entrepreneurial corporation.

The effect of a strong orientation towards managing change is that 'thriver' firms are learning organizations that recognize the simple ecological fact that, unless the rate of learning in the organization is equal to or greater than the rate of change in the environment, the firm is moving towards extinction. It is no wonder that best practice firms in our sample outspend their rivals at the Lagos Business School and have an internal climate and culture that is conducive to sharing information and ideas. A level of trust is fundamental here and firms that have more trust accept the change message more quickly.

Being change-sensitive also means that the firm recognizes that people in organizations tend to resist change for a variety of reasons such as fear of the unknown; the nature of bureaucracy which depends on specialization, routinization, control etc. to increase efficiency; the effect of a possible loss of present power or benefits; skills inadequacy in the new dispensation; fear of loss of job; etc. The change sensitive firm develops in its people the capacity to envision future states that justify change and to communicate this vision to the stakeholders in as graphic a form as is necessary to engender shared meaning of reality.

The other critical nature of 'thriver' firms is their entrepreneurial disposition. The building of an opportunity ladder and the passion for climbing that ladder in the entrepreneurial corporation marks out a thriver firm. This has not been the case with many companies. From a review of corporate performance, the work some of my colleagues at LBS have done on the EVA of leading firms show clearly that some of the traditional leading trading companies, with negative EVA, are essentially, in the words with which Ghoshal and Bartlett describe some traditional western corporations, "creeping along a state of satisfactory underperformance." This state of satisfactory underperformance is possible usually because companies that are essentially brain dead can often coast along for years, showing acceptable accounting profit until some frustrated banker pulls the life support system. It is noteworthy that some of the less than entrepreneurial diversified companies which dominated the Nigerian formal sector and are experiencing decline are organized along the multi-divisional lines pioneered by Alfred Sloan at General Motors, an organizational pattern copied by many western corporations which is cited by Ghoshal and Bartlett as institutionalizing structures that become a block to continuous intrapreneuring.

Clearly a number of trading companies in Nigeria are modelled on divisionalization. Where there has been consulting intervention by one of the leading management consulting firms in Lagos there has been an effort to deal with the problem of autonomy of divisions through Strategic Business Units (SBUs). The SBU revolution has however not eliminated the problem of core competencies being compartmentalized in a way that limits entrepreneurial possibilities that flow from a portfolio of core competencies. It is not surprising that these companies are not adding as much economic value or creating wealth to justify the capital in them. From the earlier cited work of my colleagues, some actually have a negative EVA, that is to say, they are destroying wealth and losing shareholder value. While John Holt and PZ have positive EVA it is clear that the more focussed non-divisionalized companies like Lever Brothers of Nigeria and NB Plc return the highest positive EVA.

From some of the best practice companies we have cited, especially companies like ADC, the banks and NB Plc, continuous innovation has certainly become ingrained in the culture of the organization. This has no doubt helped them to overcome the vagaries of uncertainty and to circumnavigate the trouble points of a chaotic environment.

References

Fortune Magazine, 20th September, 1993, "The Real Key to Creating Wealth."
Garrat, B. *Learning to Lead,* (Fontana, London, 1990).
Hamel and Prahalad. "Strategic Intent" in *Harvard Business Review,* May-June, 1989.
Prahalad, C. K. "How HR Can Help to Win the Future" in *People Management,* 12th January, 1995.
Prahalad and Hamel. "The Core Competence of the Corporation" in *Harvard Business Review,* May-June, 1990.
Utomi, P. "Nigeria: The Dilemma of a Private Sector" in *LBS Case/Note,* SPEB
Wildavsky, A. *Politics of the Budgetary Process*, (Boston, Little, Brown & Co., 1979).

8

Institutional Aspect of the Stabilization of the Nigerian Economy*

Let me begin by thanking Dr Chu S P Okongwu for the opportunity to ventilate my thoughts on a matter that should be the defining subject of his life, Economic Stabilisation in Nigeria. I am also grateful that the topic assigned to me, which is to dwell on the institutional aspects, is perhaps one of the most salient, given recent experience and extant challenges.

It is clearly my opinion that the only way to fully appreciate what happened with effort to attain fiscal viability and resume growth in the 1980s and 1990s is to understand how institutions evolve, and the failure of our stabilisation programmes of recent years to create institutional frameworks for sustainability of the policy choices. I therefore consider this an appropriate venue to elaborately give airing to this matter on which I have been engaged in my research and writings in the area of Competition and Strategy for business enterprises.

My approach here will be to first identify what we mean by stabilisation, then to review cursorily the history of attempts at stabilisation of the Nigerian economy, isolating for discussion some elements I consider critical for the success or failure of those programmes. After the historical review, I will introduce the concept of institutions and the phenomenological linkages consequent upon that. Our analysis will then shift to how the nature of institutions can provide sustainability to what really is an organic need for continuous adjusting of the structure of the economy, so that it can stay in equilibrium with a dynamic and changing platform, especially in this age of globalisation and technology driven pace of change which is rapid.

What is Economic Stabilization?

In a sense, it seems like an irony to talk of stability for an economy in which the object is forward movement. The story of economic

---

*Address to the Centre for Public Policy

86

development in newly emerging poor countries of the Third World has really been the challenge of increasing productivity in an accelerated manner to bridge the gap between the quality of life in the industrial democracies of the West and North East Asia and that in countries like Nigeria. It is Peter Drucker who makes the correct point that at the beginning of this century the lifestyles of the poor of Northern Europe and of those of Africa differed marginally. But the productivity gains from the Industrial Revolution which saw increases in the two hundred or so years since James Watt redesigned the steam engine outstrip the gains of ten millennia before, and that ensured that in the first 70 years of this century, the world has been truly divided into the rich north and the poor south. It seems to me therefore that the notion of stabilisation, when we are in the heat of trying to play catch up, will confuse those unfamiliar with the concept. Fortunately, I can turn to Chu Okongwu for help in defining stabilisation.

In a January 1985 lecture, fourth in the Public Service Lecture series of Anambra State, Okongwu addressed the subject of stabilisation of the Nigerian economy. In the analytical resume of the stabilisation problem which he proffered, he defined a stable system as "a feedback system whose performance tends to equilibrium with time, regardless of its initial state; for through feedback, it controls the very force to guide it back to equilibrium" (Okongwu, 1985, p2). The return to stability is triggered by an information feedback network that evaluates the gap between preferred state and extant reality.

In the logic of this metaphor, the preferred state, which is a stable state, is one of orderly growth and development of the Nigerian economy which can be thrown out of alignment by shocks. The general problem of stabilisation will consist therefore in reconstructing the motion of the system, to return to stable behaviour. The challenge of problem solving here should be in the identification of appropriate stabilisers to bring the system into the stable state– the state of equilibrium.

Given that Nigeria has been a shock-prone economy, the challenge for policy makers has been more than just the emplacement of stabilisers but also the correction of the fundamental structure of the economy such that it is less vulnerable to shocks than it has been. Surely we cannot invent a shock-proof economy as pharmaceutical firms can invent a tamper-proof caplet after analgesic capsules were tampered with, sending shock waves to consumers in the United States in 1982, but we can build an economic structure that is robust enough to have high quality shock absorbers. Evidence available to us suggests, however, that we have, by omission or commission, missed opportunities to diversify the base of the economy building in the needed shock absorbers in the process.

The need for such shock absorbers should of necessity be accompanied by a paradigm shift away from trusting on government to solve problems. This value system has usually led to expansion of the size of government which makes contraction difficult as soon as a shock reduces income flows, causing deficits with consequences for inflation and dissavings.

A Short History of Stabilization

The Nigerian economy was but a collection of subsistence agriculture communities at the time of the imposition of colonial hegemony. Raw material needs of the colonisers created a cash crop economy in which trading companies exported produce. Risk to shipment of produce by German U-boats during World War I led the trading companies to a lower disposition to trade. To reduce the risk, the colonial regime took responsibility for shipping produce – the beginnings of the marketing boards (Utomi, 1998). These marketing boards were later to play a price stabilisation and market development role.

As Pius Okigbo points out in his review of public accounts, in this era he makes the point of the build-up of surplus in the accounts of the marketing boards in London up till the advent of self-government. These reserves quickly disappeared between 1957 and independence (Okigbo, 1973, 1988).

It would seem that these accumulated reserves were drawn down by the regional governments to 'modernise' their capital cities (witness the building of Cocoa House in Ibadan, expansion of GRA's in other capital cities etc). Some of the resources were also dispensed in the pursuit of industrial development goals. As the World Bank Policy Research Report "Adjustment in Africa" points out "agriculture, rather than being stoked as the engine of growth, was taxed to provide resources to build a modern industrial sector... but government got over-extended, particularly relative to their weak institutional capacities as they tried to build unity and deliver on the promises of independence" (World Bank, 1994, p. 21).

The Ikeja industrial estate is a monument to this trend that ate into the reserves. Of this trend, current National Planning Minister Rasheed Gbadamosi has commented in a keynote address to the Ogunsheye Foundation Seminar on the national development process: "Plan distortion was a common occurrence and the public expenditure was more in favour of administration as compared to economic and social sectors. As such a lot of public expenditure was unproductive"(Gbadamosi, April 1998).

The 1960s closed with the end of the civil war and the rapid growth of the oil sector following 1956 commercial finds in Oloibiri in the Niger-Delta. By 1973 the Yom Kippur war had produced a quadrupling of oil prices touching off unprecedented budgetary expansion, the seeds of Dutch disease and structural distortions as strong exchange rates spelt doom for traditional exports and led the country into a dependence on oil exports which today account for 97 percent of the county's export earnings.

With the inability to manage down expanded budgets in the face of the collapse of the price of a mineral commodity (Dutch disease), Nigeria was suddenly unable to meet its trade debt as they fell due. By 1984 lines of credit were being frozen by correspondent banks of Nigerian banks overseas. Shortages of consumer commodities came with this, giving us the 'essential commodities' (essenco) era. Nigeria could not continue playing the ostrich. It would either put on a stabilisation programme or drop out of international trade with consequent high transaction costs.

The effort, unsteady as it were, with adjustment had as outcome appalling GDP growth rates of 2.2 per cent in 1995, 3.2 per cent in 1996, 3.11 per cent in 1997 and 2.34 per cent in 1998 (Obadan, 1999, Ogunseye Lecture), outcomes that are far from the preferred rate of 10 per cent per annum agreed to by the Vision 2010 project. This means that a lot more work has to be done if the country is to be brought into the equilibrium state of orderly growth with low inflation, higher levels of investment and growth and an export and earnings profile not so skewed in favour of the oil sector to the detriment of sectorally balanced development.

The Roots of Disequilibrium

To come to terms with the sources of disequilibrium that can further our understanding of institutional aspects of stabilisation, it should be helpful to outline and discuss, albeit cursorily, some sources of instability in the dynamics of economic intercourse in Nigeria. They include dependence on oil and oil price shocks, undue fiscal expansion which is related to the 'economically engaged state' (expansion of the scope of government's economic activity) and the perpetuation of enclave economies. Other sources of disequilibrium include sectoral disharmony, the absence of elite consensus or shared paradigm on economic thrust, the import substitution industrialisation strategy, lack of financial deepening, foreign borrowing, infrastructure deficiencies, weak human capital situation and low capacity for policy implementation in the public service.

Over-Dependence on Oil

No discussion of stabilisation of the Nigerian economy can take place without a front row seat going to vulnerability to shocks because about 97 percent of the export earnings of the country comes from the oil sector which operates within the OPEC cartel faced with a market that results often in swings of fortune. Persistent externally generated shocks from the oil sector reverberate across the economy as the import sector which displays a high consumption profile is based on the performance of the oil sector; ditto for other sectors.

Undue Fiscal Expansion

There is a dominant political culture that sees government as a tool for solving problems directly. This tends towards big government. Even during the course of adjustments, the creation of so many bureaucratic agencies to aid adjustment proves the point. We shall refer later on to the Directorate of Roads and Rural Infrastructure (DFFRI) and NALDA among others when we discuss agriculture and sectoral imbalances but these agencies and the National Directorate of Employment are good examples of how an adjustment programme can itself repeat the problems that caused government to pursue a stabilisation programme. What to bear in mind particularly is that as government grows in boom times to provide the instrumentality for a good life for the citizenry, government backs itself against the wall in terms of flexibility when incomes suddenly shrink. Resulting deficits destabilise the economy from its trajectory of orderly growth.

The Perpetuation of Enclave Economies

One of the factors militating against orderly growth of the Nigerian economy is a tendency towards enclaves which denies the broader economy the benefits of the multiplier effects of intense production activity within the enclave. Oil, of course, is the mother of all enclave economies. Almost wholly external in its orientation, the productivity of the sector is mainly dependent on foreign hands. The industry employs less than 100,000 people to generate 97 percent of our export earnings. Attempts at domesticating the sector have suffered from the fact that they are government driven, a matter that has attracted economic rent seeking behaviour as the defining characteristic of domestication. This takes away from possibilities of learning and transfer of productivity enhancing capacities from that sector to other sectors of the economy.

The pattern of intervention by government has also, in my opinion, prevented the downstream possibilities of the sector from being harnessed as it should be.

There is a tendency to thinking of oil as the only enclave economy. In the 1998 budget review organised by the Central Bank of Nigeria, the Nigerian Economic Society and the National Centre of Economic Management and Administration (NCEMA), I spoke a little about another enclave economy. Anybody who has been out of Lagos for a few years would surely have difficulty recognising parts of Victoria Island. Peaceful neighbourhoods have been transformed into shopping malls. These malls cater mainly for an expatriate population and employ a few Nigerians. It is hard to think of an enclave economy in retail trade and the hospitality industry. The many new restaurants in Victoria Island tell a different story. These enclave economies prevent flows of income to individuals in the personal sector in a way that dampens consumption and hampers investment. This leads to the question of the pattern of income flows that is whole.

Sectoral Disharmony

In referring to what I have chosen to call sectoral disharmony, I am using sectors in two different senses. In the first sense, I am referring to a balance between business, personal, external and government sectors in terms of the circular flows of income. In the second sense, I am concerned with a balance between agriculture, manufacturing, oil and gas and services. For some reason, we tend to be a one-sector economy. By that I mean that one sector always tends to dominate.

Partly at the root of the purchasing power crisis of the last few years is the fact that the government sector has been sucking in incomes from the personal sector and the business sector. With new taxes like the VAT, which I consider our best tax because as a consumption tax it captures a broader base, and all the levies of the ports, on education, PTF, etc., government has ballooned in relation to the other sectors. Being a very inefficient sector marked largely by rent seeking behaviour, a clear effect of this is that income flows are restricted, resulting in full warehouses. My colleague at the Lagos Business School, Ayo Teriba, shows clearly that with the retrenchment of the external sector as Nigeria acquired pariah status under the last regime, the trend in resource flows explains "the stagnation of production, sales, consumer purchasing power and even investment" (Teriba, 1998 p. 74).

In the same way the dominance of the petroleum sector as export earner resulted in the rise in the value of the Naira way above our purchasing power parity line such that agriculture and other export sectors became unattractive. At the same time, our manufacturing sector had a great incentive to be outward in its raw materials supply orientation. The decline of local agriculture and the relative cheapness of imported inputs made local industry dependent and uncompetitive, especially when infrastructure deficiencies are factored in. The need to give them significant tariff protection arose there from providing them a curtain behind which to fall further back in their capacity to compete with foreign rivals.

ISI and Disequilibrium

I have written and spoken much about the structural problems created by not making a quick transition from the industrial development strategy prescribed in the Prebisch thesis and would not have to repeat myself here. Unlike our Asian friends who started out drawing inspiration from Raul Prebisch's work at the Economic Commission for Latin America and moved to an export led growth, we have been stuck with the import substitution strategy. The shortcomings of ISI have been compounded by a culture of Bureaucratic-Prebendalism (Joseph, 1998) in which the sharing of the so-called national cake has meant the dispersion of inappropriate industries to zones where their uncompetitiveness is heightened. A typical example is the location of truck assembly plants so far from the seaports. Instead of locating factories as per the factor endowments of these regions of the country, the need to get the same things evenly spread has stymied possibilities of growth and development.

Infrastructure Deficiency and Absorptive Capacity

Yet another major spur of structural defects and destabilisation is the problem of absorptive capacity and infrastructure deficiency. When the budgetary expansion that led up to Dutch disease began, little attention was paid to the absorptive capacity of the economy. Besides the cement armada which made Nigeria a nightmare destination for shippers, the failure to reckon with the country's absorptive capacity led to ineffective utilisation of the gains of the oil boom. Part of the telling consequences of that failure is that whereas the Kuwaits of this world who invested some of the petro-dollar in Europe and North America can draw on the returns from those investments to absorb shocks, Nigeria is totally vulnerable.

The impact of infrastructure deficiencies, some of which create the absorption problems we have seen, is even more compelling a source of anxiety. At the Ogunsheye Foundation Lecture of 13 April, 1999, I tried to explore this challenge in a paper titled "The Paradox of Purchasing Power Parity." The summary of our presentation was that if we consider the so-called law of one price by comparing the prices of identical products denominated in different currencies, one could determine the real or PPP exchange rate that should exist if markets were efficient. Where labour is cheaper, it should take a lower income in Nigeria to have a similar consumption and quality of life. Our experience has been that for middle class people, the reverse can obtain largely because of infrastructure deficiencies.

Given the income levels and their effect on prices as cost drivers, it ordinarily will cost more for products in which countries being compared have favourable factor endowments. The logical derivative of this relationship between wage levels and cost is that the person with a lower income in the low wage economy, using the nominal exchange rate values, could have as high or higher quality of life because he can purchase a similar basket of goods for less.

The interpretation of the essence of Purchasing Power Parity as a marker for living standards ordinarily holds true when you describe the underclass, the poor Nigerians' condition. On nominal GDP, a per capita of US$250 or less, there are surely many Nigerians that fit that mould of the underclass. But a fair number of Nigerians, the traditional middle class and successful professionals, fit the bill differently. For this class the living standards are largely defined by infrastructure deficiencies in the economy. Ironically, the state of infrastructure is much worse than resource endowments should ordinarily allow because of corrupt practices, many of which involve those same middle class people. Being much dependent on consumer items requiring such infrastructure as roads, power and telecommunications, the middle class find that they inevitably have to make arrangements for some infrastructure. These private arrangements which lose the economies of scale advantage when individuals make such provisions therefore impose severe cost penalties on such a class of citizens.

The private provision of water which costs the average person in many neighbourhood, for example, about ₦3,000 a week; and of power, the supplement to NEPA's electric supply adds so much to the budget profile that the difference in dollar denominated income required to maintain similar living standards in the United States and Nigeria balloons dramatically. I am just at the initial stage of a study designed to track the actual cost of private infrastructure provisions for the family use of a sample of middle class people. If some of what my own experience informs is anything to go by, I expect to find that somebody who earns ₦8million per annum has a similar quality of life as someone who earns USD25,000 in the state of Texas for example. If you consider that incomes are generally higher for similar types of work in nominal US Dollar terms, one finds the enormous disadvantage to which the Nigerian middle class is subjected because of infrastructure weaknesses.

Corruption

Large scale goal displacement in which private goals substitute for public interest has exacerbated the problem of destabilising factors, increasing the structural distortions that follow from these destabilisers moving the economy off the equilibrium course. It is perhaps ironical that some of the more rampant rent seeking behaviour (the democratisation of corruption, some have called it) took place during adjustment programmes designed to restore the economy to its natural trajectory. Few doubt that the rampant corruption after 1988, which may have peaked in 1991 producing a budget deficit of 12.4 percent of GDP in the year of the Gulf War windfall, may have inflicted some of the worst structural damage to the economy. It is such damage that makes it important to look at the institutions that supported the effort at stabilisation and at why such damage was not contained or sanctioned by these institutions.

The Vehicles of Stabilization

Even though the adjustment of an economy is a continuing process, the most prolonged effort at correcting the journey down the path of stagnation by the Nigerian economy has been the adjustment programme introduced in 1986. Cornered and unable to manoeuvre much, Nigeria was forced by its creditors and trading partners to adjust its economy. The path to adjustment, beginning with a debate on IMF conditionalities on the streets of Nigeria to the self-imposed SAP, had to confront the uncompetitiveness of the sectors caused by an over-valued currency.

Devaluation

The imperative of devaluation was handled through stop-and-go strategies that were at times brilliant and at other times disingenuous. The starting point of a two-tier foreign exchange market, logical in its intent, became a source of arbitrage that created the most lucrative of rent sources. In the rents of the two-tier foreign exchange market were the roots of later financial sector distress at a time adjustment goals desperately required financial deepening for lending and investment capacity to stimulate preferred sectors returning to competitiveness.

Once the banks were hooked on rents, it drove the strategies of many of them who responded to shocks like the withdrawal of parastatal deposits to Central Bank on federal government orders by turning in desperation to the interbank markets. The 'unreal' exchange rates of the interbank market eventually resulted in default and systematic distress. It has to be borne in mind here that the shock of withdrawal of parastatal funds came from reaction to inflationary consequences of a USD600million budget reflation by government (Zanini, 1990). This reflation in my opinion was a panic reaction to General Olusegun Obasanjo's remark at a lunch of General Joe Garba's book; that "SAP with a human face" speech obviously influenced the injection of so much new money into the system. The response to the inflation that followed was to constrict money supply by withdrawing parastatal funds from the commercial banks.

Founding Institutions

During the adjustment season, new institutions were founded as stabilisers. They range from NERFUND as a forced savings scheme and those that support the renewal of agriculture like NALDA, DFRRI, and the NSITF. These institutions had varying levels of success in helping to attain a return to equilibrium. In the main, most of them were far from pursuing their set goals. The forced savings agents never managed to be as effective as Singapore forced savings agents in generating investments. Most of the institutions were abused for personal benefit and set the economy back rather than bring it to equilibrium. It has in fact been argued (Prof. Jade Akande at NIALS Workshop in April, 1999) that the Babangida regime created these institutions as a smokescreen to divert attention from its real agenda.

A Critique of Sap

Let me draw from a recent discussion of why economic stabilisation programmes have not succeeded as envisaged by policy makers. Financial deepening is a critical object of SAP because it assumes that deepening facilitates the channelling of capital from surplus to deficit areas. Deepening without a culture of venturing and entrepreneurial skills would surely produce much slower economic renewal. In not quickly producing growth, given lags that delay effects, the tendency is for opponents of adjustment to put enough pressure on the policy process to cause changes in policy. This is why I argue that a more proactive approach to stimulating investments and entrepreneurship is required in emerging economies, especially when they are adjusting from government-led growth to private sector-driven development. To achieve the 10 percent of GDP per annum, it is proposed that particular attention be paid to investment stimulation and promotion, industriousness (entrepreneurship), and institutions which reduce uncertainty and the comfort level of ventures to certain risks.

The social engineering of these three variables is important, as we have noted, because of the lag between policy implementation and the ultimately desired effect, and because modern economics in its bias towards quantitative measures has a tendency to neglect critical qualitative variables.

On the former variable, we have already seen in the Nigerian experience impatience with the lags. A good example is seen with the response to a market based exchange rate. While proponents of a foreign exchange market acted the J-curve to explain that a lag existed between the policy choice and the response of the non-oil exports, opponents were quick to point out that published results of companies show they were making 'extraordinary' profits while people were groaning under the weight of devaluation. The 'paper profits' of replacement cost pricing had overshadowed the falling levels of inflation. This gave rise to policy reversals regarding manufacturing, based on these spurious observations about the reforms not working. The final consequence would be policy sabotaging more robust outcomes of adjustment.

Even where the people are patient with adjustment policies and the incentives for industries based on factor endowments and the export sector begins to pick up, levels of growth such as that experienced by East Asian economies in the miracle years or as desired by Vision 2010 will be difficult to reach. The need to pay particular attention to investments, industriousness and institutions is as such an imperative for economies desirous of rapid growth. With population growing at 3 percent per annum, Nigeria needs to have a pre-crisis Asian level of growth.

Investment

Investment flows show that little new money has come into Nigeria in the 1990s. Even multinationals already in Nigeria are reluctant to invest their returns. An analysis of capital flows will show that most of what little money came in went to an enclave sector with only marginal linkages to the bigger Nigerian economy, the oil sector. Surely you cannot have growth without investments. It is my opinion that a facultative role for government exists, especially where there is an entrepreneurial regime not bound by bureaucratic excesses in which the pursuit of power overtakes purpose. With an entrepreneurial regime, an industrial policy and cooperation with the private sector to generate investment incentives, the encouragement of venture capital companies and even development banks for long term finance can be pursued. The performance history of development banks in Nigeria should seem discouraging of such strategies. Experience from elsewhere, systematically analysed by David Hulme and Paul Mosley in their book *Finance Against Poverty,* shows that the World Bank and others building on the work of the so-called Ohio School may have been quick to write off traditional modes of financing to stimulate growth in poor countries. Schemes through which government provides matching funds to venture capital firms with a track record could be another intervention track.

Beyond a careful intervention to stimulate investments, the promotion of the country as a safe place to invest for high returns is the business of the state that is required to build momentum for investments and spur growth. Success with promoting new investments is itself dependent on institutions that provide support.

Institutions

The importance of institutions in reducing uncertainty and facilitating economic discourse is now the subject of a significant body of literature (North, 1990; Utomi, 1998). In the area of investment support, such institutions as a one-stop entry agencies, property rights and the rule of law which generate settled habits in the population that give confidence to local and foreign businesses that they can trust things to go in a certain way, are of high priority. It is these institutions that make businesses confident enough to plan because they can estimate the probabilities of outcome from their inputs.

Our investment support institutions need to evolve beyond where they are at present. The Industrial Development Coordinating Committee set up as an interministerial one-stop agency did not work as envisaged. A National Investment Commission has since been set up but it is not clear if the bureaucratic bottlenecks that discourage most investors from expressing interests to having a going venture will be eliminated here. Perhaps the model of the Technical Committee on Privatisation and Commercialisation (TCPC), with a new staffing from the public and private sectors and fairly clear goals, would help in moving forward here.

Dealing with property rights and rejuvenating a judiciary that suffered much setback during the years of military rule are critical anchors to getting investors to feel more comfortable with Nigeria. Institutions that ensured the reduction of on-costs for manufacturing in East Asia through the development of industrial parks with adequate infrastructure made industry clusters build up easily. Such institutions will be helpful in ensuring new growth because they will reduce the challenges that those who are industrious come up against.

Allow me, even though I am trying to keep this discussion short, to dwell a little further on institutions of the financial sector. This is because the other two legs of investment and industriousness depend much on financial intermediation. While recognising that labour markets are critical, it is my opinion that the mobile labour we have had often has been unable to raise productivity and wealth creation because of the weak capacity for financial intermediation. The need for financial deepening and broadening is for me a major dependent variable for stimulating growth and development. This deepening, I believe, has remained elusive because of weak institutions in that sector. The consequence has been moral hazard cases and unwillingness to engage because of uncertainty. Considering International Finance Corporation studies that show the new rapidly developing economies to be dependent up to the tune of 90 percent on domestic savings for development, we cannot afford to downplay the need for financial deepening (IFC Lessons from Experience No 6, 1998). World Bank studies indeed show that "10 percent increase in financial depth (liquid liabilities) is associated with an increase in per capita GDP of 2.8 percent, a remarkable increase" (IFC, 1998, p. 11).

Unless we can have appropriate frameworks of rules that are properly implemented to guide local securities markets and venture capital companies, we are going to be unable to be a competitive economy. Appropriate systems and institutions should boost local savings and, consequently, investment rates.

Industriousness

Industriousness in an indigenous enterprise class is for me a key variable in seeking productive growth. As evidence from the Samsung Corporation and many South Korean enterprises show, (witness the process of becoming a leading exporter of microwave ovens, *Harvard Business Review,* Jan-Feb, 1988), industriousness had as much to do with the making of the so-called miracle as the conditions that attracted investments. The value of building up a culture of entrepreneurship, hard work and creativity in an indigenous class is also evident in the fact that few countries that have grown rapidly have done so primarily on foreign investments. We can therefore expect that facilitating the emergence of a strong indigenous entrepreneurial group is a major variable in moving the economy forward.

Contrary to myths that exist, entrepreneurs are not born, they are made. Entrepreneurship development programmes, continuous training and peer experience sessions can facilitate the emergence of an enterprise class that can take advantage of conditions created by the two variables earlier discussed to move things forward. Yet they are variables not emphasised much in prescriptions of multilateral development agencies. Our task here is to show that special proactive consideration for these three variables are necessary and that these factors along with how the enterprises proceed, form their strategies.

The exploration of this interface between national strategy, as in the engineering of the environment via the three variables we discussed, and business strategy of forms is thus the real contribution we hope to make here. It is therefore in order to review the factors that drive strategy in business enterprises. These competitive forces which drive strategy in emerging economies have been explicated substantially in my earlier contribution in the book, *Managing Uncertainty:Competition and Strategy in Emerging Economies* (Utomi, 1998).

The most salient point for me in this critique is that SAP missed the final objective of stabilising the economy and putting in the path of orderly growth because the rules of the game, the institutions, were weak and often excuses for executing personal agenda other than restoring the economy to equilibrium. The failure of the Babangida adjustment is for me perhaps the biggest endorsement of the importance of institutions for economic stabilisation to be effective. If you consider the promise and possibilities of adjustment between 1987 and 1990, in spite of the manner of its implementation and the final outcome, you cannot but see why premium value should be placed on the role of institutions in social and economic intercourse.

The promise of SAP was such that regime leaders could have gone down in history as heroes of Nigeria's economic transformation and emancipation. Sadly their own conduct, because of the absence of institutions to set limits to their behaviour, has resulted in extant debate being whether they should be demonised for all times or be abandoned to a footnote of history on economic management. It is with the gravity of this in mind that we turn to an attempt at understanding institutions.

Institutions and Stabilization

I have in the past found it convenient to leave the task of setting the stage for my discussion of institutions to a man who has done seminal work in this area, Douglas North. I will do so again. "Institutions provide the basic structure by which human beings throughout history have created order and attempted to reduce uncertainty in exchange. Together with the technology employed, they determine transaction and transformation costs and hence the profitability and feasibility of engaging in economic activity. They connect the past with the present and the future so that history is largely an incremental story of institutional evolution in which the historical performance of economies can only be understood as part of a sequential story. And they are key to understanding the relationship between the polity and the consequences of their inter-relationship for economic growth (or stagnation and decline). But just why some forms of exchange are stable while others lead to more complex and productive forms of exchange?"

It is a measure of the fact that the Bretton Woods institutions are not necessarily the ultimate deposit of wisdom on economic development that they did not seem to recognise the very critical nature of institutions in the development process until lately. The written thoughts of Mamadu Dia (1996), Arturo Israel (1987) and Philip Knack (Knack and Keeler, 1995) in the 1990s indicate the beginning of the discovery of institutions in Washington. As Israel points at research evidence, "A high correlation was found between the initial level of institutional performance, the degree of progress in the institutional development component, and the success of the overall investment project" (Israel, 1987).

The point of the foregoing is that institutions are rules that set limits to conducts, bring sanctions on those who violate the rules and provide incentives for behaving in manners agreed to. It is also important to recognise, as Oliver Williamson points out, that such institutions can emerge from the 'opportunistic' conduct of those who have first-mover advantage (Williamson, 1975 and 1979). We can see this in the maturing of the Nigerian private sector from seeking tariff protection that was unhealthy for their later competitiveness to a new orientation (gradually still) towards wanting a level playing field.

SAP was largely troubled because the pattern of evolving institutional arrangements from organic needs of development were sacrificed at the altar of institution creation for the sheer glamour of it or for undisclosed reasons. The outcome was many parallel governments. From DFRRI to NDE etc., these duplications of the bureaucracy of government took away from the need to reform government and the fact that we grow institutions at the margins of currently settled habits of the community. It is not difficult to see why these new institutions were loaded full of problems of moral hazard, economic rent seeking and ease of abuse that did more to sabotage than to sustain SAP.

We can go on to a broader review of institutions but time will not permit. I however want to point to the fact that the conduct of the command nature of military rule resulted in much serious damage to property rights, the degradation of the judiciary and therefrom of the capacity for contract enforcement, thus making Nigeria less attractive for investments. Given the importance of financial deepening to the Central Bank and the Nigerian Deposit Insurance Corporation, investments have not received the institution building support that they require.

I am convinced that the systemic distress banking has experienced comes from the absence of adequate failure resolution mechanisms and the structure and focus of the NDIC. The recent 'autonomy' that has come to Central Bank should be a part of the framework for using monetary policy more effectively to contain inflation. The fact that fiscal and monetary policy responsibilities were domiciled in the same place has obviously not helped matters. Weakness of institutional framework, I believe, also made little of the introduction of Open Market Operations and Discount Houses as stabilisation securities were used frequently, creating as many problems as they aimed to resolve.

It is possible to continue to review the institutions of stabilisation. It should suffice to state that there is already ample evidence from the foregoing that stabilisation has not gone as well as it could because the institutions of stabilisation have been weak or non-existent.

References

Dia, Mamadou 1996. *Africa's Management in the 1990's and Beyond: Reconciling Indigenous and Transplanted Institutions.* Washington D.C.: The World Bank.

"The Financial Sector's Impact on Growth" in *Financial Institutions, IFC's Lessons of Experience* No. 6, 1998.

Gbadamosi, Rasheed 1998. Keynote address to the Ogunseye Foundation Seminar on National Development Process, April 1998.

Israel, Arturo 1987. *Institutional Development: Incentives to Performance.* World Bank Publication. Baltimore: The John Hopkins University Press.

Joseph, Richard 1987. *Democracy and Prebendal Politics in Nigeria: The Rise and Fall of the Second Republic.* Cambridge: Cambridge University Press.

Knack, Stephen and Philip Keefer 1995. "Institutions and Economic Performance: Cross Country Tests using Alternative Institutional Measures" in *Economics and Politics*, Vol. 7.

North, Douglas 1990. *Institutions, Institutional Change and Economic Performance.* New York: Cambridge University Press.

Okigbo, Pius 1987. *Essays in the Public Philosophy of Development.* Enugu: Fourth Dimension Publishers.

Okongwo, Chu 1985. "Stabilization of the Nigerian Economy." Public Service Lecture. Anambra State, Nigeria.

Teriba, A.O. 1997. "Business Outlook for 1998" in *Lagos Business School Management Review* Vol. 2 No. 2:67-77.

9

Reified Myths: Voodoo Economics and Jujunomics*

Let me begin by complimenting your President for putting the appropriate level of pressure to make me override a regret letter I had dispatched in response to your invitation. Let there be no doubt, I always wanted to come to Calabar; unfortunately my schedule has been getting the better of me.

Nothing quite captures the imagination of modern man as the tale of the triumph of the human spirit as it battles the forces of nature and society to create conditions of a greater well-being for citizens of a nation. The process of constructing a framework of economic intercourse that leads to wealth creating and a higher quality of life in Nigeria has, unfortunately, been characterized by much strange dogma. These dogmas, arising from some 'benefits' that might not hold up under scrutiny, have shaped public choice in a way that is deserving of a major debate. My objective today is to discuss a few of these myths that lead us to economic decisions that sometimes seem like a 'babalawo' is being consulted as he chants incantations in the back rooms of the finance and national planning ministries. Jujunomics seems to be the big game in town.

Among the many tendencies in this portfolio of myths that have been repeated so often that they are reality in many minds, in effect reified to the point that policy making is sometimes truly classic voodoo economics, due apologies to President George Bush who so characterized candidate Ronald Reagan's ideas during Republican primaries of 1980. The myths include the desirability and consequences of devaluation, the effects of wage increases on inflation, the place of privatization in economic reconstruction and state creation and bringing development close to the people. Also worthy of consideration are myths about how to put a human face on economic reforms, the use of price controls and

---

*Address to the Calabar Chamber of Commerce on 4/9/98

other regulations, and the Nigerian assessment of the importance of his country in the scheme of things. There is also the assumed relationship between denominations of currency and inflation. To this list can be added the belief that wealth is a function of natural resources.

The foregoing are but a few areas in which policy making tends to proceed from a presumed base that is somehow accepted as received wisdom yet without basis in empirical evidence. We shall attempt to discuss all these, albeit cursorily, given the constraints of time. Appropriately, though, we shall begin with the mother of all myths: that the Nigerian economy does not respond to normal economic laws. The myth of the extraordinary peculiarity of the Nigerian economy, often offered as an excuse for not doing the right thing, has been reinforced and reified over the years by several pronouncements of policy makers. Perhaps among the more often cited of these expressions is President Ibrahim Babangida's response to an interview question in which he indicated surprise that the economy had not collapsed; some mischievous people tend to add "in spite of his efforts to damage it." This whole mindset of a peculiar economy pervaded the debate about whether or not Nigeria should accept an IMF loan and its restructuring conditionalities when the economy ran into trouble following the collapse of oil prices in the early 1980s. The thinking also influenced the evaluation of the adjustment programme that was subsequently adopted instead of the IMF loan.

The Idea of a Peculiar Economy

This subject of why the IMF conditionalities were not suited to Nigeria's peculiar circumstances is so important in terms of the evolution of economic policy thinking in Nigeria that a recapitulation of why we needed an IMF facility and the reactions to the idea do bear recapitulation. As the familiar refrain goes, Nigeria emerged as an independent nation dependent on a number of agricultural commodities – cocoa, groundnuts, rubber, palm produce etc. – which were managed by the produce marketing boards to generate growth in excess of three percent per annum until the advent of military rule. This, inspite of the fact that the milking of the boards resources to fund parties at the regions rapidly depleted the huge resources the marketing boards had built up between the period the regions took over the marketing boards and the time of independence.

On the strength of the economic fundamentals at a time in which deficit budgeting was hardly an issue discussed with any seriousness, Nigeria was able to prosecute a costly civil war without falling into debt. The country was also able to begin a programme of Reconstruction and Rehabilitation as part of the post-war Rehabilitation (3R) without much anxiety. After the war, oil which had been discovered in commercial quantities in 1956 began to be produced in more significant volumes – when oil prices profited from the Yom Kippur Arab-Israeli War, as the Arab chose to use oil as a weapon. The consequent quadrupling of oil prices increased Nigeria's purchasing power and following the rules of economics, its exchange rate went up. This happened naturally even though Nigeria had a bloc currency that was fixed by the Central Bank rather than being market determined. For as long as Nigeria earned all that money there was no problem with the exchange rate except that other commodities that were produced in the local 'Naira economy' would see the value of their earnings translate to modest Naira income. This low Naira value of the efforts of the cocoa farmer and the groundnut merchant kept making the enterprise less attractive. Responding to the economic nature of man the farmers saw greater incentives in being messengers in the expanding bureaucracy of government ministries than in tilling the land with very little to show for it. Following the principles of economics, groundnut pyramids began to disappear and cocoa exports continued to fade. Then oil prices did something that was very predictable by the principles of economic intercourse but that we had neglected: they crashed.

Why was this predictable? Crude oil is a commodity with minimal value added. A dramatic increase in its price would mean incentives to produce it wherever nature had stored it. Even if the place or nature of storage is more difficult to tame and access, like the North Sea, the higher prices increase the incentives to invest more to reach the commodity. There is also the fact of substitutes. Once prices go up enough, certain substitutes not attractive in earlier periods become more attractive. Having been resident in an oil consuming industrialized country, the United States, when oil prices peaked during the Iranian revolution in 1979, I could see more tolerance for nuclear energy, encouragement of exploration of difficult fields in continental USA and Americans beginning to 'surprise' Detroit by moving from the huge gas guzzling road cars to mid-size sedans that Europeans and Japanese already showed preference for. The crash of oil prices was simply a matter of time. The inevitable collapse of the price of such a mineral commodity, with consequences for budgets that have already expanded on the strength of rapidly growing income, had already come to be described as Dutch disease by economists because natural gas finds had put the Netherlands in such a predicament in the early 1960s.

The predictable crash came by 1982. It is still not clear if policy makers thought the price crash was a temporary thing or that it would hurt the middle class and *nouveau riche* too much to devalue and encourage resumption of interest in other exports. This crash would make their indulgence in consuming electronics, champagne, etc., which was not matched by their productivity, come down. What is certain is that business as usual continued with the exception of the introduction of stricter import licensing as a way of managing imports, many of which were easily available through open general licenses.

Given the profits available in a regime of scarcity, control would predictably produce rent seeking behavior– in this case a euphemism for debilitating corruption. Waiting to happen was a debt crisis. Soon foreign banks began to cut off lines of credit to Nigerian correspondent banks. Nigeria was stuck in international trade and all the austerity measures of the Buhari regime were not likely to produce growth that would sustain a higher quality of life for the citizens, the essence of economic policy.

Trapped as we were, those who said Nigeria did not respond to economic laws continued to live in denial, a fact that triggered the infamous IMF debate during which some of us were called all kinds of names for seeking a structural reorientation that could lead to an exit from the trap. A politically clever General Babangida escaped the trap he set by calling for a debate, by adjusting some other way. The Structural Adjustment Programme (SAP) freed us from becoming Albania (an 18th century economy in the 20th century) but the believers in Nigeria's peculiar nature missed that point and held on to the arbitrage possibilities of a two-tier exchange rate which the culture of corruption that characterized the post-1985 Nigeria brought in. The truth remains that the numbers on growth rates show that the peak years of SAP (1987-1991) produced the most remarkable economic progress since the late 1970s, the effort of that regime to sabotage its own policies for self aggrandizement, policy flip flops driven by lack of commitment to those policies, notwithstanding. Clearly, the jury is in on the peculiarity of Nigeria. The fact that cocoa exports took off in response to the devaluations of 1986-87, even if they were frustrated by problems of policy consistency and sequencing of adjustment policies, illustrates amply the point raised here. It is certain for me that these experiences and the reversal of economic progress in 1994, when the Abacha regime turned to controls before stability returned following abandonment of 1994 policies, prove that Nigeria responds to economic laws like any other country. This means that the imperative for you, ladies and gentlemen of the business community, is to truly educate yourselves on how the modern changing economy runs and to be a strong part of civil society acting and speaking up to ensure the right policies are in place.

I raise this point about your making an effort to truly understand economic policy drivers and being part of civil society because I am familiar with the territory. In the many years I have sat on the council of your sister chamber, the Lagos Chamber of Commerce and Industry, I have seen colleagues shoot themselves in the foot by proposing ideas that seemed to further their self-interest but turned out to hurt them. One of the more obvious was manufacturers being joyful that they would have preferential access to foreign exchange in 1994. As we all know they found that in the goal displacement common in bureaucratic controls they had a far worse situation in terms of access to foreign exchange than was the case before.

Wage Increases and Inflation

Having disposed of this myth about Nigeria being so peculiar that it is inappropriate to apply policies that work elsewhere in Nigeria, we can take on some of the other myths that have spurred a portfolio of policy initiatives that have left us reeling in the soporific effects of voodoo economics. Let us turn to the effect of wage increases on inflation.

One of the more difficult things to understand is that the government of Nigeria can go for six years without reviewing what it pays its workers. Considering that several of those years witnessed inflation approaching the three-digit mark it boggles the imagination to guestimate the real income of those workers. If we bear in mind the fact that government has been the biggest employer of labour and the failure of government to pay much of what it owes local businesses (domestic debt), causing **significant retrenchment of the private sector, the challenge of purchasing** power in the economy can only be more daunting. Very obviously this would mean that goods and services produced in the private sector would be outside the reach of consumers. With warehouses full, companies retrench and the vicious cycle goes on. Surely this is enough to make government review its wage policy? Not if there is a myth that any time there is a wage review market women raise their prices and inflation takes off.

This myth is repeated so often, yet no government official has made available a model of the economy that shows the inflationary effect of wage adjustment. The ultimate justification of the myth is the frequent finger pointing at the Udoji awards and subsequent inflation following that major hike with long back payment of the increases. Often conveniently forgotten is that the back pay made the amount of money injected into the system at once very significant, but more importantly nobody paid attention to the supply side. With little of what was desired available, too much money chased too few goods. The problems of absorptive capacity that led to bottlenecks at the ports ensured that the desired consumer goods could not come in quickly enough. Inflationary outcomes were inevitable under these circumstances.

Under current circumstances it seems to me that wage adjustments will reduce inventory in warehouses, cause capacity utilization to go up, thus yielding lower costs from economies of scale advantages. This should lead in the opposite direction from inflation. That wage increases automatically feed inflation surely is one reified myth that our economics could deal with differently, especially as we can tell that there are many other consequent variables such as supply and the level of the wage adjustment. There is also the issue of productivity. Some argue that the civil service has such a low level of productivity that wage increases will therefore result in money entering circulation that is not backed by output. This argument makes sense to the extent that policy makers retrench as they increase wages. We need fewer people on the public service. To pay fewer much better gets the job done. If we want a welfare function I will dare say it is better to dash out the money than make people a disturbance to work flow in the name of keeping them employed. That productivity is low today is due partly to the fact that many are so badly paid that they cannot afford the transportation costs to work five days a week. Some therefore come to work three days in a week.

Privatization

Another issue that has also come up frequently in the discussion of economic reform in Nigeria is privatization. The often emotion-laden discussions of privatization include such views as the process being one of giving away the family silver to a few wealthy and powerful people; privatization will only be the replacement of a government monopoly with a private monopoly, as subscription to the services of privatized balloon, with consequences for the poor, and for inflation in the economy. There are several other issues related to privatization that I have discussed extensively in published papers so I will not bother to raise them here. Perhaps an appropriate way to begin a reflection on the giving away of the family silver is an experience I had while doing research for the book *Managing Uncertainty: Competition and Strategy in Emerging Economies*. I had asked a former Managing Director of Nigerian National Petroleum Corporation (NNPC) about NNPC strategy and he sarcastically retorted to the effect that the problem with NNPC was that it was long ago privatized, except that the private owners of the NNPC did not pay for their purchase and the corporation was still considered public property in public discussions while in reality a few people did with it as they pleased. It was an informed albeit cynical response to the reality of many so-called public enterprises. People are afraid of giving away the family silver but in truth the family silver was long "given" to a few individuals. As these individuals have not paid for what they have full access to milking, the enterprises are managed as plunder, resulting in inefficiency and much higher costs which the people bear either directly in high rates of tariff or indirectly through taxation from which the subventions come. The clear examples of telephone calls to Nigeria from the United States being so much cheaper than those from Nigeria prove the point. How come services offered by private companies in the United States are cheaper? The answer is simple. Competition generates pressures to become more efficient and the need to build market share leads to part of the savings being passed on to consumers. More market share means economies of scale advantages that make it possible to further reduce prices. A virtuous cycle is established as opposed to the vicious cycle at the Nigerian end where the inefficiencies create opportunity for corruption.

What does corruption do to costs and the environment? A 1997 survey by the World Bank found that with a few exceptions corruption was found to be among the three most important obstacles to conducting business in developing countries. This survey of a sample of more than four thousand entrepreneurs in 69 countries confirms the fact that corruption creates an environment that puts obstacles to growth. Quite a bit of all that corruption flows from public ownership of enterprises. So deep is the effect of corruption that on a balance it would even be better to give three parastatals to a few individuals for free so long as the field would then be opened to competition from others. No one is suggesting they should be given away. There are means of ensuring that ordinary people get access to share ownership today or at a future date. The point of showing that people are still better off even if the family silver were given away is to give perspective to the challenge. The real question to ask is, should the children starve to death that the family silver be preserved? If no father will wish to keep the family silver in the face of famished children, surely the fact that ways of ensuring that some of the silver can stay in the family while getting desperately needed nourishment for the children should make the option imperative. For me therefore, the family silver analogy is a myth that has substituted for reality in the understanding of policy makers. Besides the foregoing, I have suggested elsewhere that one way of equitably transferring share is to recognize that civil servants have been cheated for years in terms of their wages. They could therefore receive shares in privatized corporations in lieu of salary arrears or as part of their pension scheme.

The other widely held point of view is that privatization will mean moving from a public monopoly to a private monopoly with the same problems persisting for the consumers. This is true only when competition is not allowed or where and when certain economies of scale are imperative. In the case of need for certain scale economies appropriate institutions do exist for consumer protection. If a privatized agency were to behave in a monopolistic manner, the fact that there are other players who can undercut its market share through pricing or higher quality service would check its conduct. Were liberalization to take place and competition allowed against a government agency, that government agency could use access to the regulators for predatory competitive behaviour. With a private enterprise and appropriate institutions for regulating the sector, the playing field would be more of level ground.

Indeed there are times when optimal scale economies require that you have a private monopoly. What has been done elsewhere in the world and so can be done here is to have a monopolies commission. A rates panel charged with approving rate hikes, with membership that includes consumers and other agencies, is also one way of ensuring that private monopolies operate in the interest of the common good. As I say frequently, if we can create in Nigeria a state that operates as efficiently as Singapore, I will not suggest that we try privatization and possibly end up with private monopoly. The truth is that nothing in our current realities suggests that as feasible. Being realistic therefore we need to turn to the other option.

The other big myth about privatization is that it can fuel inflation as the new owners raise rates of commercial levels or embark on new investments which have to be passed on to the consumer. As I have indicated earlier, it is possible that in the short run high rates may result, even though that is not necessarily the case if costs associated with the traditional inefficiency can be cut, but in the long run competition inevitably results in a better deal for the consumer. It is clear therefore that the myth of an inflationary consequence from privatization is exactly what we have said, a myth.

State Creation and Bringing Development to the Grassroots

Another big myth that has shaped the Nigerian political economy is that the closer government gets to the grassroots in terms of numbers of state governments and location of state capitals the more the pace of development is accelerated. This myth has led to persistent agitation for the creation of new states. What has been delivered is probably less of an improved quality of life as a multiplication of government bureaucracies that are bloated, and consuming resources that could have sustained wealth-creating activities.

Whereas in 1964 the premier of the Northern region, the Sardauna had an official fleet of three cars, today the military administrator of Adamawa state, a very small fraction of what the Sardauna used to govern, has more than twenty cars servicing the government house. With this kind of tradition it is not surprising that today's policy environment is marked by far less channelling of resources to wealth creation. With the focus on consuming what little there is in the maintenance of the multiplication of bureaucracies, growth and consequently development are denied the people. Indeed what we find with the proliferation of states and local governments is that most of the revenue allocated to these tiers of government go to the payment of salaries leaving paltry little for infrastructure development upon which real growth and true development are anchored.

It would seem from the foregoing that our concept of bringing government close to the people has not meant developing the people, and enhancing the quality of their life. Nobody listening to the debates preceding states creation would ever come to this conclusion, because the myth has assumed the dimension of reality in the consciences of many.

Economic Controls and the Protection of the Common Man

There is a very strong tendency to turn to controls when the people get under pressure from developments in the economy. The most frequently sought after of these controls is price control. The Lagos State government brought back these memories recently with the rent control edict. The announcement of rent control is always popular but in reality it never achieves its objectives. Consider the cost of building a block of four flats in Isolo, Lagos, or anywhere else for that matter. At the very least today, that would be ₦7 million. If rent control limits rent to ₦20,000 per flat per annum, it will take the landlord nearly 50 years to amortize his loan, if you add maintenance. If the opportunity cost of the money invested in putting up the building is measured from his investing the same money in the stock market, it will make no sense to invest in developing rental property. Most rational people will therefore not go that route. The consequence will be declining housing stock.

The truth is that many people who invest in building houses in Nigeria do so partly on less than fully rational choice, because a house looks like a solid investment they can see. Rent control edicts, unfortunately, have a way of reminding them of the reality of the non-rational choice in building a house, causing them to behave in a way that reduces the housing available. Governors seem for some reason not to have learnt from past experience. It never quite works anyway. It only creates tensions between landlords and tenants and eventually both parties find it better to ignore the edict.

Rent control makes moral and economic sense only when the houses have been bought from a subsidized government project or when they have been handed down for generations like in Europe and exposure amortized already. In this case, what rent controls aims at is checking predatory speculation or the use of price for keeping neighborhoods ethnically pure.

The bottom line for the experience with rent control is that people become less inclined to building rental 'iomes under such a regime of controls. The shortage of supply relative to demand triggers an upswing in rental values, the exact opposite of the intentions of rent control proponents. The problem of housing is better tackled through government building for sale, creating institutions to sustain the mortgage finance industry and through reducing inputs costs.

The Illusion of Importance

The policymaker in Nigeria is also often challenged to put proper perspective on Nigeria's value to the investor. In recent years, especially with Nigeria's decline to pariah status during the Abacha years, some sense of proportion about Nigeria's real value began to creep into the consciousness of Nigerians. The experience before now has been that Nigerians look at their population and the oil deposits and conclude that Nigeria is so important that investors will literally come crawling. Often absent from the estimation of the real worth of Nigeria to an investor is the real purchasing power available in this oil producing economy of more than one hundred million people. The truth, as the Human Development Index of UNDP and other reports tells us, is that Nigeria is one of the poorest countries on earth and that our policies keep making the policy worse.

This exaggerated understanding of the real attraction of the economy has often led policymakers, civil servants and state institutions to conduct affairs in a way that puts off potential partners. Nigeria is a country of tremendous potential but the truth is that it is a poor country that has been consistently mismanaged by incompetent leaders without a sense for their place in history.

Currency and Value Inflation

Another big myth we have to deal with in policy making is that the bigger denominations of currency drive inflation. We have reached a stage in which coins have literally gone out of use in Nigeria because the values of the coins have been made irrelevant by inflation. Yet higher denominations of coins would not be minted and currency notes have become the base units of commerce. With the five Naira note as the lowest unit of measurement in actual use we find prices have been moving in five Naira steps.

To moderate inflation, higher denominations of currency have not been introduced yet the five Naira as the base unit has meant that inflation is accelerated as prices shift in those magnitudes. In reality what we achieve is the opposite of our intentions. Add to that the nightmare of logging around cartons of Naira notes in a cash economy like Nigeria and you will see the great disservice this myth has done to us.

My colleague Ayo Teriba has, in his work, provided more than ample evidence that commerce is inhibited by these currency policies and that it makes economic sense from the typical life span of coins, currencies and costs of producing them to coin the present currency denominations of ₦5, ₦10, ₦20 and ₦50 which at the exchange rate of October 1998 have USD value of about 6 cents, 12 cents, 24 cents and 60 cents respectively.

In my travels around the world, I have found that coins have much higher values than our top currency denomination. Surely the 500 yen coin in Japan has a USD value of about three dollars and fifty cents. As Teriba also shows in his research, the poor countries that have embarked on currency reform and printed much higher currency values like Kenya have not necessarily had a rate of inflation worse than what Nigeria has had. Many, in fact, have lower rates of inflation.

The Human Face Illusion

Finally, let us consider the illusion that the way to put a human face on the structure of the economy is to maintain subsidies which distort value and create wrong incentive structures.

In the early years of SAP former head of State General Olusegun Obasanjo criticized the programme for not having a human face. Perhaps there was a basis for criticizing the fact that the Gini coefficient, the measure of the gap between the most well off and the poorest, was widening, especially because rent-seeking opportunities which were not necessarily part of adjustment were allowed by the Babangida government. But that was not Obasanjo's criticism at the launching of General Joe Garba's book. The general's human face criticism led a regime anxious to retain popularity to embark on a USD 600 million 'reflation' of the economy. The outcome was resumption of inflation that was being brought under control. Who paid the price of inflation? The common man who was being 'protected' by the new policy thrust.

The truth, as I see it, is that you can see this poor 'common man' suffer in the face of many policies ostensibly designed to subsidize existence. Billions of dollars have been poured into NAFCON, the fertilizer company. The subsidy stretches into transportation and distribution of the fertilizer. Yet everyone knows that the farmer does not pay the subsidy price. The entire subsidy ends up in the pockets of middlemen, civil servants and State Military Administrators. What most farmers who can manage to get the stuff pay is often less than if private firms imported it and sold it at market prices.

The same story can be repeated for other subsidies including the emotional subject of petrol pricing. We have now reached a point that frequent petrol shortages mean that people are paying more than commercial prices in the black market, yet oil-marketing companies are not in a position to replace their fuel pumps and the infrastructure for distributing fuel is on the edge of collapse.

Conclusion

The Nigerian economy is about the life of more than a hundred million people and deserves, at the least, to be managed with a bigger sense of responsibility than has been the case so far. The way myths have been the basis for policy choice is a major case in point. In the foregoing we have tried to show how many myths have been reified into the platform of decision making.

The challenge that you ladies and gentlemen of the Calabar Chamber of Commerce must see and rise to is how you can as part of civil society help develop institutions that constrain the making of policies on such myths.

SECTION II

THE ENVIRONMENT OF BANKING AND FINANCE

10

Sources of Uncertainty in Nigerian Banking: Implications for Transaction Costs and Role of Institutions*

When the idea of starting a series of Annual Conferences focussing on several sectors of the economy came alive at LBS I was engaged in the study of competitive strategy in five sectors of the economy. One of them was the banking sector. What I learned from the study about the effects of the level of uncertainty on the strategy that banks pursued, and some of the deductions from influence of regulations and their enforcement on transaction costs, led me into exploring Institutional Economics.

The increase in my understanding of this relatively young school in economics made me anxious to create an opportunity for policy makers, those who man institutions in the banking sector, bankers and mere academic observers of the scene like myself, to jointly explore how institution building can help reduce transaction costs. Surely, if transaction costs come down, the quantum of activity will go up, financial deepening will increase and the capacity of the system to sustain new investments and economic development will be enhanced. I am pleased therefore that this Annual Sector Conference series is beginning with the banking sector. This will provide us the opportunity to explore issues that do not so often get discussed without inhibitions. I am convinced that the outcome, followed through in good faith, will have a salutary effect on creating a level playing field and strengthening institutions so as to lower transaction costs.

My intention is first to explicate the concept of uncertainty. I will then turn to another critical concept, decision making. This is because uncertainty is important here to the extent that it affects how decisions are made. After a discussion of decision making we will examine some of the issues that generate uncertainty in the industry, the nature of institutions and how institutions can lower transaction costs in Nigerian banking.

---

* Session given at LBS Sector Conference in Banking

119

Uncertainty

What is uncertainty? Uncertainty, in essence, is about knowledge related to state of outcomes. Whenever there is lack of knowledge about the consequence of action it can be said that there is uncertainty. The absence of knowledge regarding decision outcomes is a matter of degree. What is critical is the degree of knowledge available to the decision-maker concerning outcome of a particular course of action chosen. For uncertainty to be the characteristic of a decision situation, more than one outcome should be possible for each alternative action and the probabilities of those outcomes not be known.

Let us illustrate the point. By October many Nigerian companies become reluctant to open letters of credit to import raw materials inputs from abroad. The reason is that the goods very likely will not arrive before January 1 and on the first day of January a budget document is usually released which could ban the importation of that input. In the case of a ban of imports of that item the company would bear the loss from that transaction or the duty could be increased making the final product too expensive in a time of declining purchasing power. It could also happen that the tariffs on the finished products are lowered such that the on-cost of the local producer, given infrastructure weakness, makes the local producer extremely uncompetitive. Other possibilities of outcomes from the budget which changes several policy thrusts every year can be projected. Clearly we are faced here with more than one outcome and the probability of any outcome is not possible to calculate without more information being made available.

Uncertainty, described above, differs from risk in the sense of degree of the knowledge that is available about outcome. In the case of risk there exists a lot more objective evidence so that it can be treated in terms of objective probability. Actuarial science on which the insurance industry is founded is about computing the probability of outcome. Here the probability of outcome is determined objectively. They therefore deal with risks. In the banking industry actuarial science is present in the form of derivatives, products designed to help firms manage such calculable risks as foreign currency exposure and interest rate fluctuations.

Uncertainty and risk are not a dichotomy, rather they are located at different points on a continuum where risk is at the point at which all possible outcomes are known and the probability of their occurring can be computed while uncertainty is at the end where information is lacking. The difference is essentially the same kind of difference between a small business like a neighbourhood grocery store and an entrepreneurial venture. The grocery store idea has been done by thousands of housewives and so enough knowledge of the enterprise exists. It does not mean that the neighborhood grocer does not encounter the possibility of losing money and failing. If information about outcomes were perfect then it would not be just people with some kind of gut who go into business while others become bureaucrats and professional managers. The grocer runs a risk. But the businessman who tries to create something that satisfies a customer's need, where no such product existed nor the need for it obviously discernable, will face challenges because outcomes are all too difficult to predict because of lack of knowledge of how customers could respond to the service or product. This is the territory of the entrepreneur and his challenge is to gather more and more information on possible outcomes as the enterprise progresses so that uncertainty fades away until it becomes a matter of risk at the stage of full implementation of the entrepreneurial process.

Lack of knowledge relating to the probability of outcomes for many economic activities in which banks in Nigeria are involved means that banks have to develop coping mechanism that provide them some comfort in the case of the unpreferred outcome. One typical coping mechanism is to make haste slowly regarding an opportunity lest regulations change with catastrophic loss consequences. The opportunity cost of questing opportunities lost can be seen in the stunted developments of banks. Yet another example will be the lack of knowledge on probabilities of outcome with compliance to specified lending by policy to a preferred sectors. We have found enormous moral hazard challenges from NEXIM and NERFUND type lending. With little sensitivity to the problems of the banks when the deductions from the accounts of the banks are made at the Central Bank for loans not being serviced by the borrower, this power based relationship has significant transaction cost consequences as banks strive to protect themselves from these hazardous kinds of lending.

It is therefore not surprising that Douglas North, in his seminal study of institutions and change, posits that "the inability of societies to develop effective, low cost enforcement of contracts is the most important source of both historical stagnation and contemporary underdevelopment in the

Third World." We shall talk some more about Douglas North whose outstanding insights into the role of institutions in economic development underlined the arrival of the school of Institutional Economics and won him a Nobel prize in economics. But first we have to pursue ways and means of achieving low cost enforcement of contracts in the Nigerian banking system. These contracts include relationships and expectations set out by policy in terms of how banks should act as licensed agent of the authorities; and agreements between banks and their customers on both the deposit and lending sides of the business.

Decision Making

Where there are contending possibilities of action to achieve a given objective, people and organizations are challenged with how best to proceed with the course of action and achieve the desired objective, usually at the least cost. Sometimes people or even businesses do not proceed along the path of the least cost either for reasons of altruism, not wanting to create incidental cost to others, or because the chosen path perhaps brings ego gratification to those making the decision for an organization. Most times the additional cost of that alternative path is either negligible to the organization or can actually be computed in a way that makes the organization add it up as a benefit rather than a cost.

The people who make decisions for the Shell Petroleum Development Company in Nigeria as wealth maximizers trying to arrive at the objective of exploring oil in the Niger basin should, ordinarily, probably not bother with the communities around the oil wells so long as they do not inflict costs such as environment degradation through oil spillage; after all, community welfare is government business and Shell pays its taxes. Any Shell manager who lived through the Ogoni crisis and the huge international costs that it inflicted on Shell's reputation will probably choose to add more costs by oiling community relations, perhaps through providing services it is not obligated to provide. Such was the damage that Shell might indeed consider contributing to projects that could strengthen democratic institutions and save her the trouble of any future repeat of talk about international trade sanctions against a Nigeria ruled by military dictators. In these kinds of response an observer not familiar with Shell's experience may analyze Shell's action and say its social responsibility spending is incongruent with the least cost attribute of effective decision making. That, of course, would be inaccurate measuring of cost.

Choice behaviour is very important to human beings even though a significant percentage, perhaps more than 90 percent, of our choices do not involve extensive processing. Most choices between alternatives are basically Pavlovian responses. In all these instances, be it an extended processing decision or a thoughtless act, a commitment of resources takes place.

Most corporate entities pursue objectives that require several levels and types of decisions to be made all the time. Some functions that require basic decisions that keep the machine of the organization rolling are made frequently and repetitively, so for consistency and control purposes these activities are routinized. This bureaucratic activity of decision making, though useful, is a little further down the scale of what is necessary for sustaining above average performance for the organizations into the long term.

The kind of decisions that make our firms develop advantages over rivals are of a strategic nature. Usually, other decisions of significance depend on those earlier decisions of a strategic nature. Pervasive uncertainty naturally makes us reluctant to commit to decisions that are so fundamental that so much more ride on them. The effect of uncertainty on decision-making, therefore, is that the time horizons are very short. The consequence of short time horizons is the absence of a strategic orientation and the inability of banks to develop sustainable competitive advantage attributes. This is because the building of competence that drive competitive advantage involves investments of a significant nature which nobody will make unless they can hope to recoup the investments over an appropriate time horizon.

Bearing these conceptual issues in mind let us now turn to specific causes and sources of uncertainty in Nigerian banks.

Sources of Uncertainty in Nigerian Banking

I have chosen to make available, along with this paper, an essay I wrote in January 1996 for the LBS Management Review Vol. 1, No. 2. The essay "Institutions and the Evolution of Competition in Nigerian Banking Industry" illustrates the evolution of my thinking on Uncertainty in Nigerian Banking. A reading of that research report will give greater meaning to the points I am trying to make here and save us the trouble of more detailed explication of the relationships between an array of phenomena involved in uncertainty and the role of institutions in banking.

With support from that earlier effort, let me point to a few sources of uncertainty that we will discuss, even if only summarily. These include a dearth of information for decision making regarding transactions in banking; issues of ethics in the industry; level of knowledge, skills or competence in Nigerian banks; dominance of the industry by three big players, all of which are not necessarily driven by the most rational economic consideration because of antecedent factors; the role of government with respect to stabilization securities, inadequate development of the government securities market since open market operations (OMO) came into play and general instability in the macroeconomic policy arena. The absence of strong business associations have also been a source of uncertainty in banking.

Dearth Of Information For Decision Making

In my discussion recently of the Nigerian Interbank Offered Rate (NIBOR) I dwelt quite a bit on this subject of information, decision making and transaction costs. The subject is important enough for us to explore it again without repeating much. The point was already made last week that the non-transparent manner in which banks price financial assets on the one hand and the absence of adequate information to systematically rank the risk of exposure to particular companies makes the system most inefficient. The transaction costs consequent upon this include the process of providing collateral securities which are expensive to execute and often hard to realize. It is no wonder that, inspite of the high cost of providing these assets, the rate of provisioning since the prudential guidelines were introduced has been such that if a compromise was not reached most of the big banks would have lost such much that the consequent ruin would result in technical bankruptcy. Managed as it was, some suffered a nearly 50 percent collapse of their market capitalization.

Another set of examples of the impact of inadequate information on transaction costs is the collapse of the Interbank Market and the so-called flight to safety from new or small banks into sometimes costly inefficiency of banks whose size leave the impression of greater safety. In the case of the Interbank Market, lack of information, combined with the distortion that Foreign Exchange sales brought into the market as Naira was desperately sought to pay Fx, pushed up Interbank rates to unreasonable proportions. Without adequate information to assess, the borrowing banks may host money badly in transactions with troubled banks. The ultimate transaction cost came with the collapse of the Interbank market.

Other sources of uncertainty include lack of trust of the evaluation of the health of banks by examining officials who have been known to be influenced by more than just what they see. To this list can be added:

Level of Knowledge

There is consensus among industry watchers that the growth in the number of banks created numerous opportunities for a few skilled bankers. The outcome was the frequent moves by young officers who reached very senior positions before they were really prepared for that level of work. Some have in fact observed that we have more skilled women bankers because they were generally more patient than the men who jumped at every opportunity for a pay increase or a bigger title.

Not being able to trust the judgement of overpaid Executive Directors who should be junior managers has added to uncertainty in decision making.

Dominance of The Big Three

Until recent efforts at privatizing the big three banks, First Bank, Union Bank and UBA have been managed by people who owe their position not to shareholders but to government officials who appointed them. Their motivation in certain choices could be from reference frames that are not easy to estimate from a commercial point of view.

Ethics

With arbitrage possibilities in a two-tier foreign exchange market the banking industry came to attract an unfortunate notoriety for poor ethical conduct. Problematic ethics lead often to suboptimization and the introduction of extraneous variables to decision making. The effect is, of course, increased uncertainty about choice behaviour.

Conclusion

I have made this summary presentation essentially to introduce the sets of phenomena which we expect the presentation of the regulators and practitioners to elucidate, amplify and expand. In the discussions consequent upon these presentations that will surely be much informed than mine I expect that we will see value that can positively affect how institutional development is facilitated in the Nigerian banking industry.

11

NIBOR: Issue to Bear in Mind*

It gives me a great pleasure to be part of this effort to throw some light on the idea of a Nigerian Inter-Bank Offer Rate (NIBOR). As NIBOR is designed to come on-stream shortly, I believe this exercise is worthwhile so that it is not that yet another idea is inaugurated, then challenges that should have been foreseen trigger a crisis shortly after commencement of the programme.

Funke Osibodu and Bunmi Oni have provided perspectives from both the lender and the borrower sides of the business of mobilizing savings from areas of surplus to intermediate needs in capital deficit parts of the economy. What is left for me as a student of the process is to highlight a few areas that the process has to be more sensitive to if the objective, a benchmark or interest rate reference framework, is to be realized for the mutual benefit of both borrowers and lenders.

Let me put forward a caveat before I get into the body of my presentation. I have already given notice that I am an academic. Understandably, therefore, my thrust will be to seek relationships between phenomena, which sometimes lead to an approach some may consider academic. Instead of apologizing for sounding academic, even when you have been warned that I am a teacher, what I try to do, as I shall today, is to present relationships between phenomena in a manner that will hopefully contribute to a framework for understanding matters, theory, while being mindful that the audience is made up of business people who want to know how the issues in question affect the decisions they will have to make when they return to their offices.

NIBOR is about setting a benchmark rate for pricing financial assets through a basket of 12 banks with the highest two and lowest two perceived rates eliminated in favour of the average from the other eight. Our task is to see that it leads to a more developed financial products market.

With that piece of housekeeping out of the way, let me identify the key issues I want to draw attention to. These include the efficiency of

---

* Session given at LBS Sector Conference in Banking

banks that make it into the benchmark basket; the problem of information asymmetries in exchange transactions; the things that drive transaction costs which influence the spread between rates to depositors and rates at which banks lend to borrowers; and the state of the Interbank Market. Other matters that will arise in this short presentation will include how strategies of banks are affected by the economic fundamentals and how the strategies on their part affect the cost of funds; the institutional arrangements in the sector which affect the availability of long term funds and the question of matching of tenor. I will also raise the issue of the effect of regulatory agencies action if NIBOR is to work even though I will be reserving the bulk of my comments on the role of institutions and transaction costs until next week when that is central subject of the other half of the sector Conference on Banking.

Why a Nibor?

There are those who will ask why a Nigerian Inter-Bank Offer Rate benchmark. Is it because we have become used to the concept of a LIBOR and we must imitate everything done in London? Has the market not managed to function so far without a NIBOR? These are not foolish questions but I think there are adequate answers to justify NIBOR.

It seems to me that our recognition of markets as information processing systems makes explanation of the need for NIBOR easier. Where information helps approximate rationality more in the choice between offerings, the market gets more efficient and the pricing of interest rates becomes such that economic activities increase and wealth is created. This is part of the objective of financial liberalization which aims to bring about greater financial deepening.

The problem with the goal of financial deepening in Nigeria is that information asymmetries, which are rampant in the economy, result in power based relationships that introduce distortions hampering the pace of economic intercourse. By introducing a benchmark which comes from a basket of banks, we in effect provide information that guides participants.

Eventually, the reference rates that emerge from more information being available will reduce the level of uncertainty in the market such that the risks are more measurable, leading the market to develop beyond the current short tenors. The resulting longer term investment can be supported by financial services products from the banking industry with consequent enhancement of the wealth creating capacity of the economy.

It is also noteworthy, here, that as available information reduces uncertainty to the level of risk, derivatives, hedging products of various types, will become more available and will drive the development of the financial system.

The foregoing suggests that there is clearly a major value in the idea of a NIBOR. Our challenge, therefore, is not to show that NIBOR is a step in the right direction but to raise issues to which to be sensitive so that the full benefits can be derived.

In this regard, we must pay attention not only to extremes of situations of imperfect information in the market but also to the very significant disparity in the level of knowledge in different banks. Hopefully, part of the challenge of NIBOR will be to help in building up a knowledge base and getting the industry to operate more on a level playing field with information becoming more accessible, not just regarding the risk profile of customers but also regarding the competitive forces that shape the strategies of banks. This is where a critical role comes in for institutions whose place it is to ensure a level playing field and the availability of information which then reduces uncertainty.

The Reference Banks

It is my understanding that the benchmark from which interest rate risks will be priced will come from a basket of reference banks. Twelve banks will form this pool. From the perceived rate that each of these reference banks supply, the money mart secretariat for various tenors, an average will emerge. These NIBOR quotes from the reference banks, which will be specific and in four decimal places, will be sorted with the two highest input and lowest-rates eliminated for each tenor. The average of the remaining eight will be the NIBOR for the next week.

This modus operandi suggests that critical attention need be paid to the reference banks because their perceived rates will be a function of the strategy of the individual banks and the fundamentals of the economy.

If we start from the fundamental premise that the deposit structure drives the pricing of assets for banks, it is important to then consider how both the fundamentals of the economy and the strategies of banks affect their perception of rates which translates into the benchmark from the basket. Ideally, the perception of rates should flow from the response to such economic fundamentals as rate of inflation, level of government deficits etc., Central Bank rediscount rates and the strategy that allows the bank to develop a healthy base of savings. There are of course other factors such as government securities reserve requirements, credit ceiling and what equipment keeping guidelines allow, but the real issue in our environment is that deposit base does not necessarily reflect the typical competitive forces which drive strategy in an environment where you have NIBOR. Here a very inefficient bank with the right networking can attract preferential treatment in anything such as collecting revenue for government.

When in the NIBOR environment we find that it is the primary five forces of the Michael Porter model (existing rivalry between firms; threat of substitute products; threat of new entrants; bargaining power of buyers; and, bargaining power of suppliers) that drive pricing and firm performance, we must add for the emerging economy environment megafactors from the 3E framework that I have proposed. By the time you deal with the level of development of institutions, the dominant role of government and the sometimes predatory role of government officials, you find other factors that drive strategy and, naturally, the perception of pricing within the context of the particular bank. If business associations do not emerge in banking that brings enough pressure to bear on shaping the institutions that shape the parameters of acceptable conduct, then a playing field that is not level will continue to be the marked feature of the industry. That would badly affect the possibility of a true market which makes a benchmark rate a valuable compass around which the risk involved in lending to a particular clientele can be plotted.

Transaction Cost Drivers

We have already identified the level of information available as a driver of transaction costs, but there are other drivers of transaction costs which are important to raise because one of the areas of difficulty will be in the pricing of deposits or liabilities when a benchmark rate for asset pricing is available. The contentious issue of spread which the regulatory agencies have tried to manage by bureaucratic means at some points in our history is very much dependent on what drives transaction costs. The nature of sources of deposits, sudden changes in regulatory requirements and how they impact differently on strategic choices of banks provisioning etc may result in transaction costs that could excite troubled bargaining in the pricing of liabilities. The good thing however is that this will pressure banks into becoming more efficient.

Confidence and the State of the Interbank Market

We are discussing here the rates that banks price their assets in transactions with other banks which then go on to be benchmarks for calibrating premium on risks represented by other borrowers. It is imperative in this circumstance to reflect on the state of the Interbank market. We know this market literally disappeared because of problems of confidence following systemic distress in which banks got caught not knowing the state of health of other banks.

For confidence to be high and allow the Interbank market to return and be a true market, institutions, including regulatory agencies, need to be fully developed and responsive. It is our hope that the inauguration of a NIBOR will stimulate the emergence of more institutions that add to confidence and encourage the regulatory institutions to seek to be even more responsive to the challenge of creating confidence, a challenge that next week's conference will focus more closely on.

Strategies of Banks

At this time when many are calling for universal banking, the impression is created that bankers are not keen on developing strategies that can give them sustainable competitive advantage over rivals that are based on a focus. The feeling you get as an observer is that everyone wants a shot at whatever seems possible to stay afloat today. Unfortunately, this means that they do not develop the core competences that enable them grow a niche. There are of course some banks whose focus you can see clearly so that the call for universal banking may be overblown from what the casual observer sees. While it is a good idea that policy restricting banks is probably not the best way to free the market, the nature of markets do not suggest that universal banking is the necessary outcome of liberalization. This point is important because trying to be all things to all people makes banks less than efficient and the costs that so build, reflected in their perceived rate, do not make for a truly efficient market. When banks do not have the competence to craft unique positioning their inefficiencies are reflected in the quality of their assets which eventually translate into their cost profile and their perception of rates.

Information About Borrowers

I have spent most of the time talking about the banks essentially because my academic interest is in institutions and transaction costs. The other side of the information challenge for this market is knowledge about the risk represented by each borrower. We do not have a great tradition of ratings agencies, and firms are not willing to give out information about themselves. Until this situation changes, how we determine whether you are NIBOR + 2 or NIBOR + 10 will be left to the discretion of managers who may not even be well equipped to guess well. Part of the issue today is to ask the Bunmi Onis and their colleagues in managing firms that create wealth in Nigeria to become less reticent about making information available about themselves because in the end the good firms will profit from totally transparent systems.

Conclusion

I have tried to highlight some issues that the NIBOR idea leads me to thinking about. It seems to me that if we can pay proper attention to these issues we will create a market, through NIBOR, that will facilitate wealth creation in Nigeria.

12

Environmental Factors and the Development of Insurance in Nigeria: Challenges for the New Millennium*

The last time I spoke to the insurance community, I laid claim to honorary membership of the clan since the repeat invitations were beginning to come quite frequently. With the invitation to today's conference, I am getting ready for a frequent flyer type programme with the industry. On a more serious note, I am pleased with the growing association with the industry because I recognize its importance in economic development. If in sharing my thoughts with you, the practitioners, I can in some way, no matter how modestly, arouse a higher drive for achieving goals that propel the engine of growth, I will be truly fulfilled. It is therefore a matter of honour for me that I have been given yet another chance to feel that I am making a contribution to the future by bringing to your attention some factors in the environment which, if properly addressed, could lead to the industry assuming its rightful place as a key part of the engine of growth and development.

The specific subject I have been asked to address today is "Environmental Factors and the Development of Insurance in Nigeria: Challenges for the New Millennium." To carry out the task in a manageable way, I have broken the discussion into four parts beginning with an introduction, followed by a review of the evolution of the insurance industry. The third part deals with changes that will shape the future while the fourth part focusses albeit summarily on strategies for winning in this brave new future.

Introduction

It seems trite to say that we live in a rapidly changing environment. The assumption that the reality of rapid change is something all executives

---

* Address to the Nigerian Insurance Association 19/3/98

are sensitive to is unfortunately not borne out by how we manage our companies. If indeed we recognize the profound nature of these changes then surely we will develop a capacity for learning in our companies that allows us to keep pace with the environment. Such sensitivity to change should also induce us to develop patterns of adaptation that keep us effective and strongly competitive. The insurance industry in Nigeria will have to learn to adapt to a variety of looming changes in its environment if it is to survive in the next millennium which is but only a breath away. Among the areas from which these environment challenges will come on is technology, awareness about the value of insurance, the general level of uncertainty and perception of risk in the environment and skills available within the insurance industry. Other areas where changing factors that impact on the industry will come from include corporate globalization, the evolution of institutions that affect trends in economic intercourse and the transformation of regional markets. These factors will surely affect the performance of insurance companies in Nigeria in the new millennium. We will do well therefore to discuss these factors and develop scenarios about how they are likely to affect performance in the insurance industry. To develop an appropriate base for discussing these scenarios it should serve us well to look at where we are coming from.

The Evolution of the Nigerian Insurance Industry

The Nigerian insurance industry did not develop in isolation of the global trend in sharing risk. It is useful therefore to consider its evolution in the context of the earlier traditions of insurance as we know it. Surely, the moral economy of peasant Nigeria, before colonial rule, had forms of social insurance, especially in the extended family system where in-laws were your hedge against adversity. Insurance as a professional enterprise of pooling premiums to spread risks was alien to Nigeria until colonial times. Insurance came to Nigeria by way of Britain, the colonial metropolis, even though its earliest modern roots were in the United States of America.

Earliest Origins of Insurance Practice

In its modern form insurance practice locates its roots in pre-independent America. There, precisely in Philadelphia in 1759, the Presbyterian Ministers Fund with the corporation for the relief of poor and distressed

Presbyterians and the Distressed Widows of the Presbyterian Church became the first formally incorporated Life Insurance undertakings in the world. As we will show later the impact of Insurance Companies in financial intermediation which spurs growth and development, it is important to bear in mind that this insurance venture predated the first commercial bank in the United States by two decades. The latter was birthed in 1782. Property and Casualty Insurance even predates life insurance by three decades.

It is remarkable that one of the earliest life insurance products was low premium, modest sum assured policies sold door to door through weekly or monthly collection. This product archetype known as industrial life has not had a great run here even though our conditions today resemble early 19th century United States. It seemed to work in the early days after independence and was at the core of the strategy of the British American Insurance Company. To the best of my knowledge, BAICO, which succeeded British-American, has literally abandoned industrial life. The excuse, or shall we say the reason, many insurance companies give for not staying solely in life insurance and primarily in industrial life is that purchasing power has declined so much the ordinary customer for industrial life is more concerned about surviving today than about protecting tomorrow. Do we really know this for sure? How much research have we done to understand what the customer really wants? Could it not be laziness in doing our environmental scanning or even the exaggerated ability to know what is good for the customer that is driving the choices we are making which in turn are affecting the performance of our individual companies and the whole insurance industry? We shall return to this subject later. Let it suffice for now that the Nigerian insurance industry has lagged far behind its counterparts elsewhere, when they were at our current stage of development, and that these failings could probably be located in how well the industry does its environment scanning, the level of creativity and innovation in the industry and the general challenge of competence building in a sector that should be a leading source of financial intermediation, setting the course of the development of the Nigerian economy.

It is important to make the point that many of the challenges that face the Nigerian insurance industry also confronted the American industry some one hundred and fifty years ago. They (the problems) were confronted and overcame, producing clear lessons that should enable us leapfrog these stages of development. There are adaptation and acculturation challenges, surely, but we do not have to re-invent the wheel. Let us take an example. By early 19th century the mutual forms of insurance companies were already making their way into the market place. As a member of one of the biggest mutual life insurance companies in the United States for the last sixteen years, I can tell you that I find in that form of corporate organization ample opportunity for breaking a good deal of the resistance to the insurance habit in Nigeria. Mutuals succeeded because those early insurance firms exposed themselves to learning from their experiences and their environment. My fear is that many of us in the Nigerian Insurance Industry are too bureaucratic and too steeped in routine to draw from our learning and convert such into improving corporate performance. If we were not so disposed, we would have made a lot more progress. Let us use a specific example from the early days of America's insurance industry.

When mutuals began to emerge in fire insurance in the 1820s and 1830s, an engineer who had written extensively on solar light and gravitation joined the trend. Zachariah Allen in 1835 incorporated 'The Manufacturers Mutual.' It was the first mutual to write fire insurance for cotton mills which were subject to a lot of fire incidents back in those days. His close study of fire prevention required insured mills to adhere to strict requirements and submit to frequent detailed inspections. These efforts went so well that mill insurance rates soon dropped by 30 percent. Dropping rates in the face of greater Use-Value being created for the customer should translate into market share. This happened in the early days in the United States. I do not believe we can speak of a similar phenomenon in the evolution of the Nigerian Insurance Industry.

The direct antecedents of the Nigerian Insurance Industry are of course not the American tradition but the European heritage through colonial contact. There in Europe gambling annuities from the Middle Ages matured into the Society of Equitable Assurances of Lives and Survivors which was founded in 1762. About one hundred and sixty years after, the Royal Exchange and Assurance Company was incorporated in 1921 in Nigeria. The field was dominated by subsidiaries of foreign insurers for many years after REAN blazed the trail even though its headquarters was in London. Lack of commitment to an ambitious role in national development was therefore understandable. Nigerians were active primarily as brokers and agents until the civil war of 1967. Shortly after the war indigenous entrepreneurial capacity saw the beginning of the climbing of ladders of opportunity from brokerage into underwriting. I have found the example of Leadway particularly interesting because the provincial roots represent for me an example that geographic and product niches are possible to develop if we are ready to work hard. It is in my opinion the result of failure to draw that lesson that leads many in the industry to want to be in all forms of insurance.

The Okigbo commission on the Nigerian Financial System in 1976 reviewed the role of financial institutions in economic development. The acquisition of a majority of shareholding from the foreign partners by the government as a result of the work of the Okigbo commission and the Nigerian Enterprises Promotion Decree essentially indigenized the insurance industry. With the structural adjustment programme in the late 1980s there was a rush of new entrants into insurance just as it had happened a few years earlier with banking. These changes were to affect industry structure profoundly.

Regulations Institutions and Insurance Development

In the decade before independence the leading insurance companies in Nigeria, the Royal Exchange and Assurance, Union Fire Insurance Society and Tobacco Insurance Company were essentially guided by the Companies Act of 1922 and the Motor Vehicle (Third Party Insurance) Act of 1950. The laws remained generally stable for many years because the environment did not change dramatically and because the industry did not seek to play a more central role in the economy. At least it failed to capture the financial intermediation high ground its counterparts in the US and elsewhere hold.

The reason for the slow pace of evolution of insurance in Nigeria can be partly explained by the fact that multinational company operations had limited scope and were not challenged to rise to the financial intermediation role insurance has played so well elsewhere. That explanation has limitations, however, considering the fact that banking was also largely multinational even though we had two bursts of indigenous entrepreneurial incursions into banking in the 1920s and the early 1950s.

Even government was not moved to regulate insurance practice in

Nigeria in the interest of the public until much later than with banking. Perhaps the systemic distress in banking in the 1920s and early 1950s caused government to respond with the banking ordinance of 1952 and the Central Bank Act of 1958. Insurance had to wait until 1961 for government to offer the first comprehensive insurance legislation.

The 1961 Act obviously was intended to help an indigenous insurance industry to emerge. It discriminated in favour of indigenous insurance companies in terms of minimum paid up capital among other issues. It also began to create a framework for self regulation and trade group promotion by making the Insurance Consultative body of the Lagos Chamber of Commerce gain credence and become the nucleus of the Nigeria Insurance Association. The act also institutionalized the practice of annual reporting to the responsible government agency and provision of solvency margins that guide the asset and liability ratio build up of companies.

In 1976 government action, in the middle of the oil boom and the consequent consumption and importation frenzy, was to prove a boost to the local insurance industry. The 1976 law required that Nigerian insurance companies insure maritime trade risks. This advantage was in many cases offset by problems created by the cement armada in the face of low absorptive capacity which made ships wait for weeks to berth in Nigerian ports. As a result many ships did desperate things to get out of the long wait to enter Nigeria harbours. This environmental shortcoming translated into claims that eroded the profitability potential of Nigerian insurance companies that had been given such an advantage.

An indicator of growing challenges in the Insurance Sector was the increasing rapidity with which the enabling laws were tampered with. In 1991 an omnibus decree was promulgated raising minimum share capital, reintroducing solvency rates that had disappeared as requirement in 1976 and mandating membership of the NIA for all insurance companies. Six years later a new decree created the National Insurance Commission (NAICOM) as a regulatory body. The 1997 decree had the effect of increasing minimum paid up capital.

It would seem to me that efforts to regulate the industry have consisted mainly of increases in minimum capital and reporting requirements for insurance companies. Surely, these capital increases bear very little relationship to the particular strategy pursued by insurance companies.

While capital adequacy is important to protect the customer from sudden failure of insurance companies, the trade-off is against entrepreneurship in the sector. A similar regulatory mindset exists in the banking industry now and neither serves well the growth needs of the financial services sector. Those with ideas who have opted for a strategic position in a niche that does not require as much capital find that a big entry barrier has been erected. It is my opinion that the great challenge is one of more effective monitoring with solvency ratios based on the nature of the particular risks being covered. This may seem like a lot of work, and many of us could use less work. But the reality is that it will better profit the economy.

The Paradox of Focus and General Insurance

The journey so far in the Nigerian insurance scene is that it is characterized by a high degree of gravitation towards General Insurance, the coverage of all risks. Perhaps with such a trend one broad minimum capital base, with the goal post moving up ever so often, seems understandable. I have made the point elsewhere that I understand African Alliance is probably the only Life Assurance Company left in Nigeria. I recognize a few small players exist here and there. This again is like the clamour for universal banking. How easy is it to be all things to all people. Can we build competencies in all areas of insurance practice such that these competencies give us a sustainable advantage over rivals? The debate between focus and diversification strategies is far from settled but it is noteworthy that very focussed enterprises tend to return a higher rate on the investment than broadly diversified operations which, in struggling to defend various flanks, soon get into unchecked retreat and fall into the trap that leads to corporate surrender.

It is my view that the limited development of the Nigerian insurance Industry which keeps it far below its potential comes from lack of focus, and it should seriously consider investing in the competencies that allow the companies to create customer value thereby growing their market share and improving corporate performance.

The challenge of leadership within Insurance Companies today seems to me to be the challenge of broadening horizons of its managers and executives to recognize that this is not about technical competence in actuarial science but about understanding the customer and creating Use-Value which is appropriately perceived by the customer. To become capable at the business of creating such value, focus certainly will come in handy.

Investment Competence and the Insurance Industry

The profitability of insurance companies essentially comes from surplus of premium income over claims settlement and operating costs, and from investments, using the cash flow they generate. The latter source of income makes the insurance industry a big source of financial intermediation in the economy. This is where a thriving insurance industry becomes a major source of national savings and movement of capital from surplus to deficit areas where entrepreneurial acumen helps use the capital to create wealth and national well-being.

There is a fair amount of consensus here that the Nigerian insurance industry is very deficient in investment competencies. The fortunes of the management of many of the world's leading corporations are in the hands of the insurance industry because a tradition of being leading institutional investors has enabled them to dominate decision-making about executives that deliver or fail to perform in public companies in which they have significant stakes. We seldom see many of our insurance companies in such roles.

Insurance companies derive funds that they channel to investment outlets from three main sources: policy holders' surplus, unearned premium reserves and loss reserves. To invest such funds one needs the skill to evaluate investments so that the company is liquid enough when claims come. At the same time ensuring a high enough return will probably require a portfolio mix of safe and high risk investments. Given economies of scale that can be so generated, it is often possible to have a portfolio that includes venture capital investments, investment in more risky high return funds for emerging markets as well as secure investments in government securities. The competence comes in the structure of the portfolio and continuing management of the portfolio in a rapidly changing world. Here we have not done well at all. It is not surprising that the industry has not grown much. In fairness, rigid investment prescriptions by the regulators are sometimes offered as an excuse for the limited creativity here.

Creating Value for the Customer

I am often fascinated when I talk to managers and ask them why they are in business. The most frequently offered response is "to make profit." Can you make profit if customers do not see you as creating Use-Value that helps meet a need or bridge a dissatisfaction gap in their profile? Surely not. It seems to me that the challenge in the journey so far has been the absence of studied effort on the part of the industry to understand their customers and potential users of insurance services and to make heroic effort to create value that helps meet the needs of the customers. I have a feeling that insurance management in Nigeria so far has been too much of an armchair affair. To make progress we have to get off the armchair, find out more about the customer and build the capacity to truly meet his need.

Trust and Reliability

The Nigerian insurance industry has also suffered from a prolonged perception of not being reliable, especially with promptness of payment of claims. Many in the industry are often angered by this charge and proceed in vigorous defense of the industry. Trust is critical for any industry to grow. What is even more interesting is that trust is a matter of what people perceive. If we are not perceived as trustworthy and it is hurting our business, is it not worth our while to pool resources to reconstruct the reputation of our industry? I recall advising on a subtle trade group campaign on growing the insurance habit some fifteen years ago to a friend of mine who was active in NIA. Three years ago, at the initiative of current Chartered Insurance Institute of Nigeria (CIIN) President Ogola Osoka, I also tried to encourage Nigeria Re-Insurance Corporation to lead such a campaign for the industry. I am surprised that trade marketing is still strange to the Nigerian insurance industry. I have read somewhere that a committee has been in penalties to make suggestions on how to address the problem of the reputation of the industry. Such a committee deserves much support because I can see locked in the bowel of successful education of the people on the value of insurance, a rapid growth industry. Can anyone afford to wait? We may pay claims promptly. But if the people do not believe it, then it is our duty to show them some evidence.

Inflation

Just as trust has hurt the industry, the persistence of high inflation in the

1980s and 1990s has had very adverse effects on the insurance culture, especially with life insurance. Most rational people can easily see that what they get for many years of forced savings in premium payments quickly comes to nothing when they collect, because of inflation. This has been a major disincentive to the public especially as products that help hedge the value of the sum assured against inflation have not been generally available.

Social Norms and the Insurance Habit

It is important to bear in mind that in subsistence peasant economies that we are only striving to transform, insurance came in the form of the extended family and it was sometimes taboo to think of death and such other losses that come from what is seen as the will of God. This has slowed the insurance habit from taking hold. Breaking it depends very much on what the companies commit to educating the people.

The foregoing are but a few of the characteristics of the journey so far for the Nigerian insurance industry. We will do well to now turn to the challenges of the future.

Challenges of the Future

The future that confronts the insurance industry in Nigeria is one in which there are many changes taking place at a pace that those unable to learn quickly enough to adapt will not survive. The challenge of the future is to develop within our insurance companies the capacity to learn at a rate that is equal to or greater than the rate of change in the environment. Not to do so will leave us as dinosaurs. Given our track record for learning in the industry I would dare say that this is an area of hard work and strong leadership for the new breed of chief executives that are taking over the reigns in insurance.

The great challenges in the near future will include overcoming the paradox in the tendency towards fragmentation, smaller size new companies, at a time when consolidation between the biggest companies in Europe and North America is still proceeding with increasing economies of scale and synergies. Also among the challenges are: the impact of changing technologies; the effects of corporate globalization; the opening up of world markets in the post-Uruguay round world in which the World

Trade Organization is lowering barriers; and the changing nature of work. Also likely to affect the environment for insurance will be changing attitudes towards managing risk and patterns of investment in a financial global village.

In dealing with this on-rushing changes the industry first needs to recognize the attitude of people in organizations towards change. While change is certain and constant man and his organizations have a tendency that favours stability and predictability. This leads them to resisting change. To break this tendency towards inertia, those who lead should stand up as visionary leaders who have captured a view of the future towards which they lead in a committed way. Critical to getting the followership to be part of that journey is developing the skills that enable effective communication of the future so clearly envisioned.

Technological Changes

Technology is making information much easier to access. With the computer revolution it should be easier to develop a data bank that allows you to know the customer better and to create Use-Value that he perceives as meeting his needs. Technology will also make a difference as we can use it to reach dispersed customers at low cost. We talked earlier about industrial life policies. Surely it costs a bit to have people pounding the streets at today's transportation costs. With Internet access people can be billed and remit their premiums at such negligible costs that an industrial life strategy can become quite profitable again.

Globalization

I have spoken to the insurance community on a previous occasion about corporate globalization and will not repeat myself. Suffice it to say that the convergence of three streams of technology–computing, telecommunications and broadcasting – has made the world a global village. With information and communications technology, firms are competing on a global basis now. There is nothing to say that AXA will not be on your front door very soon. This means that companies unable to build competitive advantage will be in big trouble in no time.

Norms of Work

Changing patterns of work increasingly means that life-long employment is becoming less and less fashionable. This creates some opportunities for the insurance industry. Surely it will increase the popularity of individual pension schemes. Secondly, it means that working through agents, a traditional outlet for insurance marketing in which the industry has built some competencies, will be increasingly the way to do business.

Purchasing Power and Growth

If the policy environment should stabilize in the near future growth will resume in Nigeria. One consequence of renewed growth will be higher disposable income. This should be beneficial to the insurance industry, especially, if the confidence issues are handled quickly enough. The future could therefore be one of growth which tends to attract intense competition.

Aids and Life Insurance

Another factor in the environment that is bound to affect the insurance business in the near future is the increasing spread of AIDS. The state of the scourge of this pandemic is captured in the following comment by the head of an NGO that works to educate the grassroots on the virus.

"According to the Joint United Nations Programme on HIV/AIDS (UNAIDS) and the World Health Organization (WHO), co-sponsors of the joint programme, over 30 million people were infected with HIV, the virus that causes AIDS, and 11.7 million people around the world had already lost their lives to the disease. More than two-thirds of all the people now living with HIV in the world, nearly 21 million men, women and children live in Africa south of the Sahara desert, and 83 percent of the world's AIDS deaths have been in this region. Since the very start of the epidemic, HIV in sub-Saharan Africa has mostly spread through sex between men and women. This means that women are more heavily affected in Africa than in other regions, where the virus initially spread most quickly among men by male-to-male sex or drug injecting. Four out of five HIV-positive women in the world live in Africa."

An even higher proportion of the children living with HIV in the world are in Africa – an estimated 87 percent. There are a number of reasons for this. Firstly, more women of child-bearing age are HIV – infected in Africa than elsewhere. Secondly, African women have more children on average than those in other continents, so one infected woman may pass the virus on to a higher than average number of children. Thirdly, nearly all children in Africa are breast-fed. Breast-feeding is thought to account for between a third and half of all HIV transmission from mother to child. Finally, new drugs which help reduce transmission from mother to child before and around childbirth are far less readily available in developing countries especially those in Africa, than in the industrialized world.

Given the attitude of Nigerians to the HIV test many may suddenly become ineligible to take out life insurance. Insurance companies need to find new creative ways of sifting out AIDS-infected customers from those free of the virus.

Industrial Structure and Challenges of the Future

The future challenges the Nigerian insurance industry faces can be identified in certain factors that affect the structure of the industry and the performance of the constituent enterprises. To aid our identification of these challenges we will be served well to use a framework or model that shows systematic linkages between phenomena in the field. The traditional industry structure analysis framework proposed by Harvard Business School professor, Michael Porter, should ordinarily be what we turn to. I have, however, been able to propose another framework from my work. This model, the 3E framework, proposes megafactors that affect the structure of industry groups in emerging economies. It highlights factors in the environment of developing countries which are generally not captured by the Five Forces model of Porter.

Among the megafactors which impact on the competitive environment are government action and the predatory conduct of government officials, institutions, and the role of business associations.

Government action and the predatory acts of government officials which affect industry structure can be seen clearly in issues such as the monopolistic positions that NICON and Nigeria Re enjoy with official blessing. Surely there are many disadvantages to other players that these policy choices create. Winning the future for insurance companies would have to include reducing the negative effects of these near-monopolies.

Many of us here today were in Abuja last week for the Nigerian Economic Summit. The NES prescription which the Vision 2010 basically adopted includes the elimination of such mandated monopoly situations as are represented by the position of NICON and Nigeria Re. Freeing the industry from legislated dominance of some players could stimulate creativity which I believe is so far in very short supply in the industry.

The other megafactor in the model is institutional development. Institutions, which include regulatory frameworks, and settled habits of community which set limits to acceptable conduct, tend to reduce transaction costs and encourage economic activity. There are many who are convinced that the major problem of the industry is the increasingly overbearing nature of the regulatory framework. To return to the example of near-monopoly of some of the key players, we find that there are practitioners convinced that this life business is prevented from growing by the reinsurance obligation to deal, to a significant extent, with Nigeria Re. This denies them support for new product development from foreign reinsurers whose strategy is increasingly defined by how they support the business strategy of those whose business they depend on.

There is also the charge that weak institutions encourage broker abuse of the system. Companies that are insuring risks need the premium to invest so they can meet premium payments and have a healthy return on the investment for shareholders. If brokers do not remit what they collect, then they get the investment income but bear no risks of their own. The future will be dire if this capacity of brokers to defect goes on unchecked. As we are told there are already efforts to cut out brokers in India and even at Lloyds beginning in the year 2000. Brokers have a place of value in the value chain of selling insurance but if they continue to operate at the expense of the insurance companies, there will be no future for the industry and they will have played their own dirge.

The third megafactor is about the role of business associations in stimulating the evolution of institutions. Where groups like the NIA play their part well, the playing field will be level and creativity will rise, growing the industry. A strong future for the industry will benefit from the effectiveness of the NIA which should commit strongly to dealing with the poor reputation challenge. Also a megafactor in the 3E framework is the portfolio of competences the firm has built up to support competitive innovation.

In examining some of the five forces that will shape strategy in the industry a few miscellaneous items came up as worthy of mention regarding how the environment is shaping strategy. Low entry barriers into the industry have encouraged players that are not competitive. Increasing paid up capital requirements should raise entry barriers and the credibility of the firms active in industry, it is argued. That can only stifle creativity. In any risk business failure should be expected. What is critical is a well worked-out failure resolution mechanism that prevents failure from becoming systemic or hurting badly the smaller saver customer.

Strategic Imperatives for the Insurance Industry

The strategic imperative of all of the foregoing is that the Nigerian Insurance Industry cannot continue in isolation. This also means that now is the time to begin benchmarking at the global level. It means more concentrated investment in developing human capital and in thinking through strategies more deeply than has hitherto been the case.

Already there are encouraging signs. The future is a daunting challenge. But it is one that can be tamed. All it takes is the will to give it our best. The nucleus for success is on ground. I see it in the quality of men and women in this hall. I see it in the managers from insurance who come to the LBS. This is the evidence for my hope.

SECTION III

POLITICAL ECONOMY ISSUES AND THE MACRO-ECONOMY CHALLENGE TO BUSINESS

13

Nigeria's Economic and Political Profile in the Next Five Years

I have been asked to share my thoughts on the most difficult of issues, the long term future of Nigeria's economic and political life. Five years certainly is long time in a country that can have three heads of state in one year. Nigeria is without doubt a forecaster's nightmare. In spite of this, it is possible to discern trends that can allow us to suggest possible country profile options for Nigeria five years hence.

I believe it appropriate to begin with a cursory sketch of the historical path of Nigeria's political economic development. The natural starting point is the colonial era, since the Nigerian state is essentially a colonial creation.

The primary purpose of British contact with the African people that later agglomerated into Nigeria was trade. The traders first came to the oil rivers in search of input into their soap-making industries in the wake of the industrial revolution. There are many intervening variables like the 'civilizing' mission of the Rudyard Kiplings and the christianizing mission of the church missionaries but in the end the need to protect British trade interests led to the establishment of colonial hegemony.

The primary purpose of governance was to create infrastructure, structures and cultures conducive for order, to enable British traders peacefully export produce for use in British industry. To raise taxes and run minimum government responsible for good inland to seaport railway systems and law and order, a system of 'indirect rule' seemed most efficient. Traditional government systems made it ideally suited for Northern Nigeria. In the East where the monarchy tendencies were less prevalent Lord Lugard and his successors as British governors of Nigeria had more difficulty. An attempt to create such institutions through the warrant chief system proved unsuccessful and the Aba women's riot of 1929 remains the symbol of the rejection of that system.

These differences in cultures have often been used by those who say Nigeria is not a nation-state and therefore should not continue as such. I offer as counterpoint the fact that most modern nation-states are fusions of desperate peoples either through conquest or cultural and trade links over a period of time. Anyhow, Nigerian continued under colonialism until 1960 when agitation for independence by nationalists resulted in the birth of a new nation. In the very nature of colonial struggle lay one of the problems that would challenge the new nation. Nationalists accused the colonial administrators of not meeting so many needs of local people. With independence, they proclaimed, all will be made available. As a result expectations were raised far beyond the resource endowment capabilities of the state and the managerial capacity of both the politicians and bureaucrats to deliver.

Since the political base of the new leaders was in the regions and resources were increasingly more at the centre, after independence, competitive communalism became more a feature of the political economy of Nigeria. At this time manufacturing industries were few and far between, motivated primarily by the desire of European trading companies not to ship unnecessary bulk from Europe back to Nigeria to retail. So, instead of shipping so much water to Nigeria in beer bottles, breweries were established and barley imported; instead of shipping fresh air in bus imports, truck chassis were imported and mammy wagons built locally. These were the few industries at independence.

As resources increased at the centre, especially with increasing oil revenues, competitive communalism took on the form an American scholar, Richard Joseph, calls 'bureaucratic prebendalism,' the concept of sharing the national cake. So deep-rooted was this instinct to come to the centre and collect your prebend from the vicar that the idea of baking the cake, creating wealth, somehow drifted away from the consciousness of the Nigerian elite. In time the idea of getting the share of the community the elite represented suffered mutation and getting the share for the individual actor became sovereign. This fuelled the mindless acquisitiveness of the later 1970s and 80s and which reached a climax in the 1990s.

In the meantime, policies terribly negligent of the rural areas from which both the agricultural and mineral wealth of the nation came resulted in the depletion of the wealth base and debilitating rural-urban migration. With the elite consumption profile foreign in flavour and way out of line with its productive capacity, major disequilibrium in balance of payments had developed and been compounded by unfavourable terms of trade.

The state, now habitually hijacked by self-serving soldiers who lie through their teeth about intervening to stave off one cataclysm or the other, was in deep crisis of foreign and domestic debt, compounded lately by crises of legitimacy and open cynicism. It is against this backdrop that we must project into the future and draw a profile of Nigeria in the next five years.

One cannot go on to the future, however, without addressing the ameliorative efforts of the mid-1980s. This period, you will recall, was the genesis of structural adjustment. Some who have expressed concern about my impassioned stance against the Babangida regime in the face of the contrived political schisms of 1992 remember this era and say to me, "but you were a friend to these people." Indeed I was and remain a passionate advocate of restructuring our economy.

In the wholesale rejection of the Babangida years, some have suggested that SAP was a disaster. I beg to disagree. I can go as far as saying that the early years of SAP not only arrested imminent collapse following the freezing of lines of credit but started us down the path of recovery. By 1988, inflation had dropped into single digits and the much vilified exchange rate was steady at a level we look back at with envy. I still insist that those years between 1986 and 1989 were truly the golden years of leadership in Nigeria. By 1989 something went abysmally wrong. Any orgy of rent-seeking activities was abroad on the land before you could scream IBB.

I began to object to policies of the Babangida government at this stage. This desperation for rent-seeking behaviour which pervaded economic activities was either acquiesced to by government or was apparently encouraged because of the interests of those in government. It was at this stage that I dismissed the budget process as a joke since no one in government seemed to behave as if the budget was to be a policy implementation guide. By 1991 I had left a standing instruction that my secretary respond to every invitation to a budget discussion with a polite negative. Also by 1991 debilitative malpractices had begun to bring SAP to its knees. It was only natural that 'Babangida bashing' as Tunji Olagunju and Sam Oyovbaire call it gathered momentum about this time. Between insiders who as a natural process long identified by Irving Janis even in John F. Kennedy's best and brightest team as victims of groupthink, and uncharitable opponents, the truth can be found. But in Nigeria, a culture of cynicism puts you either for or against or brands you a turncoat moving from for to against. In the tradition of populist reaction to a rejected era we have proposed a re-bureaucratization of economic management in the 1994 budget, a move I dare to predict will not serve us well, even though the heart of the policy makers point in a desired direction with more consideration to industry than to briefcase businessmen from the near East. Our projection of Nigeria's future will be based on scenarios consequent upon Nigerian elite behaviour and upon global trends. We shall begin with the latter.

There used to be a time when you heard things like strategic delinking from the world economy from policy economics scholars in the third world. In my graduate school days in the late 1970s when there was a strong Latin flavour to international political economy studies and the dependency theory held sway, people eager to defend the apparent gains of the import substitution logic which became quite popular with Raul Prebisch's tenure as Executive Secretary of the Economic Commission for Latin America, talked about delinking from the global economy.

With CNN and information networks making this a truly global village where you can play the Singapore stock market from Port Harcourt, it is clear that 'dependistas' will find delinking a difficult proposition. To succeed in today's world we cannot damn the world and we need to find a clear niche in the global intercourse of trade. Using our present location in the world arena as a base, five years from now has to be frighteningly bleak.

Perhaps I can make this scenario even more frightening. A few years ago an OECD study of the future of the world economy projected that early into the soon coming century, industrialized countries would depend primarily on biotechnology and genetic engineering for their raw materials input. All the medium technology production would come from today's rapidly industrializing economies of South East Asia, Brazil and such economies which would for the most part be subcontractors to industries in OECD countries. The rest of the world, almost all of Africa included, would be practically dead, a burden to the thinking part of the human race.

With oil declining every day in importance, policy making it impossible to invest with confidence in Nigeria, Immigration and Customs officials making it certain that genuine businessmen from abroad either never set foot in Nigeria or are frightened off at the airport, it is easy to project our place in this future concert of economies as seen from OECD eyes. Add to this the fact that our educational system has declined so remarkably that people can be in government and consider it acceptable that higher institutions be closed for months, and you see that we shall be unable to compete even in middle level biotechnology in spite of our tropical advantage and a tradition of people aggressively seeking education.

So, is it all hopeless? Shall we just roll up our sleeves, roll over and sing a requiem for Nigeria? I think not so. This is partly because I am an optimist by nature and partly because I know the will of the Nigerian people. Once it becomes clear what faces Nigeria and that bad leadership is responsible for this, there will be shakings in the land and the end result will be rejuvenation of the Nigerian spirit and economic reconstruction. If this happens, then certain economic, social and political phenomena have to be addressed.

On the political economy side it seems to be that a more pragmatic ideology of managerialism, seeking efficiency and effectiveness in the setting and pursuit of targets and objectives, will have to replace bureaucratic prebendalism. We have the people with the ability to carry this off as in cases where consultants move in to restructure a troubled company. If in an emergent culture we stress merit, bold in contempt every man who displays wealth without an export-oriented industry to show he creates wealth, give education new relevance and free up the economy from excessive regulation while guiding the path forward by dividing up the country into zones of development and providing a core area of infrastructures within each zone of development, I have no doubt that the entrepreneurial genius of the very hard working people who make up Nigeria will blossom in a way that could make the tigers of Asia seem like amateurs.

It is assumed that in this new dispensation all Nigerians will be socialized into seeking to create an enabling environment, not that those employed at entry ports become repellant to foreign partners. We will have to learn that 80-100 million people or not, there is nothing inherently attractive about Nigeria that investors will be falling over each other to come here.

Capital, like water, finds its own level and the determining variable is the return on investment. I was fascinated that in the last three weeks, five friends of mine have indicated they are travelling to Ghana to start a division of their businesses there. The range of their businesses runs from advertising through marketing of motor lubricants to cocoa processing. It is not theory any more that Ghana is attracting foreign investment. Certainly it cannot be an IMF ploy that Nigerians are investing their hard earned money in Ghana. These businesses will create jobs for Ghanaians and create new wealth with multiplier effects there.

The optimistic scenario, in my thinking, involves having the political will to take some hard decisions. In my opinion, one of those hard decisions would be to abandon the Ajaokuta Steel project. Heresy, some of you may say. Perhaps I see myself too much in the light of a management consultant trying to restructure a troubled company.

But just pause for one moment and think of a wage bill in excess of ₦20 million a month for people who for years have produced nothing. Here is a pool of very well trained people whose energies can be turned into something more rewarding, if you consider the steel glut the world economy has been plagued with for many years. Such ultranationalism as producing your own steel is extremely myopic in an independent world of the nature of what we have today. What we could do, in view of the massive civil works there and the reality that our yet-to-start production steel machinery is already obsolete, is to turn Ajaokuta into an industrial centre. This could be one core area of zones of development we have proposed elsewhere.

Another hard decision is to get Nigerians determined to reverse the culture of a toll gate economy we have. Everywhere people erect toll gates and we acquiesce. For example, I have refused to pay ₦15 instead of ₦12 to any vendor for *The Guardian* newspaper. Sometimes I forgo buying the paper for that reason. Federal toll gates deliberately never have change. It is from these small habits that foreign exchange premiums grow and lock us into a trap of a perpetually inefficient system. All of us must show resolve to overcome extortions of our economy.

For the optimistic economic scenario in Nigeria to play itself out, there has to be concomitant social and political restructuring. One would be extremely myopic not to note that the dominance of a military clique/ traditional rulers coalition has contributed to Nigeria's underdevelopment. While flashes of brilliance as described earlier may be noticeable from time to time, the nature of this coalition is that of a conquering elite and not of national leaders.

They are by nature, therefore, predatory, treating public office as spoils of war. A recent experience of dinner with three very respected African-American dignitaries proves this perception to be increasingly universal. Asked to assess Nigeria, the two who have been around for a while delivered cold pessimistic views of Nigeria's future. Said one of Nigeria, "These Obas and chiefs are still selling their people for a dime a dozen every day as they did our forefathers. If you watched the shameless parade of these people to Babangida, Shonekan and Abacha all in one year, it is easy to see how pathetic they are."

As social parasites, traditional rulers, totally irrelevant in the scheme of things, sustain themselves by harassing state governors for contracts, the centre for oil lifting and debasing the values of society by awarding meaningless chieftaincy titles to egoistic criminals. Most disturbing however is that they try to offer a cloak of legitimacy to illegitimate regimes, thus prolonging governments that act contrary to the interest of the people these traditional rulers supposedly represent. This comes clear from the fact that in the shameless harlotry of parading before the three leaders of 1993, not even a few could look these leaders in the face and counsel that their actions were diminishing Nigeria in the eyes of the world and causing severe hardships to millions of law-abiding citizens anxious for an environment to peacefully carry on life-sustaining economic activities.

A democracy is not a sure guarantee of success in governance but an open system certainly beats an autocratic one for proving uninhibited pursuit of the potential of the individual within a nation. Even if this is an exaggerated ideal, reality is that in our global village a leader in uniform does not attract much respect any more, and this prejudicially predisposes many who would have supported a country to look away. Visits across borders by parliamentarians lead to bonds of friendships that are translated into legislation that supports the cause of development. Free and fair elections within the year in Nigeria is in my opinion a pre-condition for an optimistic scenario in the next five years.

Five years hence Nigeria can either be a country struggling to free itself from economic control, an island declining from an interdependent world, or a country deep in the throes of civil disturbance and economic trauma labouring through a never ending constitutional conference; or it can be the country of the optimistic scenario with a restructured educational system and people competing medium level biotechnological development and light industries exporting to near and far markets. But this brave new world has to begin now with structures of policy monitoring, reform of the budgetary system, and a public service culture reprogramming. This is why the civil service reform proposed should not again be a matter of who is accounting officer but how to create a managerial culture responsive to effective implementation of policy in an environment of very scarce resources.

Before we go I would like all of us to stop for some seconds and examine our consciences. It is easy to blame others. But what is our contribution to the Nigerian problem? I know my lifestyle is not as expensive as that of many of you here. I know also that I do not work less hard than many of you. And I am convinced, given the population dimensions in Nigeria, that I consume far more than my contribution to the creation of real wealth in Nigeria. Think about that, long and hard.

References

North, Douglas 1990. *Institutions, Institutional Change and Economic Performance.* New York. Cambridge University Press.

Okigbo, Pius 1987. *Essays in the Public Philosophy of Development.* Enugu. Fourth Dimension Publishers.

Utomi, Patrick 1996. "Institutions and the Evolution of Competition in the Nigerian Banking Industry" in *Lagos Business School Management Review,* Vol. 1, No. 2: 71-82.

Utomi, Patrick 1997. "Business Outlook for 1998: Policy Imperatives and Implication for the Private Sector" in *Lagos Business School Management Review,* Vol. 2, No. 2: 79-85.

Utomi, Patrick 1998. *Managing Uncertainty: Competition and Strategy in Emerging Economies.* LBS Management Series. Spectrum Books.

14

The 3I And 3E Approach: A Blueprint for Stemming the Rot And Rebuilding the Nigerian Economy

The story of the Nigerian economy through the 1980s and 1990s has been that of a free fall in which the momentum of decline was punctuated ever so briefly by attempts at adjustment in the late 1980s. This prolonged recession has produced a tendency to despair regarding prospects of renewed sustainable growth and the improvement of the living standards of Nigeria's rapidly growing population. This presentation aims at indicating the context in which the rot can be stemmed and growth with sustainable development attained. The blueprint proposed here marries the macroeconomics framework, the 3I approach, to a microeconomics context, the 3E framework.

In its bare essence, the 3I (investments, industriousness and institutions) represent the 'missing' dimension in World Bank and IMF adjustment prescription which are vital to convert fiscal viability resulting from traditional stabilization programmes into platforms for rapid growth and poverty eradication in economies where structural distortions have led to a widening of the gap between the poorest and the most prosperous groups as the Gini Index trend shows clearly in Nigeria. But the value of industriousness at the macro level is diminished unless strategies that help enterprises, at the micro level, to compete effectively lead to innovation and wealth creation. My earlier work on competition and strategy which produced the 3E framework should serve well the review of the micro side.

The objective in the following sections is to offer prescriptions that create the macroeconomic soil on which entrepreneurial ventures can sprout. It is also about oiling the interface between government and the private sector such that the rhetoric of making the private sector the engine of growth becomes reality. That can happen only when the private sector is stronger than is the case in Nigeria at the closing of the twentieth century.

Public policy can indeed drive the build up of a viable, wealth creating private sector as the experience with industrialization in South Korea and elsewhere in East Asia suggests. But that has not been the Nigerian experience where government sponsored development banks have been generally grounded by moral hazard problems and a culture of seeking economic rent, outright complicity that redefines the tragedy of the commons syndrome, as both the operators of the banks and their customers 'scramble' for a piece of the national cake. Government money in development banks belong to all and therefore to none. The prescriptions below suggest institutional arrangements to reduce such problems and allow policy to help boost the private sector.

Since the prescriptions made here are based on how policies emanating from the government sector impact on venturing, value-added manufacturing for export, and domestic consumption, with consequences for local savings and therefore of additional investments, it is appropriate that our review of how Nigeria got into free-fall be based on the dynamics between the four main sectors of economic activity. It is as such that the effect of policy on resource flows between government, the business sector, the external sector and the personal sector is a useful tool for explaining why the circular flows of income between these sectors have produced stagnation rather than new wealth. Here I am drawing liberally from the concerns in the research of my colleague, Ayo Teriba, who sees growth as dependent on the right balance between the sectors which generate certain consumption and therefore production dynamics.

How it Came to Free-Fall

The modern economy came through the colonial administration of the British Empire. The colonial regime was a study in minimum government. Government focussed on ensuring law and order and in building institutions and infrastructure that support economic activity which then constituted primarily of harvesting cash crops and mining minerals for export to the metropolis. The produce marketing boards captured most of the returns from value created by the cash crop farmers. This was reflected in the reserves built up by the Nigerian Produce Marketing Board. This structure of the economy was such that the business sector was very small and underdeveloped; the external sector and the government sector were literally fused as the external sector was dominated by the colonial metropolis.

Resource flows from the external sector into colonial Nigeria were limited as most of the enterprises that came brought in little and what they brought in was invested in extractive industries or areas that generated much more significant outflows of capital than the investments. Even the income from agricultural produce exports was held back in London in foreign reserves.

On the eve of independence, therefore, we had a retrenched personal sector, a famished business sector with hardly a manufacturing investment and a 'minimum' government which was bloated at the external end because of the fusion of government and external sectors. Pius Okigbo, the quintessential student of Nigeria Public accounts in this era, makes the point that these external holdings of the marketing boards were so inviting to the political parties when self-government came that the reserves were wiped out even before independence. Between self-government in 1957 and independence in 1960 the reserves from the produce exports had been appropriated by the regional governments (Okigbo, 1987; Utomi, 1997).

Some of it was used to support an effort to diversify the base of the economy. In the Western region some of it went into developing an industrial estate in Ikeja, a move that was replicated in this competitive political era in the other regions. The quest to move a larger part of the economy into manufacturing suffered from many structural problems. Part of it came from the fact that agriculture had not developed enough to supply the raw materials inputs of manufacturers at competitively attractive prices that enabled manufacturing. Efforts to develop the agricultural sector further in the Eastern region met with great successes but could not be sustained as Nigeria was soon engaged in a civil war.

The weak personal and business sectors encouraged a line of thinking in government that progress was dependent on government driving the development process. This philosophy coincided with the adoption of the Prebisch thesis and the Import Substitution Industrialization strategy. Government was soon investing in all manners of assembly plants. Meanwhile the needed investment in agriculture to make industrial input available and ensure food security was abandoned as increasing oil prices made it easy to import raw materials.

It is not surprising that the collapse of oil prices came with a crisis of Dutch disease, a much atrophied agricultural sector, and reluctance to invest in manufacturing. It is logical therefore to assume that a return to a balanced, growing economy will involve renewal of the agricultural sector, significant new investments in manufacturing, especially if they favour exports over import substitution, and a freeing up sectors of the economy made perpetually inefficient by government ownership, with concomitant cost inflicted on those in the economy dependent on the services of such parastatals.

This simple logic of escape from decline, as obvious as it seems, was not pursued because of a tendency to get into a vicious circle in policy choice when the challenge of reform confronts the kind of managers who have kept watch over the Nigerian economy. Attempts at checking decline took place in 1982 when austerity measures were implemented, but real reform involving restructuring imports and exports in the direction that would sustain higher productivity and output was avoided. The government persisted in the maintenance of an exchange rate that had diverged markedly from the purchasing power parity position, allowing the overshooting to harden into a severe structural disincentive for exports. All this was done to 'protect' the living standards of an urban elite that had a largely import-denominated consumption profile. Time would prove that the cost of 'protecting' would be deeper and more severe erosion of their quality of life when rampant scarcity and then a plague of retrenchment all but wiped out the Nigerian middle class.

Failure to privatize either in response to those who did not want to give away the family silver to a few rich people or because of entrenched interests who profited from Ricardian rents extracted from these enterprises ensured that the on-costs borne by the real sector made Nigerian products uncompetitive. As manufacturers have to each create 'local governments' of their own to provide water, light, telecommunications, access roads etc., continuing government ownership would combine with policy instability to create a scenario of de-industrialization that has afflicted Nigeria through the 1990s.

In the face of weak economic fundamentals and government's inability to service due debt, correspondent banks had by the early 1980s begun to freeze lines of credit to Nigerian banks. The economy was soon in 'free-fall' relative to its earlier state of health. Policy could not possibly run away from adjustment even if revenue coming from oil did not make it quite the basket case that some African economies seemed like at the time. When the government of Muhammadu Buhari was ousted by the Babangida regime the form of adjustment to pursue quickly came to the fore. A national debate resulted in a rejection of the IMF adjustment facility and a so-called homegrown structural adjustment programme was put in place.

SAP was anchored on the replacement of import licensing and its perverse rent culture which will see a Chief or Alhaji with no known business get six times the value of import license granted a huge multinational manufacturer, with a foreign exchange market. The market produced an effective depreciation to the real effective exchange rate of 104 percent between September, 1986 and August, 1992. The SAP also included elements of trade liberalization.

The deregulation of interest rates and other financial reforms were aimed at achieving financial deepening. This was never truly achieved because of either lack of faith in the adjustment processes by the managers, or the effect of corruption which led to constant overspending, budget deficits, and use of instruments such as stabilization securities charged against banks, to manage money supply.

Even with all the problems of policy instability, corruption and inadequate faithfulness with implementation, SAP still resulted in growth rates in excess of 5 percent per annum up till 1991 when policy makers all but sabotaged their own programme, running unprecedented deficits even in the face of a windfall for oil prices that was triggered by the Gulf war. Notable in all the trends is that the personal sector continued to lose ground in terms of real value of wages. The business sector witnessed mixed performance. Even as some manufacturing was forced by adjustment policies, especially in areas of appropriate factor endowment, to experience higher capacity utilization, there was not a sustained reversal of the decline of manufacturing. Agriculture did pick up but it was the finance sector that seemed to grow the most. The fact of the finance sector growing much faster than the real sector is at one and same time symptomatic of the tendency of adjustment programmes to be generous to the finance sector so they can drive new growth, and an indicator of how opportunities for arbitrage had driven up financial sector activity.

What was obviously missing which kept sustainable growth away was concerted investments and a will to venture. These factors obviously do not get the specific emphasis they deserve in IMF prescribed adjustment conditionalities. It is precisely the fact that these factors are assumed as flowing from getting the fundamentals right that has stimulated this presentation of the 3I and 3E framework to show that a more conscious stimulation of these variables would make sustainable growth follow adjustment.

The 3I

Financial deepening is a critical object of SAP because it assumes that deepening facilitates the channeling of capital from surplus to deficit areas. Deepening without a culture of venturing and entrepreneurial skills would surely produce much slower economic renewal. In not quickly producing growth, given lags that delay effects, the tendency is for opponents of adjustment to put enough pressure on the policy process to cause changes in policy. This is why I argue that a more proactive approach to stimulating investments and entrepreneurship is required in emerging economies especially when they are adjusting from government-led growth to private sector-driven development. To achieve the 10 percent of GDP per annum, it is proposed that particular attention be paid to investment stimulation and promotion, industriousness (entrepreneurship), and institutions which reduce uncertainty and the comfort level of ventures to certain risks.

The social engineering of these three variables is important, as we have noted because of the lag between policy implementation and the ultimately desired effect and because modern economics, in its bias towards quantitative measures of effects, has a tendency to neglect critical qualitative variables.

On the former variable, we have already seen in the Nigerian experience impatience with the lags. A good example is seen with the response to a market based exchange rate. While proponents of a foreign exchange market used the J-curve to explain that a lag existed between the policy choice and the response of the non-oil exports, opponents were quick to point out that published results of companies showed they were making 'extraordinary' profits while people were groaning under the weight of devaluation. The 'paper profits' of replacement cost pricing had overshadowed the falling levels of inflation. This led to the accusation of manufacturers by government of profiteering. But the accusation was spurious given the need for additional working capital and the declining real value of those profits. However, government reversed policies based on these perceptions.

Even where the people are patient with adjustment policies, and the incentives for industries based on factor endowments and the export sector begin to pick up, levels of growth such as that experienced by East Asian economies in the miracle years or as desired for Nigeria by Vision 2010 will be difficult to reach. The need to pay particular attention to investments, industriousness and institutions is as such an imperative for economies desirous of rapid growth. With population growing at 3 percent per annum, Nigeria needs to have a pre-crisis Asian level of growth.

Investments

Investment flows show that little new money has come into Nigeria in the 1990s. Even multinationals already in Nigeria are reluctant to invest their returns. An analysis of capital flows will show that most of what little money came in went to an enclave sector with only marginal linkages to the bigger Nigeria economy, the oil sector. Surely you cannot have growth without investments. It is my opinion that a facultative role for government exists, especially where there is an entrepreneurial regime not bound by bureaucratic excesses in which the pursuit of power overtakes purpose. With an entrepreneurial regime, an industrial policy and cooperation with the private sector to generate investment incentives, the encouragement of venture capital companies and even development banks for long term finance can be pursued. The performance history of development banks in Nigeria would seem discouraging of such strategies. But experience from elsewhere, which has been systematically analyzed by David Hulme and Paul Mosley in their book *Finance Against Poverty,* shows that the World Bank and others building on the work of the so-called Michigan State University School may have been too quick to write off some traditional modes of financing to stimulate growth in poor countries. Schemes through which government provides matching funds to venture capital firms with a track record could be another intervention track.

Beyond a careful intervention to stimulate investments, the promotion of the country as a safe place to invest for high returns is the business of the state which is required to build momentum for investments and spur growth. Success with promoting new investments is itself dependent on institutions that provide support.

Institutions

The importance of institutions in reducing uncertainty and facilitating economic intercourse is now the subject of a significant body of literature (North, 1990; Utomi, 1996, 1998, chapter 199). In the area of investment support, such institutions as a one-stop entry agencies, property rights and the rule of law which generate settled habits in the population, giving confidence to local and foreign businesses that they can trust things to go in a certain way, are of high priority.

It is these institutions that make businesses confident enough to plan because they can estimate the probabilities of outcome from their inputs.

Our investment support institutions need to evolve beyond where they are at present. The Industrial Development Coordinating Committee set up as an interministerial one-stop agency did work as envisaged. A national investment commission has since been set up but it is not clear whether the bureaucratic bottlenecks that prevent most investors from expressing interest in having a going-venture will be eliminated here. Perhaps the model of the Technical Committee on Privatization and Commercialization (TCPC) which had new staffing from the public and private sectors and had fairly clear goals and targets, would help in moving forward here.

Dealing with property rights and rejuvenating a judiciary that suffered much setback during the years of military rule are critical anchors to getting investors to feel more comfortable with Nigeria.

Institutions that ensured the reduction of on-costs for manufacturing in East Asia through the development of industrial parks with adequate infrastructure made industry clusters build up easily. Such institutions will be helpful in ensuring new growth because it will reduce the challenges that those who are industrious come up against.

Industriousness

Industriousness in an indigenous enterprise class is for me a key variable in seeking productive growth. As evidence from the growing Corporation and many South Korea enterprise cases show (witness the process of becoming a leading exporter of microwave ovens: *Harvard Business Review*, Jan-Feb 1998), industriousness had as much to do with the making of the so-called miracle as conditions that attracted investments.

The value of building up a culture of entrepreneurship, hard work and creativity in an indigenous class is also evident in the fact that few countries that have grown rapidly have done so primarily on foreign investments. We can therefore expect that facilitating the emergence of a strong indigenous entrepreneurial group is a major variable in moving the economy forward.

Contrary to myths that exist, entrepreneurs are not born, they are made. Entrepreneurship development programmes, continuous training and peer support experience sessions can facilitate the emergence of an enterprise class that can take advantage of conditions created by the two variables earlier discussed to move things forward. Yet they are variables not emphasized much in prescriptions of multilateral development agencies.

Our task here is to show that special proactive consideration for these three variables is necessary and that these factors vary along with how the enterprises form their strategies. The exploration of this interface between national strategy, as in the engineering of the environment via the three variables we discussed, and business strategy of firms is thus the real contribution we hope to make here. It is therefore in order to review the factors that drive strategy in business enterprises. These competitive forces which drive strategy in emerging economies have been explicated substantially in my earlier contribution in the book, *Managing Uncertainty: Competition and Strategy in Emerging Economies* (Utomi, 1998).

The 3E Framework

The framework essentially integrates variables from the structure-conduct-performance paradigm in structural economies with elements from the competing core competencies perspective of the resource-based theory of the firm and megafactors in the environment of poor countries.

If policy were to be geared to push the 3I, the entrepreneur would be in a better position to manage the elements of the 3E framework to produce outcomes that result in wealth creation in the economy and value added exports. In such a scenario ambitious growth rates can be achieved.

Growth will depend much on growing managers and entrepreneurs who can read the 3I and develop strategy within the context of the 3E framework which allows for desired outcomes. Hardly considered in this analysis is a factor in the core competencies of the firm, managing the abuses of weak institutions-corruption. We shall however reserve that discussion of corruption for another time.

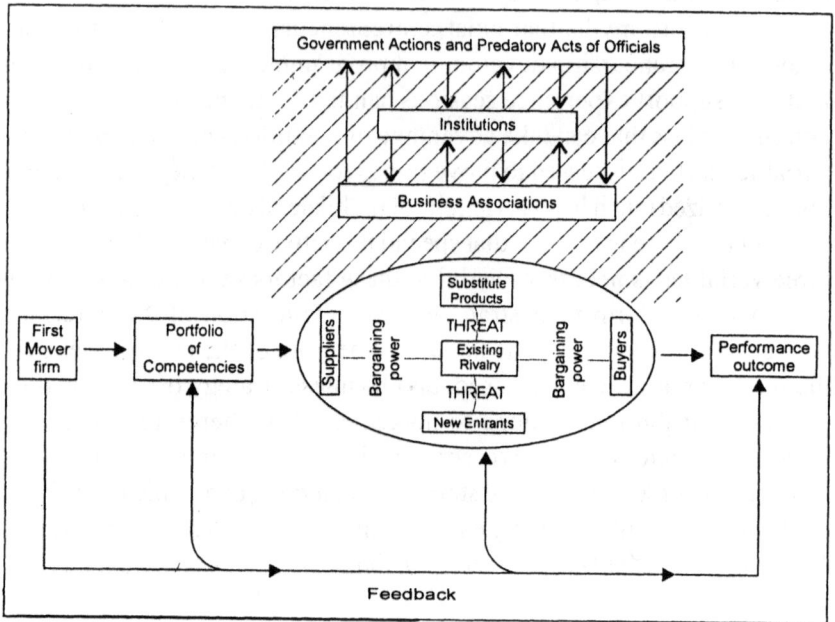

Conclusion

In the foregoing we have tried to establish that certain salient issues in the macro-economic environment have not received the attention they deserve if rapid growth is to be one of the fruits of embracing economic liberalization. These issues we have identified as being focussed on increasing the capacity for investments, industriousness and building institutions to reduce uncertainty and transaction costs (the 3I). Being proactive in boosting the 3I from a macro-economic policy level will move the country forward more quickly if, at the level of the firm, the micro level strategy is driven by a better understanding of how elements of the 3E framework affect the building of competitive advantage by the entrepreneur.

We have tried to suggest that it is at the level of the convergence of the 3E framework and 3I that growth and development are optimized.

15

Privatization, the Emerging Market and the Nigerian Economy*

I feel quite honoured to be asked to share some of my thoughts on this very important albeit controversial subject of Privatization, the Emerging Market and the Nigerian Economy. In the main, I am sure that our interaction will prove of value to decisions we may be making as participants of some significance in the Nigerian economy.

Privatization and Emerging Markets

It is in my experience all too easy to reduce a discussion on a subject such as this to very economistic levels such that the key human elements are lost. On the other hand we can also get so focussed on the politics of privatization that we forget that it is about how to free resources from encumbrances that prevent them from being efficiently utilized to create wealth. What is critical for our purpose is the recognition that at the root of the subject is prosperity and the quality of life citizens enjoy.

At the beginning of this century, the difference between the quality of life of the average European and the average African was marginal. Today, the difference is phenomenal. As Peter Drucker and many others point out, routinely, the source of this divergence has been in productivity trends. How we organize work and ownership of the means of production has without doubt played a role in the emergence of economies into prosperity.

Douglas North, whose work on institutions and economic development earned him a Nobel prize in economics, explores the transition of economies from poverty to prosperity and shows us that property rights and evolving institutions provided the catalyst for the rapid development of the United States economy in the 19th century. Privatization in command economies seems to hold the key that can unlock the institutions that support rapid wealth creation and have thus become important in assessing the emerging markets.

---

* Address to the Nigerian Shareholders' Association

Our objective in the following pages is to establish the context that now makes privatization imperative for Nigeria to become a serious emerging market. The nature of the economy of a big emerging market country is diagnosed. Here, insights from the East Asia experience will be instructive. In the main, however, we hope to track the reason the Nigerian economy got to a point in which privatization became a central issue, why the process of privatization seems to have come so far and become paralyzed and the implications of the state of privatization for capital flows through Nigeria, and therefore, of the economic development potential of the country.

The Imperative of Privatization

In 1920 Argentina was one of the 10 most developed economies of the world. In the ensuing years the populist political culture drove a policy regime that encouraged widespread nationalization. By the 1970s Argentina's fortunes had plummeted to the level of GDP growth comparable to the stagnated levels of West African economies. Argentina, that had become one of the world's poorer countries, began by the late 1980s to react with passion to its condition. A massive privatization programme that many, even at the World Bank, considered too much too quickly, was embarked upon. It privatized virtually all state-owned companies including its national energy company and national airline from 1990 onward. One result is that it has gone from being one of the typical examples of the failure of state-run closed economies to being one of ten Big Emerging Markets (BEMs) identified by the Clinton administration as markets of the future in which it needs to support American companies playing mutually beneficial roles in the expected rapid growth. The dean of the Yale School of Management, who served as Under-Secretary for International Trade in the Clinton Administration when this policy was enunciated, names other BEMs as: The Chinese Economic Area (China, Hong Kong and Taiwan) South Korea, Indonesia, India, South Africa, Poland, Turkey, Mexico, Brazil and Argentina.

Clearly the case of Argentina begins to suggest to us that future prosperity and becoming an emerging market should be related to the privatization of the economies of many countries who, because of state domination of economic activity, have somehow not managed to raise productivity to the extent that the quality of life of the people improves considerably.

There are, however, those who will look at a few Asian economies like Singapore and the other Asian tigers studied by the World Bank in the famous East Asia miracle undertaking and say there is a fallacy in arguing the imperative of privatization. It is important therefore that we examine the underlying factors and differences, if any, between the circumstances of their rapid development and ours. In many of the East Asian examples there was significant government intervention in the production of goods and services.

Howard Stein represents the school of thought which disagrees with part of the World Bank view that believes that markets are necessarily substitutes for state intervention in economic activity. A lengthy quote from his book on Asian Industrialization and Africa should sum up his position:

"As noted above, a focus of structural adjustment is to encourage the movement of production decisions from public into private hands. Following neo-classical economics, there is no need to be concerned about the nature of business organizations. In contrast, the case studies indicate the important relationship between State policy and industrial organization and economic growth and innovation."

"In general, business organizations are social institutions which provide a refuge from the vicissitude of the market. In addition to reducing transaction costs, they embody habits and routines which allow companies to handle the complexity of production and exchange and develop expectation in a world of uncertainty. Different organizational forms will breed greater operational success." While authors like Oliver Williamson (1985) have stressed the role of governance structures within firms as a means of limiting opportunism and therefore transaction costs, what has been more important to success in Asian countries has been organizations that are able to encourage loyalty and trust leading to transaction cost reductions.

"As in Africa today there were few entrepreneurs with the experience to build large-scale industrial firms. Faced with this absence, government in Asia set out to foster entrepreneurship" (Stein, 1996).

In my opinion the arguments of Professor Stein, though generally valid, in no way invalidate the criticism of the interventionist approach by the World Bank. Yes, government involvement in East Asian economies increased trust, thus reducing transaction costs and boosting venturing in business. A perspective in which markets are pushed as substitutes to government intervention does not necessarily discount institutions which reduce transaction costs. A close reading of the arguments of Douglas North shows that institutions evolved not necessarily from the activities of governments but in the selfish interest of those involved in transactions of economic exchange. Governments only tend to reinforce these institutes because the wealth that results from the limits they set to acceptable behaviour is for the common good.

In a similar vein as Howard Stein, Machuko Nissanke and Ernest Ayeertey posit that "instead of viewing the role of government and that of the market as mutually exclusive substitutes, the emerging perspective is one of complementarity between the two for the resolutions of market failures and coordination problems" (Nissanke and Ayeertey, 1997). The real challenge for me in this question of whether or not government can lower transaction costs through its institutions is our extant experience. It would seem, sadly, that the hallmark of Nigerian institutions is the pursuit of power rather than purpose. Often the desire for power so completely overwhelms purpose that a process of goal displacement produces a new purpose contrary to or opposite in intent to the original purpose of the institution. You can see this in some CBN and NDIC issues as clearly as you can see it in the NUCs approach to higher education.

I am convinced from the foregoing that markets, even though they may have their imperfections, are more likely to bring growth and development to Nigeria than government intervention.

To explore the subject of privatization in Nigeria it would seem appropriate to show how Nigeria got to have so many state-owned enterprises.

Background to State-Dominated Economy

Developing countries in post-Second World War era saw a need to supplement inadequate entrepreneurial skills and limited private capital with state investments. Nigeria followed the trend. This pattern was, in fact reinforced, in my view, by the fact that the leading bureaucrats of the independence era came out of British Schools when Fabian socialism was in the ascendance.

As oil prices went up, putting much resources at the disposal of government, these bureaucrats, Ayida, Asiodu and company talked about government assuming the commanding heights of the economy. Import substitution industrialization firms or ventures attracted a good portion of the investment from government. When oil prices collapsed, Nigeria was hit by Dutch disease. Policy did not realign purchasing power parity with the exchange rate. The situation was clearly not sustainable. Devaluation then came as a remedy.

Before the medicine of devaluation, the apparatus of SOEs had mushroomed into a portfolio of investments which by 1990 had a value of more than 36 million (Zayyad, 1992). This interest profile of the state stood at more than 1,000 billion Naira at 1994 replacement cost, according to Dr Hamza Zayyad, Chairman of TCPC (later BPE). He said in a paper presented at the UNCTAD Secretariat that this huge investment had a return on investment of 2 percent. Most of the return came from surpluses of CBN. In reality therefore they were almost all loss leaders putting a burden on tax-payers. In the face of this reality the Nigerian government under Gen. I. Babangida announced in 1988 a rather bold effort at privatization.

Decree No. 25 of 1988 was essentially part of the package of Structural Adjustment Programme in Nigeria. SAP had as primary premise the need to stimulate economic growth through more efficient and responsible use of resources with the market as determinant of efficient allocation. Financial liberalization was thus expected to result in financial deepening; market determined exchange rates were to help the relevant sectors who mobilize resources from deeper financial markets to access foreign exchange and facilitate the process of creating wealth. For government to avoid the effect of subventions to poorly performing SOE with consequences for deficit budgeting and efficiency of productive enterprises, it needed to embark on a privatization programme.

Decree No. 25 of 1988 specified 100 enterprises to be fully or partially privatized. Another 35 enterprises were to be wholly or partially commercialized. The concept of commercialization was fairly new, with hardly any known precedent. It was designed to put the enterprises on a commercial footing without ownership moving from public to private hands.

Outcome of Effort So Far

The results have been mixed. Commercialization has certainly not lived up to billing. Commercialized parastatals have mainly increased rates and salaries of staff without commensurate improvement in services. The biggest success was with a sector not initially listed at all – banking. By the time the carry-over from government appointed boards in banking all disappear we should be able to see more of the impact of privatization on the industry.

For a variety of reasons, both political and the result of pure inertia, the process stalled towards the last Babangida days and was consigned to the back burner in 1994. Last year at the annual meetings of the World Bank/IMF there seemed to be a change of heart in the announcement of wholesale privatization by Finance Minister, Chief Anthony Ani. An excited world a little weary of bad news from Nigeria welcomed the opportunity of Nigeria joining the league of serious emerging markets. If Ghana could, just with the offer of Ashanti Goldfields, have a capital market attracting world attention, surely privatizing government interests in the oil industry and the electricity and communication monopolies would set up Nigeria for very serious emerging markets league. The ovation had hardly died down from the announcement made on October 1, 1996 when the 1997 budget came, revealing a reluctance to pursue that line of action.

Implication of Outlook on Privatisation

Our love-hate relationship with privatization has many implications. First, in a world that increasingly believes there is no alternative (TINA) to such a move, we will become more isolated. This cannot be good for the growth and development of any economy. Then there is the implication for capital flows if we reject privatization. It would seem that international capital goes where the risks of precipitate action by government and high transaction costs occasioned by the inefficiencies of SOE are not prevalent. If we continue to reject the idea of privatization our potential to become a significant emerging market into which capital flows will likely come to nothing.

There are those who respond to the question of capital inflows by arguing that there is abundant evidence suggesting a tenuous relationship between capital and development. One article appearing this week in *The Guardian* argues this as a criticism of privatization. In my opinion arguments that the key relationship for development is human skill and adaptation of technology truly begs the question. Whereas these, along with the nature of institutions, are very critical, the pace at which they alone can drive growth will, in my thinking, be gravely affected by a situation of acute capital scarcity. If we look at the Asian growth experience we find that in the 1960s most of the capital flows through East Asia came from the United States. Today 75 percent of capital flowing through East Asia are of Asian origin. Capital did help accelerated growth there and the capital came from outside the region. That tonic has enabled things such that today the region is able to sustain regenerative investments from regional savings.

Another reason why it is imperative that we go the way of policies that do not isolate us is that we are operating in the age of corporate globalization. The convergence of telecommunication and computing has effectively changed the way companies operate around the world. Firms used to externalize local competition thereby internationalizing their operations. Today they globalize operations because of the efficiencies inherent in such an approach as they are locked in a race with rivals to increase productivity. In this new global order the economy that does not fit a global framework will be ignored. The current de-industrialization of Nigeria is not unrelated to such undercurrents. If we bear in mind that most of our smaller neighbours have restructured and have better reputations than Nigeria, it is easy to see why some multinationals who have Nigeria as their target are locating in Ghana and elsewhere in the region. Given the benefits of the Uruguay round of GATT and tariff barriers falling, the incentive is high for them to produce elsewhere and ship to Nigeria for sale.

Such strategies, adopted by companies in response to our ambivalence on issues related to macroeconomic fundamentals, of which the logic of privatization is a derivative, could prolong economic stagnation. Along with stagnation comes the exacerbation of chronic poverty, already a phenomenon of our national life that is made worse by serious problems of income distribution as the slide of the Gini coefficient during the last decade indicates (World Bank Poverty Assessment, 1996). This of course is an invitation to social upheavals.

Instead of these sad prospects, Nigeria could finally live up to its potential, becoming a Big Emerging Market by privatizing and following the trend of BEMs in terms of the macroeconomic fundamentals. Perhaps we should conclude by citing this characteristic exhibited in the 10 BEMs identified by the Clinton administration for building partnerships.

Reforms In BEMs

The following are reforms from BEMs:

India (Eased foreign investment restrictions, lowered income tax rates, reduced tariffs, made currency convertible.)

South Africa (Adopted unified exchange rate, reduced export subsidies, reduced tariffs.)

Turkey (Accelerated privatization program, eased foreign investment restrictions, reduced import charges/fees.)

China (Pledged IPR protection, reduced tariffs, systematized tax/ trade laws.)

Indonesia (Eased foreign investment restrictions, reduced tariffs for agricultural products, reformed banking sector.)

Poland (Eased foreign investment restrictions, liberalized foreign exchange rules, reformed social welfare system.)

Brazil (Eliminated most tariff trade barriers, reduced tariffs, reduced government economic regulation.)

Argentina (Eliminated price controls, privatized public sector companies, reduced tariffs and import quota.)

Mexico (Privatized public sector companies, liberalized financial sector regulation, reduced trade barriers via NAFTA, imposed strict government credit controls.)

Chinese Economic Area

Hong Kong (Improved securities fraud enforcement, centralized bank supervision, created new telecom policy authority.)

South Korea (Relaxed foreign exchange control, eased foreign investment restrictions, downsized bureaucracy.)

Taiwan (Improved IPR protection, liberalized insurance market, simplified import licensing.)

I have no doubt that if we too go this way Nigeria will soon be classified a BEM. This will no doubt result in considerable opportunities for all of us present here today.

References

Ayeertey Ernest, Nissanke Machiko et al., 1997. "Financial Market Fragmentation and Reforms" in *The World Bank Economic Review*

Vol. 11, No.2.

Stein, Howard and Lewis, 1996, "Shifting Fortunes: The Political Economy of Financial Liberalization in Nigeria." *Discussion Paper Series A* No. 318. The Institute of Economic Research, Hitotsubashi University, Japan.

Williamson, Olive E., 1985. *The Economic Institutions of Capitalism.* New York. Free Press.

Zayyad, Hamza, Chairman of the Technical Committee on Privatization and Commercialization (TCPC) now Bureau of Public Enterprises in a speech at the UNCTAC Secretariat, 1992.

16

Poverty Reduction Challenges and Opportunities in Nigeria:The Role of Public and Private Sectors As Well As the Civil Society*

Let me begin by thanking most sincerely the UNDP for the work they have been doing to keep the world sensitive to the biggest shame of our era: the widespread poverty in parts of a world that has made so much progress in productivity improvements since James Watt redesigned the steam engine that it truly has the capacity to eliminate poverty from the planet Earth. My thanks also goes to the organizers of this symposium, the UNDP Nigerian office, for asking me to participate in this discussion of a subject truly dear to my heart.

I am convinced that if we can conclude these sessions with a clear agenda for action to which all of us as stakeholders can commit, and not in the way many Nigerian talk shops seem to end, an exercise in verbal prowess, the trouble of coming to Abuja will be well worth our while. In this discussion, I will try to identify what poverty means to and for the private sector, civil society and public policy makers. With this we will look at how the challenge of poverty has evolved in Nigeria, review political economy trends from colonial times to the present and see how each epoch has affected the human condition. From there, we will show the possibilities for reform in terms of attitudes of the three partners in poverty alleviation and what outcomes we might expect. In this process, I hope to offer some kind of agenda for action, advocacy and value sharing that can bring all the recognized mutual benefit in poverty alleviation. In doing the foregoing, I will not only rely on analysis but will draw from personal experience.

Understanding Poverty

We shall make an effort at understanding what poverty means from a few different perspectives. These perspectives include those of the private

---

* Address to Peoples' Bank Forum at a Symposium organised by the UNDP Nigerian office on 17/1/97.

178

sector, that of social order, and the perspective of governance. These are the domains of private enterprise, civil society and the public sector.

Poverty and the Private Sector

The private sector is exposed to the problems of poverty more directly in the form of purchasing power problems, threat to property through antisocial behaviour of some responding to the frustrations of poverty and through lack of investments derived from the vicious cycle of a poor country that is considered unattractive for investment, leading portfolio managers to look elsewhere to invest. In the process of investing elsewhere, better conditions are created in the new investment havens leading to capital flight away from the already poverty-stricken country to those new destinations for capital flows. The private sector also is directly affected by poverty in terms of the quality of manpower available in the competitive race to build advantage over similar industries in other economies trying for a share in a sector of reduced options to the poor, in what has become a global market place. There is also the impact of taking away entrepreneurial capacity that would drive competition among possible suppliers.

On purchasing power, there is more than ample evidence of the impact of poverty. A friend of mine who is Chief Executive of a major, quoted, public company in the food and beverages sector told me early in March, shortly after I returned from a sabbatical, that not one case of any product had moved from their warehouse since the beginning of the year. He said this trying to explain the dilemma of low interest rates not leading to a rush of borrowing. How could he borrow to invest, he lamented, if he could not even sell the stock he had produced? The simple answer is that low purchasing power had finally begun to hurt industry in a very serious way.

This problem of real declining purchasing power came home to me towards the end of 1994. An economic counsellor in one of the embassies in Lagos called me to find out my opinion on why Coca Cola was having difficulty with sales. I tried to do a little field research on the matter and finally came up with an answer. People could not afford purchase even after a bit of price cutting by the carbonated soft drinks bottlers of the time. Why did the effect of low purchasing power surprise industry? I suspect that part of the reason is that in the lag between declining real incomes and consumer behaviour the impact on consumption first came to the poorest groups in society and industry, not being particularly sensitive to this segment, did not quite see it coming until it began to manifest itself in middle income people. Then suddenly the full impact of poverty creeping up on us began to manifest itself. The same goes for the current controversy in the capital markets about 'declining performance' in the brewing sector. The industry leaders are flustered by stockbrokers blaming them for profit decline and argue that if the brokers were competent enough they would have found that the industry had been in decline since the peak of 1983. Nigerian Breweries has, during the years since 1983, grown at the expense of so many smaller brewers who have become extinct. Thus the market was reduced from more than 40 brands of lager beer to less than ten brands and serious brewing firms from nearly 30 to no more than half a dozen.

These considerations on purchasing power are enough to stimulate an interest in poverty alleviation in the private sector. Still ,the private sector has to deal with more poverty issues. One such is the quality of manpower. Productivity increase which is the essence of the firm is made possible by education and attitude to work among other variables. The poor lack the means, or the inclination because of ignorance, to acquire the education that can enhance their contribution to work in the way that increases productivity. One interesting illustration of this comes from a multinational company that tried to grow tea on a commercial basis in the Mambila plateau. In the early days one of the biggest challenges to productivity was the attitude of the local people they hired. On many occasions they would simply not show up for work and did not care to give 'cogent' reasons. They just did not want to come to work on that day. The culture they were used to did not organize work around the schedule the multinational was used to, and there was no intervention of education to re-orient them for the brave new world that had come upon them.

We can bring examples to give life to the other ways we have identified but I believe that these two should suffice and that some of the other ways we have identified as impacting on the private sector from the poverty condition of Nigerians are self explanatory. Let us then turn to civil society before getting to the public sector which should play a key but redefined role in this quest to rid Nigeria of poverty.

Poverty and the Civil Society

Poverty feeds on lack of knowledge, absence of social will to recognize that it can be eliminated in the common interest, and paucity of horizontal social linkages committed to doing something about it. It is clear in my mind that, given the tragedy of the commons embedded in government action and the need advocacy to monitor both the impact of policy choices in the private and public sectors as they affect the human condition, NGOs and institutions of civil society have a major role to play. This means that we need to identify how poverty affects civil society to stimulate appropriate response from civil society structures.

Poverty affects civil society in many ways including the blighting of the impact on democracy. Democracy is of value because it allows for the interest of all to be represented in the making of authoritative and binding allocation of values. The structures of democratic institutions with complex redundancy (Wildavsky, 1977) lead to more effective, if not necessarily the most efficient, public choices. But democracy can hardly work in conditions where the people are poor or ignorant. As we see in Nigeria with ₦50 notes stuck in loaves of bread that are distributed on election day the poor and the illiterate can easily sell their birthright for peanuts. These and many other impacts of poverty on the civic responsibilities we all have, give meaning to what poverty represents for civil society.

Poverty and the Public Sector

The process of governance is about making life better for people who, philosophically speaking, have given up part of their liberty to a sovereign for the benefit derived from collective provision of non-appropriability goods consumed by most of society. Poverty is therefore of concern here in terms of the fact that part of the benefits expected from the sovereign is attacked by the condition of poverty. This includes good health, an environment that allows one to provide himself and his dependents food, shelter and security, and opportunities for seeking self-fulfillment. These factors on the hierarchy of human needs identified by Abraham Maslow and others who developed his thesis are deprecated by poverty conditions.

Not only does the public sector have the obligation to eliminate conditions that make the attainment of these human needs difficult, it also has responsibility for reducing the cost of managing these to attain these objectives in a world of limited resources. Thus when government does not succeed in fighting poverty, it has higher costs in providing health care, policing a society with so many deprived people and providing infrastructure that gets ripped off as the railings on Eko Bridge and the Lagos-Ibadan Expressway.

The Challenge of Poverty Alleviation

One of the major errors of the commonly held views about poverty eradication is that it is a matter of morality of a good conscience. The truth is that poverty is a scourge affecting the capacity of the private sector to grow to its potential. It also affects the extent of commitment of limited government resources to combat diseases, crime and antisocial behaviour consequent upon a human condition of neglect and denial of the basics of decent quality life to parts of the population by a lack of will to tackle the problem of poverty. Poverty is also about social discord that results from absence of appropriate civil culture because of the lack of education of the poor. Democracy and its many benefits to social order are hardly possible with poverty.

Those who hold the view that the poor are as they are because they do not try hard enough and so do not deserve the 'charity' of the effort of others to eliminate poverty come from this perspective that poverty eradication is a matter of morality. Where it is a matter of morality the challenge is couched in charity terms of donation, of taking away from one group and giving to another. Abundant experience suggests, however, that it is possible to provide enough and eradicate poverty by policy choices in both the private and public sector which do not take away from anybody. Indeed these choices which do not take away from those who see poverty eradication as charity at their expense can improve on their own quality of life just by changing how they think of policy choices. I illustrate this problem with two metaphors.

The first is Tawney's metaphor of being so deep in water that even a ripple could drown him. This is really the state of many of our very poor. It is a condition that freezes options, making the very poor so taken up by the sheer struggle to stay alive that they do not even know what they could do to be of value to the more productive half who are searching for people with specific skills to add to the workforce.

The other metaphor is about the man who found the goose that laid the golden eggs. Very anxious to get more golden eggs he cuts up the poor goose and there is no more laying of golden eggs. In my opinion there is a tendency for the elite in a country like Nigeria to seek the golden eggs in a way that leaves the poor bird good only for dinner. Just as the choice of how to obtain golden eggs differs, we can have policies that take a perspective of gauging its impact on the quality of life of the people while seeking growth. We can have, in the alternative, policies that seek growth without enough thought to how they impact on the quality of people's lives. Unfortunately, either because of laziness, or graft, there is a tendency for the latter choice to be dominant in what we see. A good part of our population, the poor, cut up the goose or as part of the goose, is unable to be part of contributing to laying more golden eggs. As they are denied the options of a more productive life the pie we bake is smaller. Much energy is then dispensed by the elite in a bitter struggle over the smaller pie.

This suboptimal approach to economic development which comes out of how these metaphors describe our extant reality in Nigeria can be clearer from an understanding of the political economy history of Nigeria.

Nigeria's Political Economy and the Challenge of Poverty

When the colonialists arrived in Nigeria we had peasant subsistence farming as the dominant occupation. Living conditions fit Tawney's metaphor. Colonial intervention introduced a cash crop economy. Commodity marketing boards were later introduced to ensure that marketing of the commodity was more efficiently done and that a system of guaranteed prices was an incentive for farmers. This was quite a tonic to the quality of life of many of the rural poor engaged in farming. When self government came to the regions of Nigeria in the middle 1950s a political culture of 'competitive communalism' set in.

In the competition between the regions the earnings from the commodities were appropriated by the regional governments through the marketing boards and channelled into the development of urban areas. As Dr Pius Okigbo, then the Economic Adviser to Prime Minister Tafawa Balewa, pointed out in a 1973 address to the Annual Conference of Food and Agricultural Association of Nigeria, the reserves built up by the marketing boards were guzzled up in a very short period of time (Okigbo, 1987). This clearly slowed down the pace of decline of poverty in rural cash crop-producing Nigeria. Competitive communalism did manage to produce a modest but steady growth rate of a little over 3.2 percent of

GDP over the period of civilian rule from 1956 to 1966.

Oil came in 1956 when it was discovered in commercial quantities at Oloibiri but became a source of boom from 1973 when prices were quadrupled following the Arab-Israeli war. A political culture following from the boom under a military regime with its hierarchical command structure produced a culture aptly described by American Political Scientist Richard Joseph as 'bureaucratic prebendalism.' In this cake-sharing culture, policy became less growth oriented with the behaviour of economic actors to policy more in the direction of the man who cut up the goose. Energies were focussed on sharing the national cake. The effect was that the pie was getting smaller (GDP grew from 1973-1995 an average of 0.017 percent) and those at the top were taking more of the small pie, making poverty chronic as the change in the Gini Index from 1982-1992 indicates in the 1996 World Bank Poverty Assessment report on Nigeria. We were going the way that made Argentina unable to sustain development from the 1920s when it was one of the top ten economies in the world until it dropped to West African levels of GDP in the 1970s.

The challenge of the moment is therefore to jumpstart a growth with equity approach. At the least we have the Malaysian experience to show us that economic development is more sustainable when there is equity in income and opportunities distribution. The process of changing attitudes to development to build in equity will involve collaboration between the public sector, the private sector and NGOs.

An Agenda for Action

The anxiety of some in the private sector regarding action against poverty as charity is obviously not tenable. At the same time the private sector can make decisions that have the right effects for poverty eradication without being seen to give up shareholders money, by simply thinking through the decision options it has, bearing in mind the effect of each option on alleviating poverty. Take as an example how companies source agricultural inputs. The NTC small-holder extension service support based approach to sourcing its raw materials rather than embarking in large-scale growing of tobacco has done much to increase incomes in tobacco - growing states. Afprint when it needed cotton set up Afcot and invested heavily in large-scale farming. When returns were not very encouraging they understudied NTC and implemented the NTC-type strategy. Last year they were able to boast about the large number of farmers that work with them who could afford a pilgrimage to Mecca.

The challenge here is for companies to be deliberate in examining strategy for win-win choices that can improve their lot and the lot of the poor. These better-off poor will eventually buy their products just as many of the cotton farmers will wear Afprint cotton prints.

For NGOs the challenge in reconstructing civil society lies in advocacy for policy choices in both private and public sector to reflect this poverty impact analysis. It is also about working for the evolution of institutions that put limits to behaviour in such a way that uncertainty in economic exchange is reduced, resulting in a higher momentum in economic activity and wealth creation (North, 1990). In addition to working institutions, civil society should aim to emphasize that poverty eradication is more than increased incomes for the poor. The weight of the full perspective of human development as opportunity to exercise the options for a better life for all should be pushed to the fore of the public agenda by civil society.

My involvement with a programme for widows from the lowest income groups has also taught me that what is required is much more than an opportunity to earn more. At the Widow Support Centre we have tried to access micro credit for the widows but we find that there are other problems related to how they perceive their self worth which is reflected in their performance. These include their ability to control their children, without a male authority figure, how to deal with in-laws etc. Sometimes this gets in the way of what they can achieve with the loans. Their repayment occasionally falls behind as a result of these problems and the shame of their not being able to meet the obligation complicates their feeling of self worth. NGOs need increasingly to take a perspective of the whole human condition rather than the fragmented approach.

On the part of the public sector there is need to identify with policies that encourage growth with equity as some countries like Malaysia, whose visioning process our Vision 2010 is imitating, have managed to do. Government needs to think more in terms of partnership with the private sector where the private sector is left to be the engine of wealth creation, but government creates the environment to ensure that wealth so created is more evenly distributed and that its own energies are channelled where they are really needed: in providing effective social services such as health care and not in running State-owned business enterprises. The imperative of privatization is key here.

References

Okigbo, Pius. *Essays in the Public Philosophy of Development.* (Enugu, Fourth Dimensions, 1987)

Wildavsky, Aaron. *The Politics of the Budgetary Process* (Boston. Little Brown and Co., 1979)

Work, Douglas. *Institutions, Institutional Change and Economic Performance.* (Cambridge, Cambridge University Press, 1990)

Maslow, Abraham. *Motivation and Personality* (New York, Harper and Row, 1954)

SECTION IV

BUDGET REVIEWS AND POLICY ADVOCACY

17

Orderly Development of SME Sector and Budget '98*

Let me begin by admitting that when I received the invitation to be here today the least I expected was having to open my mouth. It is obvious that the organizers, having sorted out my passionate commitment to developing the SME Sector, used that to corner me into saying some words today. Unfortunately for others who want me to be involved in other discussions, this puts my talk quota for 1998 past the 60% mark. It means I will not be saying much the rest of the year. Anyhow, the subject is important enough to warrant a skewed agenda for participating in public discussions as far as time I can allocate to these matters is concerned.

I am indeed concerned that even though budget '98 does identify the SME sector as a key area of emphasis I cannot see very clearly the capacity to deliver on those intentions. In a previous discussion of the budget I focussed more intensely on capacity to deliver on SMEs through FEAP at the micro enterprise level and through traditional medium scale support institutions through entities like NERFUND, NBCI etc. For me the challenge is a multifold one that goes beyond the capacity problem to encompass a difficulty with focussing on a problem and consistently pursuing prescribed solutions. It also includes a certain tendency for us not to have conceptual clarity with regard to the daunting tasks before us as we pursue nation building. To my mind, if we recognize the importance of making the SME sector work, if poverty alleviation, crime control and issues of national harmony were not to be tackled, we would not have dealt with the matter. Few goal-oriented groups will approach SME development the way we have. The idea of industrial policy has been much discussed. The industrial policy project did consider the place of SMEs, yet few people seem to remember that Rasheed Gbadamosi headed an industrial policy committee.

---

* Address to the Association of Small and Medium Enterprises

In this short address I will therefore compare a few of the experiences from North East and South East Asia. In drawing from those experiences as benchmarks for how we have derailed I intend to lay emphasis on a number of points. Among these is the fact that few economies make real progress unless they develop a substantial indigenous private sector. Nigeria hardly has an indigenous private sector. The way to develop such a sector is through focussing on SMEs and providing them a pedestal to move up in quality and competence such that they can compete in a shrinking global arena. I will also like to raise to the fore of our consciousness issues of how a failure to address the problems of today's poverty will ensure that all of us are poor tomorrow, including those who today hijack disproportionate returns to their contribution to national wealth. If time permits I will also try to show how critical institutional frameworks are for developing a savings and investments base as well as sustaining it. The issues of resource endowment and economic growth and the tragedy of corruption which continues to damage the Nigerian potential also call for our attention. Finally I turn to business and would-be entrepreneurs and accuse them of contributing to national stagnation through lack of big dream and empire building visions.

The small domestic market not only reflected the country's relatively small population and its relatively low average income level. Perhaps more importantly, its skewed distribution of income, and hence expenditure pattern, shaped the nature of effective demand, i.e. the nature of the domestic market for particular goods. Without a more equitable development strategy, which might transform the pattern of effective demand, domestic industrial production for mass consumption needs could not expand very much. In addition, the sector's employment generating capacity was limited due to the relatively capital-intensive nature of the investments as well as the weak linkages to the rest of the Malaysian economy. With the growth of big industry out-pacing small-scale enterprise, and with capital-intensive industries expanding much faster than labour-intensive ones, employment creation lagged considerably behind investment growth during the period of import substitution. By the mid-1960s the inherent limitations of the Malaysian import-substitution strategy were becoming clear. In 1965, the Federal Industrial Development Authority, or FIDA (now known as MIDA, the Malaysian Industrial Development Authority), was set up to encourage industrial investment, although it never really got going until 1967. [Jomo K.S., 1996]

If we consider how much bigger than the Nigerian economy that of Malaysia has come to be because of this switch in policy from ISI to an export orientation, we shall see where we went wrong. What has happened in the 1998 budget is that a framework for making it viable for SMEs has not been deliberately addressed.

If indeed we want to encourage SME, the issue of access to capital and markets, infrastructure to reduce cost and enhance competitiveness, institutions that reduce uncertainty in the environment, and servicing of domestic debt by government should be dealt with squarely. In the past monetary guidelines from the Central Bank have ordered certain proportions of loanable funds from banks to go to what was referred to as preferred sectors. In the age of deregulation that is not so fashionable any more, SME activity vital for development, job creation, income re-distribution etc. has also continued to be depressed because of the nature of income flows in the economy and the other factors we have just listed.

For SMEs to thrive there has to be a more stable regime of interest rates which, if inflation is low, could be considerably low. With low interest rates, availability of savings, and entrepreneurs identifying value creating enterprise opportunity, we should see an attraction of capable people into the sector. Priority in budgeting should therefore be to keep inflation low without entering deflation as our policies in 1997 have tended to do, and make the savings from pensions etc. available to fund venture capital and SMEs.

The SME sector also suffers not just because purchasing power is generally low in the economy, punishing large scale manufacturers to whom many SMEs are suppliers but also because of the kinds of spending commitments of government. Most of the expenditure of government today goes into capital projects and Petroleum Trust Fund activities. This means that monies flow into the pockets of a few businesses that are external in orientation. So money goes from PTF to those companies and then to the foreign exchange market to exit the economy. The fact that most of the money in circulation comes in capital votes also means that SMEs will not find customers who have purchasing power to sustain consumption of their products.

On the whole these issues highlight the inadequacy of 1998 provisions for the SME sector. More needs first to be done for this sector at the heart of our economic development.

Conclusion

In these brief comments our objective has been to show that while we still talk about SME as priority our policies do not reflect this consciousness. There is still so much uncertainty such as whether SME projects funded in dollars when the exchange rate was₦22 to $1 will repay at₦85 to $1. Without insurance to manage such wildly fluctuating exchange rates, entrepreneurs cannot have the confidence to dare. Not only does uncertainty challenge SME ventures but the other issues we have pointed to here contribute significantly to it.

Reference

Jomo K.S. *et al*, 1997. *South East Asia's Misunderstood Miracle: Industrial Policy and Economic Development in Thailand, Malaysia and Indonesia.* Colorado. West View Press.

18

Business Outlook for 1998: Policy Imperatives and Implications for the Private Sector*

The objective of this presentation is to analyze the economic and political risks likely to confront business enterprises in the course of 1998. The emphasis will be on the nature of the public policy process and how the variables identified here could affect public choice and subsequently the environment of business. The analysis proposed here will review the state of the policy process, the possible effects of the politics of an election or transition year and international attitudes towards Nigeria. Other factors considered include the capitalization of companies following the market corrections that started in the summer of 1997, the possible implementation of Vision 2010 suggestions and the challenge of confronting growing poverty.

Within the foregoing variables we will situate several issues that currently affect the business climate. These include the managing of inflation, the need to stimulate purchasing power, trimming the size of government and increasing public sector productivity, patterns of withdrawal of money from the circular flows of income by policy choices that have been made in recent years and the pending issue of privatization. Also of critical consequences, and so subjects of the analysis, are the impact of corporate globalization, the current regime of a dual exchange rate, the wages review expectation, and the pressing matter of how to better manage the external sector.

To put all of these in context it is important to recall the broad objectives of the managers of the Nigerian economy and the dominant paradigms for evaluating business cycles. These will enable us discern what could drive policymaker responses to the variables and issues we have hitherto outlined.

Broad Objectives of Economic Policy

The often stated broad objectives of economic policy have been: 1) to

---

* Session at LBS Budget Review

restructure and diversify the productive base of the economy, 2) to achieve fiscal and balance of payments viability, 3) to achieve sustainable non-inflationary or minimal inflationary growth, and 4) to improve government efficiency and promote private sector growth. Very little of the nature of policy outcomes suggests much progress on numbers one and four. Progress has been made on fiscal viability but the apparent approach to containing inflation has stifled growth by damaging purchasing power capability through withdrawals and sterilization of money from the system. These outcomes of the manner of pursuit of the outlined broad policy objectives have kept at the trough of the business cycles a prolonged recession.

To gain deeper insights into why policies have kept businesses in this state we need to draw from some theoretical perspectives on business cycles. One typology of business cycles identifies six groups of theories: the monetary theories, innovation theories, the multiplier-accelerator model, political theories, equilibrium-business cycle theories and the real business-cycle hypothesis.

Theories in Business Cycles

1. *Monetary* theories attribute the business cycle to the expansion and contration of money and credit (Hawtrey, Friedman).
2. *Innovation* theories attribute the cycle to the clustering of important invention such as those surrounding the railroad or the automobile (Schumpeter, Hansen).
3. The *multiplier-accelerator* model proposes that external shocks are propagated by the multiplier-accelerator, thereby generating regular, cyclical fluctuations in ouput (Samuelson).
4. *Political* theories of business cycles attribute fluctuations to politicians who manipulate fiscal and monetary policies in order to be re-elected (Kalecki, Nordhaus, Tufte).
5. *Equilibrium-business cycle* theories claim that misperceptions about price and wage movements lead people to supply too much or too little labour, which leads to cycles of output and employment (Lucas, Barro, Sargent).
6. *Real-business cycle* proponents hold that productivity shocks spread through the economy and cause fluctuations (Prescott, Long, Plosser).

Most appropriate to the extant Nigerian circumstances are the first four types of theories. Money supply has been used to manage inflation first by erratic mopping up of funds through the idea of stabilization securities charged against banks then through Open Market Operations. The latter more stable approach would seem now inadequately implemented as Discount Houses look for new ways of staying afloat other than through trading in securities. Seen from the monetarist perspective the control of inflation through sterilization of money results in households losing purchasing power, thus depressing the activity level in the circular flows of income.

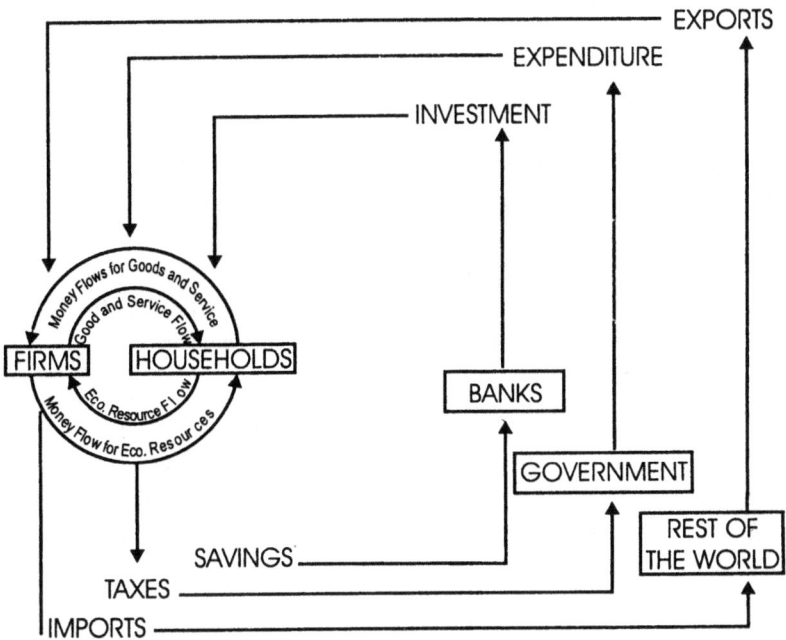

The Circular Flow of Income
Source: Villegas & Abola. *Economics: An Introduction*—Sinag-Tala Publication, Manila 1992

There was an 'outbreak' of minor innovations and a surge of entrepreneurial spirit at the onset of the Structural Adjustment Programme, part evidence of which includes the transformation of such Lagos streets as Awolowo Road, Ikoyi and Allen Avenue, Ikeja into major high streets (Utomi, 1996a). As policies shifted away from stable competitive exchange rates and fiscal balance in favour of highly inflationary deficit, spending by government experienced a lull. No major innovation producing a quantum leap in value creation has taken place to propel business out of a prolonged recession.

Crude oil on another hand has continued to generate external shocks that have generated cyclical fluctuations. Even when a windfall came during the Gulf war, it was managed in such a way that 1991 was a year of enormous fiscal deficits in Nigeria.

On political theories we find interesting possibilities especially as 1998 which we are trying to analyze is an election year. In this regard it is pertinent to note that the search for legitimacy by the new Abacha regime in 1994 led to abandoning pretences to SAP and turning to controls. When that failed a somewhat different drumbeat was turned to. The expectation from this perspective suggests that the nature of government spending in 1998 will be affected by whether or not Gen. Sani Abacha makes a move to retain power.

With these orientations in mind let us now turn to the issues that will determine policy outlook in 1998 and how this will affect the business cycle, in essence, the performance of the private sector.

Issues of Challenge in 1998

We have already indicated that the issues that will affect policies and the business environment include how government manages inflation, the trimming of the size of government, privatization etc. Let us consider each in some detail.

Inflation

A review of policy activity will suggest to most people coming from a monetary perspective that the truncated pattern of government spending characterized in 1997 by non-release of first quarter capital vote into the third quarter was a clear tactic to keep inflation down by starving circular flows of the tremendous amounts of money withdrawn through the Value Added Tax (VAT), increased petroleum pricing with the extra income going to the Petroleum Trust Fund (PTF), etc. (see Teriba, 1997). Very senior insiders in the policy arena suggest, however, that the non-release of allocations may be more a factor power play and efforts at getting ministries to account for what they collected in the past than a deliberate policy of managing inflation through money supply.

The fact that money is scarce more by default than by a deliberate debilitating monetarist strategy is more worrisome in my opinion. All the same the net effect is that inflation is already into single digits. Ayo Teriba, in fact, worries that the possibilities of crossing 0 percent, with more disastrous consequences from the deflation for firm performance than an inflationary situation, could materialize given the trend. Could this change in 1998? Probably.

The political climate remains cloudy, shrouded in the anxiety over whether or not Gen. Abacha will make a bid for the presidency. Civilian aspirants who would already have been spending a lot of money that could push inflation are circumspect, having been burnt by recent experiences in which the military encouraged them to commit vast amounts of their personal fortunes to electioneering campaigns only to move the goal post and rewrite the rules. Once it is clear Abacha has no hidden agenda they will commit resources. Evidence from careful observation suggests that a shrewd Abacha will leave the issue hanging until the last minute. This will mean that the only thing that will push inflation will be spending by the regime to create a feel-good sense in the populace to improve its own chances. The net effect of these scenarios is that the prospects for inflation are modest to moderate.

Trimming Government

The regime does seem committed to trimming the size of government. Politics permitting, it would seem that this will come soon. Policy sources suggest that the long overdue review of wages of civil servants, most of whom are not paid a living wage, is being delayed until the issue of rationalizing the workforce in the public service is effected. Three things are, however, troubling about the aspects of the exercise to which policymakers do not seem to have given much thought. These are the nature of the benefits those living the service will receive: how they can be made productive members of society; and how to increase productivity in a badly demoralized and corrupt service.

The question of benefits for civil servants to be retrenched raises a moral question of recognizing that they have been paid unfairly for many years. At present wage levels severance pay is so poor. It is almost an assurance that the social consequences of rationalizing could be very deep and may compound the problems of purchasing power that need to be dealt with if growth is to be stimulated. The same independent economists propose that wages be increased before restructuring. These economists go as far as arguing that the adjusted wages be made to take effect from 1993. The backlog and severance pay under their proposed scheme would then be somewhat adequate to begin again.

It seems appropriate, however, that a decent end-of-service package is worked out in an institutional framework for helping many of the affected who will have become unemployable to develop small scale business skills; to help them establish such ventures is imperative to get optimal outcomes from the process. None of such initiatives appears evident in the posturings from the policy arena even though these would seem natural to a worldview espoused by Prof. Sam Aluko who remains a prominent player in the economic policy formulation.

Then there is the huge task of retraining the smaller public service that will be left so that productivity increases will come. The re-orienting of the civil service will also have to focus the bureaucracy on partnership with the private sector in a way that the effect of their renewed and reinvigorated efforts will be to facilitate private sector-led growth.

Unless some of these factors, and the need to recognize that those who will survive the massive rationalization will suffer from 'survivor guilt' and will need reassurances to keep morale up, are dealt with, 1998 could be a policy implementation nightmare year. If we end up with good intentions that do not get implemented, it would be just as good as not making policy at all.

Privatization

Often easy to politicize, the issue of privatization cannot but come to the fore in 1998. This is partly because some critical parastatals are on the verge of collapse. NEPA executives recently suggested in public comments that they required several trillions of Naira to avert total collapse. In so doing they were only confirming a point some of us have made repeatedly in recent times. If Finance Minister Anthony Ani and his Petroleum Resources colleague can get into an unprecedented public squabble over funds for maintenance of the refineries, and if capital expenditure allocations for 1997 have been set on to get Ministers to explain previous spending, the likelihood that NEPA will get one of one thousand parts of its 'needs' seems remote. The worsening of NEPA service will most probably result in closer scrutiny of their cost profile and the amount of rent built in. This should no doubt accelerate a push towards privatization. This expectation of an inevitable reconsideration of the need for privatization does not discount the impact of the politics of entrenched interests. Having been one of those in the Hall who applauded Anthony Ani's declaration of plans for wholesale privatization in Washington during the 1996 World Bank IMP Annual meetings, I do have a feeling for deep rooted opposition of some interest group. At the 1997 annual meetings of the Bank and Fund in Hong Kong, I monitored Ani closely in the expectation that he would update the world on his announcement of the previous year. His avoidance of the subject spoke volumes of the problems with privatization. People at the Bureau for Public Enterprises (BPE), the successor agency to the Technical Committee for Privatization and Commercialization (TCPC), also appear somewhat cynical about the prospects of more meaningful privatization.

In spite of all of the obstacles to privatization, the near collapse that faces NEPA sends signals. There is the Iridium project and other technologies around the corner which threaten NITEL monopoly in telecommunications. With these technologies; one can have services that by-pass NITEL. Such threats to monopoly enterprises will loom large in the 1998 horizon. The fact that a second carrier to compete with NITEL has apparently been licensed should be a pointer to the way things may evolve. Should politics prevent privatization, the purchasing issue will need to be revisited because a greater portion of household income will be committed to privately generated electric power. This will limit the possibilities of consumer goods led growth.

Dual Exchange Rate

There is hardly any controversy in circles outside of government that the continued use of a dual exchange rate policy leaves loopholes for abuse, encourages an external orientation in government consumption and allows for a deceptive understating of government spending. This point is particularly critical because it impacts on the external sector as the multilateral agencies and the Paris Club are insistent on the condition of the dual exchange rate being removed. Given the devastating effect of poor management of the external sector on the circular flows of income which have been starved of foreign direct investment and portfolio investments, an overhaul of exchange rate policy is overdue. Inside government sources suggest, however, that this is one issue the regime is so emotionally committed to and would be unlikely to budge on. There is evidence from late 1995, when the dollar dropped dramatically in value on market speculation that the regime would free the exchange rate. The fact that nothing eventually happened suggests policy makers may be unreasonably stubborn on the issue. They may not shift their position in 1998.

It is clear that the external sector will not improve much in 1998 from the foregoing and the extent of the global tarnishing of Nigeria's image from the advance fee fraud (419) and human rights abuses. If the European Union, the Commonwealth and most of the world keep up with the pressure, the external sector will suffer further pressure beyond the strong impact of corporate globalization which has already manifested itself in the form of progressive de-industrialization of Nigeria as quite a few multinationals sell off and leave town.

Competing Governments

With PTF (which along with VAT accounts for some of the biggest withdrawals from circular flows of income) comes the additional problem of policy coordination. The Central Bank of Nigeria, devoid of autonomy to influence policy, has little control over competing agencies of government with such capacity to influence money supply and fiscal policy. A typical example was the scuttling of the policy intentions of the 1997 budget because PTF money placements in banks increased funds available when the real sector was not investing because inventory was high and not moving. The banks turned to the government securities market but the interest rates and the shallowness of the market proved an inadequate source of returns. They turned to the capital markets which was equally shallow. The next option was the foreign exchange market which under pressure resulted in the significant devaluation of the Naira.

In 1998 the pressure to manage competing policy centre will increase. Politics could, however, turn all these bad news to some hopeful signs. This will depend on the sense for a place in history by the incumbents or/ and whether speculations that General Abacha would run for President turn out to be right, affecting policy to facilitate such plans.

Capital Market Corrections and Environment

There are many variables that can be affected by the politics of 1998. One factor on which the direction of politics will have little impact is the on-going correction in the capital markets.

The high returns trends in the capital markets during the last few years which have been against the currents of the fundamentals of the economy and the growth rate in the economy were bound to trigger market correction at some point in time. That process started during the summer of 1997. Some analysts predict that the usual sell-off in search of liquidity for the Christmas season and school fees commitments which is followed by significant buying by February/March may not follow the pattern as dividends announced early in the new year could be unsatisfactory. This could result in panic selling and a market crash. Companies would clearly be under pressure to watch what the market does to their capitalization and to manage investor relations with more care than they had done previously.

Implementing Vision 2010

The incumbent regime has made the project of fashioning a modus vivendi for Nigeria through the Vision 2010 project, a high profile platform of its tenure. This has happened in spite of a cynical public imputing motives that the real purpose of the Vision 2010 committee was an expensive and wasteful abuse of state resources to buy time for the regime. It would seem that a desire to prove the skeptics wrong should therefore mean that a strong effort at implementing some prescriptions of the Vision 2010 Committee should be in the offing in 1998. The big question is which parts of the programme will be emphasized.

A pointer to what may happen may be found in the speculations that a cabinet reshuffle which brings in Vision 2010 participants into the Federal Cabinet will be made. Given the history of how the regime makes decisions, the possibilities of this happening remains a toss up.

Bridging Income Gaps

The phenomenon of declining real wages which has persisted for several years takes place alongside policies like the PTF programme. In the PTF approach, money withdrawn from millions of Nigerians who use transportation and energy from fossil fuels go to a few consultants and contractors who work for PTF, contracting the number of people with purchasing power. The effect is a widening of the gap between the poorest and the most privileged in the society. This can be seen clearly from the trend in the Gini Index, the measure of this gap (See table 1). The effect of this in the face of GDP stagnation is the increased possibility of deviant social behaviour. This fact comes out clearly in the UNDP 1997 Human Development Report which aims to put pressure on government to run a poverty impact test of its policies. Should this affect policy makers as the Minister of National Planning keeps pledging it will, then there could be a movement in the direction of improving purchasing power through wage adjustments and the kind of spending options considered by government.

External Sector

The last meeting of the Commonwealth Heads of States and Governments brought a mixed set of reactions to observers of how the regime has managed the external sector. Some celebrated the failure to expel Nigeria as evidence of improved management of the external sector where the trend had been that of descent into pariah status. Others saw the continued suspension of Nigeria as evidence that Nigeria remained untouchable and so would have difficulty getting support at institutions like the International Finance Corporation (IFC). If the external sector continues to be managed the way it is, with the external affairs ministry continuously alienating the international community, the problems of advance fee fraud not being seen as robustly tackled, and the understanding of the multilateral agencies (World Bank/IMF and even the Paris Club) not being better cultivated, the external sector will not contribute to growth in the way that has accounted for the South East Asia economic success story.

Globalisation

Closely related to the issue of managing the external sector is the challenge posed by the convergence of telecommunications and computing which has combined with falling shipping costs to make it easy to produce and distribute from almost anywhere in a post-Uruguay round world. The work of Vision 2010 has focussed attention enough on this subject that a change in the nature of the composition of the cabinet and its cohesion, bearing in mind that the Cabinet hardly met in 1996 and 1997, could lead to initiatives that will make things move towards improving the environment for business performance and enhancing the nature of public-private sector relations.

Conclusion

The foregoing suggests that 1998 holds opportunities and harbours serious threats. How these opportunities and threats develop is a function of the way the 'politics of self-succession' unfolds in Abuja. A particular strength firms must strive to develop is the capacity for scanning the environment. A good ear to the ground will suggest appropriate responses that could, in fact, allow a company to thrive in Nigeria's chaos.

International Poverty Incidence Comparisons
(US$1/day poverty line)

	Incidence	Depth	Severity	Gini
Nigeria, 1985	31.50	10.20	4.40	.387
Nigeria, 1992	27.10	10.80	5.70	.450
Ghana, 1989	19.68	4.93	1.86	.408
Cote d' Ivoire, 1988	17.34	4.08	1.31	.345
Morocco, 1991	1.64	0.23	0.06	.396
Sri Lanka, 1990/91	23.44	4.97	1.61	.302
China, 1990	17.76	4.12	1.32	.315
Pakistan. 1991	12.77	2.86	1.11	.312
Panama, 1989	19.64	9.52	5.93	.568
Brazil, 1989	26.00	10.90	5.64	.638
Peru. 1990	40.60	14.06	6.71	.439
Columbia, 1991	2.95	0.79	0.34	.513

Reference

Teriba, A.O. "Business Outlook for 1998" in *LBS Management Review,* Vol. 2, No. 2, July-December 1997.

SECTION V

VALUES AND MANAGEMENT EFFECTIVENESS

19

The Evolution of Institutions, Patriotism, Democracy and Accountability in Governance*

The regime that overthrew the civilian government led by Alhaji Shehu Shagari in 1983 emphasized the need for patriotism. This regime led by Generals Mohammadu Buhari and Tunde Idiagbon did so in a manner suggesting that a good deal of the problems of society that caused them to intervene could be overcome by patriotic conduct. They decreed patriotism, practically, ordered out the flag and ran television commercials condemning those joining the brain drain train (The Andrew Checking Out Commercial). At the end of the day, economic austerity increased and quest for "essential commodities" consumer good items in short supply became desperate. The result was a gradual return of sharp practices in spite of the fear of harsh penalties for indiscipline in the land.

The notorious case of 53 suitcases allegedly belonging to an Emir that were let in during the currency change when such was prohibited left the impression that sharp practices were condoned, if the right people were involved. It proved to be an excuse for those who wanted to question the credibility of the austere regime.

In the same way as the push to engender patriotism by the Buhari-Idiagbon regime proved insufficient to improve the quality of life of Nigerians, the demise of the second republic and the aborted third republic show that democracy as an ideology of governance does not necessarily result in accountability and good governance. What then, might we say, are the missing variables which are necessary for patriotism and democracy to result in accountability and good governance in Nigeria?

The role of institutions, embedded in how they evolve, is clearly a major variable influencing the value of patriotism, democracy and good governance. Our objective in this presentation, therefore, is to establish why the issues of patriotism and democracy have become important enough concerns to warrant their choice as the theme of this conference. We also

---

* Address to Conference of Nigeria's People and Organisations in Boston, Massachussets

Per Capita Output of Thailand, Indonesia, Nigeria, South Korea, and Malaysia (1970 - 1996) US**$**

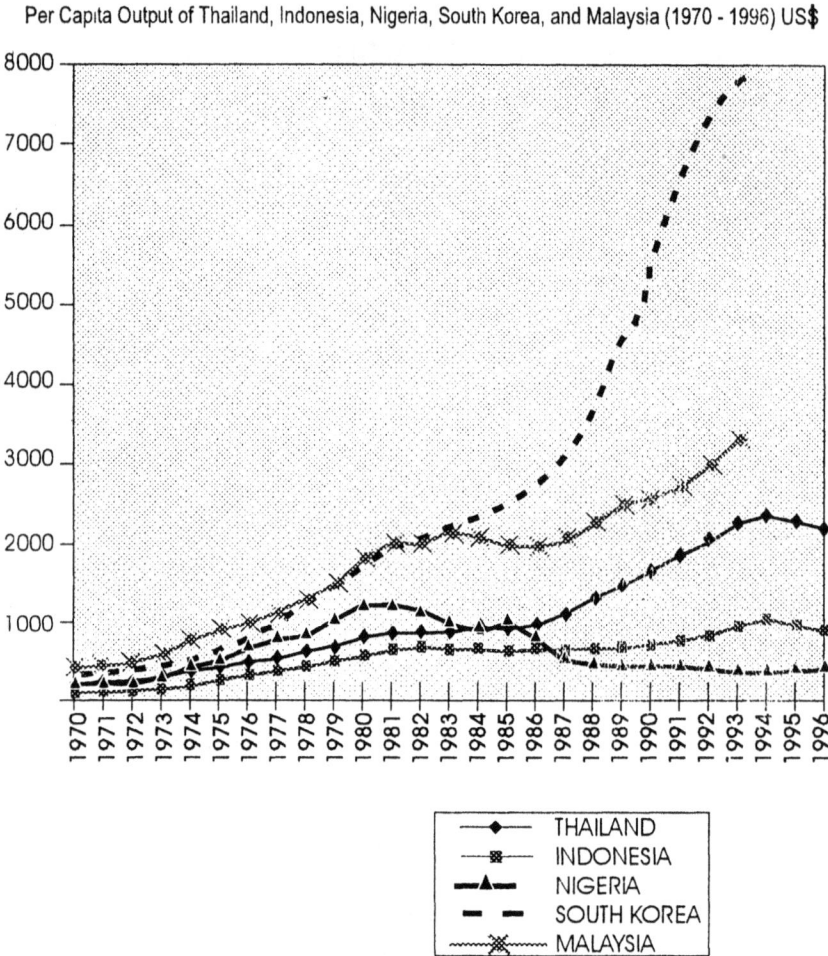

wish to establish what institutions are, how they evolve and the implications of this for constitutionalism, democracy and patriotism.

Why These Concerns

At the centre of concern about democracy, constitutionalism and patriotism is anxiety about the process of national development. Many seem to believe that with more patriotism things will go right. Decline in the quality of life brought into sharp relief by the indicators of national production such as nominal GDP per capita shows Nigeria in a horrendous slide.

The 1996 poverty assessment report of the World Bank was even greater gloom. Nigeria experienced significant growth in the first development decade after independence but in the years since oil prices quadrupled, something that should have been a boost to development, the Nigerian economy has stagnated. But for a short period in the late 1980s the Nigerian economy has actually been in steep decline (World Bank, 1996). From a GDP growth of more than 3.2 percent per annum from 1956 to 1966 the economy has grown by about 0.017 percent from 1973 when oil prices were quadrupled till today (*Economist*, 1996). Attempts to explain this decline have followed, among other traditions, the efforts to understand the nature of the state in post-colonial Africa. Within this tradition there is a clearly identified disconnection between the State and Society (Leys, 1975; Shivji, 1976).

The modern state in post-colonial Africa has often been seen as an alien establishment of colonial experience (Murphy, 1986) passed on to a local elite at independence. The local elite assumed at independence that the legitimacy they built their regime on was different from the colonial regime's legitimacy base because it came from the people. Those civilian regimes were soon to find out how isolated they were from society by the rejoicing that followed each overthrow of government. In reality, people saw a connection between the post-colonial and colonial state from how they behaved. The state continued as alien to the society in the perception of the populace. They had little by way of leverage to call government to order, that is, hold it accountable. It was as a result of this disconnection between state and society that policies pursued by government often tended to profit those that provided the narrow base of support for regimes. This gain, usually through economic rents, comes sometimes to the detriment of total society. At the least, the crisis of legitimacy which leads to compensating the narrow providers of a power base, materially, leads a regime to focus the energies of the state in extracting and sharing to privileged constituencies from which it draws legitimacy, rather than in creating an atmosphere for generating wealth. This point is made very well in the whole discussion of bureaucratic prebendalism in Nigeria (Joseph, 1987). Peter Lewis has, in fact, argued that "political coalitions will converge around the creation and allocation of rents" (Lewis, 1994).

Rent - seeking is thus related to the disconnection between state and society.

Following from this nature of the disconnected state, it is perhaps logical to expect that greater linkages between the state and society through increased participation of the populace in determining who rules should improve economic management. Clearly, the possibility of holding those so determined accountable (democracy) and in generating national pride in the population (patriotism) should lead to an improved quality of life. The interest in patriotism, democracy and accountability which is much affected by the development of institutions is a germane subject to consider at such a meeting as the CONPO annual conference.

As we have seen in the introduction with the Buhari-Idiagbon regime's effort, patriotism of its own does not lead to progress. We shall in fact show that in this paradox of which comes first, the chicken or the egg, national progress which we seek through patriotism might itself be a stimulant of patriotic fervour, if not a determinant of it. To understand how economic policy which can affect patriotism has evolved in Nigeria, we will need to look at the paradigms through which policy orientation has been drawn on in post-colonial Africa.

Development Paradigms

It is worthy of note that the quest for the redemption of the state in post-colonial Africa features competing paradigms. One paradigm, pushed strongly by the multilateral development lending agencies, is a market economy paradigm. Another paradigm into whose tradition the theme of this conference falls is the modernization paradigm. This paradigm sees a continuum in which there is incremental transformation of traditional people with the evolution of attitudes towards those of the modern western nation-state. Among the attributes of the evolution are such affective components of behaviour as patriotism in the populace. This tradition, one of the oldest in looking at emergent states since the independence movements began to mature in the 1950s, has undergone changes in approach but transformation of attitudes in the population remains central to inquiry (Geertz, 1963; Apter, 1965).

The tradition of market economy prescriptions in its broad sense forms the basis of the context within which I have chosen to examine the concepts of patriotism and democracy with the notable difference that the market economy solution as proposed by the World Bank and others is short-changed by inadequate emphasis on the place of institutions and how they evolve and play a role in the moulding of markets. These markets, in reducing capacity for elite abuse of the commonwealth, provide in my opinion a context to better understand how patriotism is enkindled and democratic traditions sustained to the benefit of accountability in governance.

Institutions, How They Evolve and the Crisis Of Institutions In Nigeria

Institutions in their bare essence are systemic frameworks, or value systems, used by society to set limits to acceptable conduct. In effect institutions exist to constrain behaviour in a way that facilitates social intercourse and economic exchange relations. The study of institutions in economics has two competing perspectives. One perspective draws from the choice theoretic approach that underlies micro-economics and is represented by the work of people like Douglas North (North, 1990). This approach sees institutions as instrumental objects evolving as exchange relations grow. With the assumption of neo-classical economics that a man acts to maximize his wealth or self interest, the tradition holds that a party to a transaction, acting as a rational self-seeking maximizer of advantage, would defect rather than cooperate if the likelihood of a repeat transaction were not there. He normally cooperates because in subsequent transaction, he would pay the price of retaliation if he did defect. In transactions one would ordinarily see defection or cooperation. The effect of second-guessing the likelihood defection would be less willingness to transact, or a high cost to the transaction. Costs are lowered through institutions evolving to bring sanctions to bear on those who defect. These constraints from institutions, or restrained behaviour, come not so much from continuous enforcement which will make transaction costs high but through rules that make informal constraints operational. People restrain themselves because a norm of behaviour evolves around the rule policed by the institution.

The competing institutionalist tradition sees institutions as less instrumental but more "as settled habits of thought common to the generality of man" (Veblen and Stein, 1994). Whichever the perspective we choose, institutions clearly are evolutionary. In both these perspectives referred to as the New Institutional Economics and the Old Institutional

Economics, whether they be habits shaped by time or responses to the need of society at a point in the nature of exchange relations, they have come incrementally, adding on with time at the margins, so to speak. For Nigeria and most post-colonial societies the challenge of institution building comes from the imposition of institutions from abroad. These new institutions were lacking in the legitimacy that evolved institutions have. While evolved institutions were incrementally grafted on, earning society's acceptance progressively, imposed institutions have limited basis of acceptance. They have thus not been successful in constraining behaviour as institutions should do, except at high enforcement cost as through the colonial police. Where these new institutions exist side by side with traditional institutions, they sometimes weaken the traditional institutions without supplementing them as effective constraint of inappropriate behaviour. Where institutions have evolved appropriately they have often stimulated social progress through enhanced exchange relations. This is why property rights feature strongly in institutional economics. As we can see, the evolution of institutions ensuring property sights correlates strongly with the blossoming of American capitalism in the 19th century (Coase, 1992; North, 1990). Third World underdevelopment has been thus associated with the state of institutional development (Knack and Keefer, 1995). We can surely hypothesize on the relationship between property rights, foreign investment and economic growth. Even though I have not seen a study on the relationship between confidence in the economy and a sense of patriotism, I have no doubt that a study will show national pride, patriotism, correlates strongly with economic success and confidence in the economy. People were more proud to say they were Nigerians during the oil boom days of the 1970s.

Given this relationship between institutions that ensure property rights and economic progress, and national pride, we can see clearly a place for the idea of evolution of institutions in the theme of this conference.

The Market Paradigm

Having introduced institutions, central to our discourse, it should be appropriate procedure to look at the approaches to development we have pursued and then evaluate them in terms of the role of institutions and how this has affected the notions of Patriotism, Democracy and Accountability. The market paradigm has been proposed to supplant the state intervention paradigm by the World Bank and has to different degrees been adopted by most African countries, including Nigeria, since the middle of the 1980s (Gibbon and Olukoshi, 1996).

The thrust of market policies is that you achieve greater efficiency through encouraging market prices that reflect the scarcity value of the product. In other words, for example, if foreign exchange is priced at its scarcity value which is equal to the opportunity cost, people will not consume imports of frivolous things but will efficiently utilize the foreign exchange to optimize on their well-being, which may mean using it for inputs that enhance production of goods and services.

This approach sees the efficiency of markets as determined by prices distorted by state intervention. The thrust of policy should therefore be to remove state interference with markets through deregulation and privatization of state owned enterprises (SOE)(Collaghy, 1990).

A classic example of how this has been implemented has been in the Nigerian financial system. To achieve an adequate pool of savings and appropriate culture of financial intermediation, it was necessary, following the Mckinon-Shaw model of financial repression, to liberalize: get the state out, and financial deepening will follow. Logically, deregulation, lowering entry barriers into banking, will lead to greater rivalry which should result in higher levels of efficiency (Stein, 1994).

What happened in Nigeria, however, was that rent-seeking behaviour which had become a habit in the state-intervention era sipped over with the arbitrage possibilities in the two-tier foreign exchange structure (Utomi, 1996b). With rent gains driving venturing into banking, possibilities of bank failures increased. In markets, failures by risk-taking enterprises like banks are inevitable. What is required to keep failure from imposing heavy costs on the systems is adopting failure resolution mechanisms or exit formula which impose minimum costs on the system. Institutions usually ensure this. Here it was clear that issues of sequencing of deregulation and appropriate effort to build institutional capacities of the Central Bank of Nigeria (CBN) and the Nigerian Insurance Deposit Corporation (NDIC) did not get enough attention early in the liberalization programme.

Once the obviously inevitable failures hit the badly managed banks, the absence of failure resolution and exit mechanisms at CBN resulted in panic and systemic distress. Deposits which had moved out of the traditional big but inefficient banks to the more efficient banks rushed back in a flight to safety as information asymmetries made it difficult for depositors to determine which banks were okay among the new generation banks.

The challenge of evolution of institutions was clearly at the root of the disaster that has befallen Nigerian banking. Society's response was to accuse those who entered banking of lack of patriotism. If one takes the self-seeking rationality view of men in neo-classical economics, Nigerian bankers were bound to behave the way many of them did in the absence of institutions that put a high cost to inappropriate behaviour. Rent - seeking opportunity presented itself and it looked like there would be no cost to defecting. That cost has come after the fact in the tribunals now set up to try bankers (*The Economist,* 1996). But the damage is already done. If you take the old institutional economics approach of institutions as settled habits of thought, then people will have been conditioned by social norms not to act in the manner that damaged confidence in the system. It should not take a feeling of patriotism to achieve such behaviour. It would seem therefore that our understanding of institutions suggests that patriotism is not the source of the trouble in banking. What is needed are institutions of the type associated with democracy as they provide an opportunity for enhanced exchange relations with the possibility of stronger economic performance which can produce an economy in which people can invest pride.

What markets with appropriate institutional development will achieve is improved exchange relations resulting in a success that increases the basis of national pride. A good example would be soccer in Nigeria. Once the football market became more of a market, talented young men found themselves sharpening their skills on a world market as professionals in Europe and elsewhere. Assembled and supported by an institutional framework of the NFA which, in spite of its weakness, can pick good coaches and make a foreign training schedule possible, a Gold medal at the Olympics was an outcome. Suddenly, patriotic fervour was aglow in the land. The challenge then for politicians is to enshrine in symbols these national successes and use them to build commitment to the national vision which they need to have clearly thought out. Patriotism generated by economic success, when tapped by political leaders, can drive further economic success.

State Intervention Perspective

The roots of the state-led development perspective, which the market approach was introduced to reform, can probably be most clearly identified in the paraphrasing of scripture by Kwame Nkrumah when he said "seek ye first the political kingdom and all else will be added unto you." The trophy captured from seeking the political kingdom was the state. In Nigeria the state's quest to solve all of society's problems, as stated by the promises of politicians, was given further impetus by the cash flow generated by oil price increases. The thesis of government occupying the commanding heights of the economy was proposed by the public service and became the thrust of policy. This generated a culture of rent-seeking by economic actors and public officials whose energies became focussed on getting a piece of the national cake baked by oil exploration. Those with greater access to power got disproportionately larger share of this cake that kept getting smaller with oil price crash and the crippling Dutch disease that followed. (Lewis and Stein, 1996). It was, naturally, difficult for those who thought they were getting an unfair portion of the cake to feel national pride and display it in the manner we call patriotism.

The desperation to appropriate more and more of this 'national cake' pushed those who could acquire power, whichever way, to invest more in trying to acquire it. Once they have acquired power much of their talent is invested in damaging institutions that frustrate the ease of access to the cake for incumbents. B. O. Nwabueze in *Military Rule and Constitutionalism* takes us through an exploratory journey on how the military destroyed much of Nigeria's institutions that constrained behaviour; be they evolving institutions from tradition or implanted institutions such as democratic constitutions (Nwabueze, 1992). The rule of law suffered so much assault in the 1980s and 1990s in Nigeria that it is getting harder to affirm the possibility that the will of the whole of society can be upheld over the deviant if the social miscreant has power or other resources such as financial muscle or the right social contacts. The end result of most of these developments is to weaken accountability in governance. Without accountability abuse tends to increase rapidly and decline sets in. The outcome is an exodus of high priced human capital. The brain drain that was attacked through television commercials calling on the patriotism sentiment had become a mark of the Nigerian condition.

Institutions, Civic Society and Accountability in Governance

Evidence from the crises in banking, the challenge of surprising deregulation in such sectors as civil aviation and communication clearly indicate the importance of institution development for enhanced exchange relations and improved quality of life (Utomi, 1996b). Evolution of institutions surely is sustained if the institution of consensus building, democracy, is in place.

The quest for democracy in Nigeria has revealed the impact of civic culture, the development of horizontal rather than purely patron-client vertical linkages. Civic society as involvement of the enlightened in joint effort to set the boundaries of leadership and social behaviours feeds patriotism and leads to more accountable governance. Horizontal linkages leads to share values which become the basis for making demands on the state. This shared basis of expression also increases the power of the group relative to those in authority.

The point of the foregoing is twofold. First, that patriotism which is desirable and contributory to effectiveness in nation building does not fill just a function of socialization and setting-up of rallying national symbols. While rallying symbols as we saw in the independence struggle mobilize patriotic sentiments, symbols alone are unable to sustain patriotism. A sense of deriving value from the object of love, the state, is critical for patriotic fervour to be robust. The second point is that national success, facilitated by appropriate institutions evolving to modulate self-seeking behaviour, provides a more sustainable platform on which patriotic fervour can rest. At the same time as they engender success because they facilitate exchange relations, institutions in their evolution embody values and these values can be directly stimulating of patriotic fervour. Just as the value that the United States will spare no effort to protect American life abroad is embodied in the institution of US foreign service and stimulates commitment of Americans to the flag abroad, we can have institutions that generate patriotism.

In a nutshell, civic society facilitates democracy and institution building which, when institutions develop appropriately, provides the value the individual derives from belonging to an imagined community and leads him to act with patriotic emotions (Anderson, 1983).

The challenge of Patriotism, Constitutionalism and Accountability in governance for Nigeria lies in creating such value from the institutions to draw their commitment. Examples like the spontaneous national response to the Olympic victory lead to the belief that with time there could be a bridging of the distance Nigerians feel between the state and its institutions. The mode of selection of the team, the consequent performance and the sense of national pride it generated are the logical flow of patriotism. The point this raised is the value of universalistic principles in developing of a nation.

Since the oil price decline, the political crises following the annulment of the June 12, 1993 presidential elections by the Babangida administration and the 1995 hanging of some Ogoni leaders following intercommunal feuding and murders, the negative international media blitz on Nigeria have reduced elements that ordinarily inspire pride. The challenge of building patriotism, and through it accountability in governance, has to include national reconciliation.

Conclusion

Patriotism, democracy and accountability in governance are desirable attributes, not as ends in themselves but as means to a just and equitable society in which the well-being of the citizenry in economic and other terms is advanced.

Patriotism, we found, was given a boost by economic performance of the state and other national achievements driven by institutions. These institutions have, however, been stunted because of the imposition of hierarchies (military rule) over markets (interest group politics). As the military have struggled to acquire legitimacy by branding as wrong everything done by the regime before them (Utomi, 1985), institutions have been damaged. This has impeded the progress that engenders patriotism. Other elements of the national character suggested as impediments to both institutional growth and patriotism include the absence of such principles as merit, which does not preclude affirmative action in the country.

To build a patriotic citizenry and accountable governance is therefore the imperative of national reconciliation, and military and institution building (Israel, 1987) cannot be overlooked. Surely how the private sector reads the moves of government and responds help build momentum for growth of institutions (Utomi, 1997) and national pride.

Bibliography

Anderson, Benedict. *Imagined Communities: Reflections on the Origin and Spread of Nationalism* (London, Vers, 1983)

Anifowoshe, Remi. *Violence and Politics in Nigeria* (New York, Nok Publishers, 1982)

Apter, Daniel. *The Politics of Modernization* (Chicago. University of Chicago Press, 1965)

Ayittey, George G. N. "Indigenous African Institutions."

Callaghy, Thomas. "Lost Between State and Market: The Politics of Economic Adjustment in Ghana, Zambia and Nigeria" in Joan Nelson (ed).

Coase, Ronald. "Institutional Structure of Production" in *American Economic Review.* (Vol. 82 No. 4. 1992)

Dia, Mamodu. *Africa Management in the 1990s and Beyond: Reconciling Indigenous and Transplanted Institutions* (Washington DC, World Bank, 1996) *The Economist,* June 8, 1996: "Nigeria Going On Down."

Geertz, C (ed). *Old Societies and New States* (New York, The Free Press, 1963)

Isaacs, Harold. *Idols of the Tribe: Group Identity and Political Change* (New York, Harper Colophon Books, 1975)

Joseph, Richard. *Democracy and Prebendal Politics in Nigeria: The Rise and Fall of the Second Republic* (Cambridge, Cambridge University Press, 1987)

Knack, Stephen and Philip, Keefer. "Institutions and Economic Reformer: Cross Country Testing Using Alternative Institutional Measures" in *Economics and Politics* (Nov. 1995)

Lewis, Peter "Economic Statism, Private Capital and the Dilemma of Accumulation in Nigeria" in *World Development* p. 424, Vol. 22, No. 3 1994.

Leys, C. *Underdevelopment in Kenya: The Political Economy of Neo-Colonialism* (London, Heinemann, 1975)

Murphy, John. "Legitimation and Paternalism: The Colonial State in Kenya" in *African Studies Review* Vol. 29, No. 3 Sept., 1986

North, Douglas. *Institutions, Institutional Change and Economic Performance* (New York, Cambridge University Press, 1990)

Nwabueze B. O. *Military Rule and Constitutionalism* (Ibadan, Spectrum Law Series, 1992)

Rothschild, Donald and Robert, Curry. *Scarcity, Choice and Public Policy in Middle Africa* (Los Angeles, UCLA Press, 1978)

Shivji. *Class Struggles in Tanzania* (London, Heinemann, 1976)

Stein, Howard "Theories of Institutions and Economic Reform in Africa" in *World Development* (Vol. 22 No. 12. Also Veblem)

Thorstein. *The Place of Science in Modern Civilization and Other Essays* (New

York, Huebsch, 1919) p. 239.

Utomi, P. "Legitimacy and Governance: One More Year of Military Rule in Nigeria" in Issue Vol. xiv, 1985"

Utomi, P. "Thriving in Nigeria's Chaos" in *LBS Management Review* (Vol. 1, No. 1, 1996)

Utomi, P. "Institutions and the Evolution of Competition in the Nigerian Banking Industry" in *LBS Management Review* (Vol. 1, No. 2, 1996)

Utomi, P. *"Managing Uncertainty Competition and Strategy in Emerging Economies* (Ibadan, Spectrum Books, 1997)

World Bank. *Adjustment in Africa. Reforms, Results and the Road Ahead* (New York, Oxford University Press, 1994)

World Bank 1996: Nigeria Poverty Assessment Report.

World Bank 1996: Nigeria Poverty Assessment Report.

20

Trust and Economy Development

"I cannot trust these people any more. I will never accept cheques again in payment for my services. Every client will pay in cash or bank draft." He made this statement with a lot of passion. I could see he had some unpleasant experiences. But I knew the nature of his business. Surely, his clients are reasonably trustworthy. He has been keen himself on developing long-term relationships with clients. What went wrong? "Another cheque has been returned unpaid," he said. Another cheque? Does this happen to him too? "He could have had the courtesy of telling me to hold on to the cheque for some time. I thought the cheque was as good as cash. As things are, I am changing the policy; cash payments or bank draft. Period."

Consequences: a few more people on the queue at the local bank with their black nylon bags waiting to collect cash. That branch will be paying out more than its usual ₦2m cash per day. Add the risk of losing the money to robbers and of course more handling of our already worn out and unhygienic currency notes, a few more coughs, 'apollo' etc.

While we were analyzing this problem, a young lady commented. "You cannot trust people these days." She went on to tell her story. She started a real estate outfit a few years ago. As the business grew she invited a former schoolmate to enter into partnership with her. Profits grew but did not reach the levels she expected. At meetings, her business partner always complained of the economic situation of the country; things are bad. He was not meeting his targets. She continued doing her best and they shared the returns. She was astonished one day when her business partner's wife visited her in the office and told her/her partner had married a new wife, bought a brand new car and other assets. He had been diverting some business and taking the proceeds. She confronted him and after a few conversations they agreed to part ways. She resolved to run her business herself. "Small is also beautiful," she said.

It is incredible how once one tongue is loosened many others are let loose. Another person bought a second-hand hair dryer for a new one at an important market in Lagos. Getting her money back was a nightmare

(I will spare you the details). Suffice it to say, she now shops at Mega Plaza and Park & Shop. There she feels sure she is buying brand new electronics. "One cannot trust those boys in the market. I prefer to pay a little bit more if necessary for the assurance that I am buying a genuine product." Those boys at Alaba market wanted to make the most of the transaction. They did not envisage a long term relationship with my young friend. After all, how often would she go back to buy a hair dryer? Moreover, there are other customers. Business will move.

Nigeria has become a low-trust society. Thirty years ago there were no 419ners, a man's/a woman's word was his/her honour. One did not need to carry so much cash around: firstly, you did not need so much to transact business; secondly, you could write and accept cheques (bouncing cheques were a rare phenomenon compared to now). Thirty years ago, we did not have many counting machines nor graduate cashiers in our banks but we were usually not short-changed. These days if you don't manually count your money after the counting machine has supposedly done so, you may be shocked to find out a few pieces are missing from many bundles. Thirty years ago you could hold your head high as you travelled to Europe or America. Now possession of the green passport brings suspicion, even harassment, at airports.

You (yes, you) and I must be ready to forgo personal benefit once in a while for the good of our community, for our country, for something bigger than ourselves. This is the way forward. Before wealth can be created, we must learn to work together. For this to happen we must build our social capital; we must increase the level of trust in our country. Nigerian history shows beyond reasonable doubt that a nation's resource endowment is not sufficient to guarantee its rapid economic development. In spite of our abundant natural and human resources, we are today one of the poorest countries in the world.

Trust – the expectation of regular, honest and cooperative behaviour – is the missing link; it must be factored into a nation's resource endowments. 419ners, sycophants, corrupt government officials and their 'friends' in the private sector who vote in favour of their dishonest actions have contributed a great deal to making Nigeria a low-trust society. What is the relationship between social capital, the prevalence of trust in a society, and economic development?

First, what are the characteristics of a high-trust society? In a high-trust society individualism (personal freedom and initiative) is combined with a sense of community. Generally speaking, members of a high-trust society willingly subject personal interests for group goals from time to time. There is also a high propensity to associate in high-trust societies. The histories of USA, America, Japan and Germany show that the level of social capital in these countries enabled them make quantum leaps in economic development in the last one hundred years. Although the level of social capital is now depleting in these countries, there is still a large and positive balance in the social capital account.

The level of trust in a society affects the size of business organizations in that society. In a low-trust society where one cannot take for granted that non-family members will be honest, loyal and cooperative, businesses are likely to be small – not larger than what the entrepreneur and his family members can control. Even where family members do not have the necessary skills, entrepreneurs are unwilling to hand over management to professionals since the people cannot be trusted. While trust may abound within the family, the level of trust between family members and outsiders is low. This has implications not only for the size of business organizations but also for their growth and survival.

The low level of social capital prevents many Nigerian businesses from enjoying economies of scale. The lack of trust outside the family makes it difficult for unrelated people to form enterprises, grow them and enjoy such economies. In a high-trust society, it is much easier for entrepreneurs to grow their business beyond the size they can control, employ professional managers, enter into partnership agreements, quote the company on the stock exchange etc.

Trust also reduces transaction costs. The cost of doing business can be measured where, for example, the supplier of a critical raw material can be relied upon to supply straight to the assembly line just in time. This will result in lower prices from the lower cost structure of the producing company. When the supplier undercuts agreed values, rework need increases leading to higher prices.

21

Privatisation of Public Enterprises and the Prospect of the Nigerian Shareholders*

⌐hose who want privatization want greater efficiency of the economy through higher effectiveness for companies who are better focussed. This they believe is not possible with government-owned enterprises because the goals of government are such that they can lead wealth creating enterprises not to create the wealth they could. Let us illustrate. If NAFCON were to make decisions, what would be the cardinal driver of choice? As a government enterprise, there will be the agricultural policies of the government, expectations of job creation by the government, the plans of the Ministry of Industry regarding industrialization, the need to earn enough profit to keep afloat etc. There are possibilities that some of these seemingly conflicting goals can influence someone to transpose unto the goal matrix of the enterprise personal goals that become difficult to detect. More importantly, it makes the measures of performance and accountability difficult to calibrate. Managing performance without clear criteria for evaluating output is a nightmare known to any management neophyte.

This is why government in business is generally problematic. It is the reason most countries of the world are going for privatization and multilateral agencies like the World Bank prescribe it as a way out of economic difficulties, especially because the lack of effectiveness results in government channelling resources it could have used for infrastructure development into sustaining enterprises that could ordinarily be profitable. With a private enterprise the demand to grow shareholder value as prime objective, notwithstanding that other stakeholders need to be satisfied to some extent, makes it easy to measure performance. Bearing in mind that these narrow interests have a way, in a competitive environment, of working in the interest of the common good because shareholder value cannot be enhanced unless use value is created for customers, it is argued that this

---

* Address to the Nigerian Shareholders' Association

is a better route to the common good.

Having made this point one would be shortsighted to assume that public ownership never works out to the common good. You indeed have the case of Singapore where the public sector is just as efficient as the public sector. The Singapores of this world are few and far between. Singapore has in fact been described as the most efficient state in modern history. The reality is that the balance of probabilities weigh heavily against our having public enterprises that are as efficient. In that sense, what is prescribed is the ideal type view of the role of government as the provider of non-appropriability goods; that is, goods from which you cannot exclude a non-paying citizen from utilizing. Other kinds of production are then left to the private sector, in this logic.

Another problem with government ownership of wealth creating enterprises is that, given the awesome power of government, those enterprises tend to be monopolies even when you allow other players. It is easy for the companies to get government to legislate in a way that creates an unleveled playing field. The non-level playing field causes private operators to flee the sector, allowing a monopoly or a quasi-monopoly to emerge. In this circumstance of monopoly, enterprises tend to be affected by the phenomenon of x-inefficiencies, as economists call it. These inefficiencies invariably get passed on to consumers and in the end people pay more for services by a government agency which ostensibly exists to make life cheaper for the common man than the prices of those private sector 'cheats.' This is why it should be interesting that it is cheaper to call Nigeria from the US on the telephone than vice versa. In fact the shame of our parastatal cheating the poor man is brought into great relief by NITEL fighting a service in which you call the US and they call you back to connect you to your US counterpart. So where is the interest of the common man we are protecting? By the way, how many really poor Nigerians have telephones or light?

The argument of protecting the common man is much abused by an elite that wants to be subsidized and by contractors/managers benefiting from the substitution of organization goals with personal benefit in these enterprises. When services are more efficient and the market grows we have economies of scale, which means that prices can come down because the marginal contributions of additional customers come with little or no additional investments.

The interest of these people benefiting from the inefficiencies is unfortunately propped up inadvertently by 'naive' economic optimists who believe we can be a Singapore. In their 'concession' they argue for liberalization and not privatizing, but there they miss the point of the level playing field and the tendency towards monopoly where an enterprise with state interest exists.

Shareholder Value

With that brief attempt at explicating the reason privatization is good for society, let me turn to its benefits for shareholders like you. I have already said that the prime driver of performance in the private sector is the need to enhance shareholder value. This means that privatization will increase the pool of firms available to pursue enhancing shareholder value. It also means opportunity for investment for players in the capital market like you.

To fully benefit from this essence of the enterprise shareholders need to be more vigilant and have guidelines that allow them to throw out non-performing management. This places additional responsibility on institutional investors with the staff and resources to more closely monitor executives. Besides the points I have already made about why shareholder value is key, one of the things likely to happen with privatization is that it will open up the economy. Given that players in some of the sectors to be privatized will be foreign enterprises with technologies, skills and managerial know-how as well as international distribution networks that could magnify the nature of the returns on investment for shareholders, this means growth. I do also expect that privatization will broaden the scope of competition in the various sectors of the economy, creating more investment opportunities.

There is additional value to shareholders in that with the broadening of opportunity the Nigerian Capital Market will grow with consequent deepening of the market to the benefit of those making longer term investments. Also of benefit to the shareholder is that more of you will get opportunities to serve on the boards of these enterprises with foreign participants. This will help us develop corporate governance skills that will facilitate the growth of enterprises in this market.

22

Declining Moral Standards and Changing Values: its Effect on National Development*

The subject of my short address today surely has come in good time considering the wave of soul searching that has swept through our country since the passing away of General Sani Abacha. When I accepted the invitation of the Catholic Youngmen Association and chose this topic, nothing my sometimes fertile imagination conjectured about the moral and ethical rot that mark the crisis of values in Nigeria could compare with the things that were actually going on, according to the stories some people have heard from key players who have been opening up since the recent death of the man who has been presiding over government in the last five years. It is therefore a moral imperative that good Christians revisit what the obligations of their faith prescribe at this time. Our discussion today will review these obligations and evaluate how they affect our development as a country.

You will permit me to be very liberal in drawing on what has been said by others regarding the issues at stake. That way I can avoid repeating myself and I can also analyze the information knowing that they are not mere products of my own biases or idiosyncrasies. The two people I intent to draw liberally from in establishing the state of Nigeria's moral decline and what the obligation of every Catholic should be in such circumstances are Monsignor Robert Lozano, the regional Vicar of *Opus Dei,* and The Rt. Revd. Dr John Onayekan, the Archbishop of Abuja. Their works that I draw from are the recent homily of Monsignor Lozano on the feast of Blessed Josemaria Escriva and Archbishop Onayekan's paper at the recent national forum organized by the Catholic Secretariat of Nigeria.

We all are witnesses of the rot that in recent times has set upon

---

* Address to U.I. women university students at Imoran Study Centre, Ibadan.

many aspects of our society. Nigeria is now a very different place compared with what it was 30 years ago when I came to this country. The family then was held in high esteem and any conjugal infidelity, when it existed, was severely condemned without hesitation; very high standards of moral behaviour were instilled in our youth who were disciplined and hard working; lecturers and workers in the universities and the public service held their heads high and were responsible and competent in the discharge of their duties; bribery was non-existent if you compare it with what obtains now.

Today, instead, we are told by a reputable international magazine that in Nigeria "politics is the art of becoming rich...", thereby summarizing in one sentence the atmosphere of political life and the intentions held by many who seek public office. Today, we often hear stories of conjugal infidelity, occasional or habitual; we hear hair-raising stories about the moral decadence of our university students; and I am not referring only to the proliferation of the so-called 'cults' or examinations malpractices, but to what obtains inside the hostels and out of them. Today abortion is rampant among both the married and the unmarried and often the killing of the unborn children is carried out by medical doctors who call themselves 'Catholic': all those who procure or perform an abortion are acting in full awareness of the Church's teaching and in open defiance of it. Thirty years ago there were no, 419ners there was hardly any instance of corporate fraud and no bank manager or purchasing officer demanded a percentage before a transaction could be closed. In those days teachers in schools didn't accept or demand any 'gratification' from their pupils who wanted to pass an exam they didn't take. We had no 'area-boys; criminality was much lower and there was no need to put barriers in streets and set up 'Operation Sweep'.

"We are not being pessimistic in calling to mind these truths. We Christians are the most optimistic people there are, because we know the power of grace and the mercy of God, but we are not naive." What we have to do is to follow the example of Jesus Christ in everything "without ever getting frightened by the paganized atmosphere we find ourselves in. We must not think that if we put into practice the radical demands of the Gospel we will become alienated from the lifestyle of our friends and companions, to such an extent that we couldn't behave naturally at work or in social relations. We mustn't let ourselves be dragged along by the false consideration that if absolutely everybody behaves in a certain fashion, we will appear somewhat peculiar if we don't do the same." That if we can't beat them, we have no choice but to join them.

Yes, we ought to follow the example of Christ himself: "His behaviour constantly offers us lessons because he is God with us. He loved all people, even those who had strayed from the law of God, even from the natural law, but he did not compromise with error. He made himself all things to all men, but lifted up the fallen, and exhorted them to break radically with evil. He sought out the sick, the lepers, without permitting their infirmities to touch him. He welcomed people with dissolute lives – like the Samaritan woman, or the woman taken in adultery – but warned them to sin no more. He took part in the celebrations of his acquaintances and friends, but rejected all frivolity or worldly behaviour." What should be our reaction, the reaction of a Catholic layman or woman, when confronted with the ills of our time, these times in which we are afflicted by "social, economic and political problems," as we say in the "Prayer for Nigeria in Distress." "The attitude of a Christian towards others should largely be one of surprise" says Msgr. Cormac Burke, a priest of *Opus Dei* working in the Vatican. He should be surprised, truly astonished, at the lack of ideals he sees in so many people around him or at the false ideals they at times pursue. A sign of the weakness of the faith and ideals of so many Christians today is the fact that they are unchristian but are not even human. After all, if a person does not react with amazement at the absurdity at the intellectual poverty and the human degradation- of the postures held by some Christians, he may eventually come to regard them as reasonable or respectable...

"It is surprising, really surprising, if a person states that he does not believe in God, or if he maintains as a reasonable proposition the idea that the world emerged, unaided, from nothing. But it would be more surprising if we were to treat his statement as if it were a reasonable and intelligent position, and began to argue seriously about it. It is not a serious position. It is absurd. It is surprising if a person who says he is a Catholic does not pray or go to Mass on Sundays. It is absurd. It is surprising if a person proclaims himself to be more 'liberated' because he rejects the need for any self-control in sexual matters. It is absurd because he is clearly enslaving himself. It is surprising when somebody defends abortion in the name of humanity!!! This is an absurd proposition, it is a proposition that is a contradiction in terms. It is surprising if a communist or a tyrannical dictator puts himself forward as a defender of freedom and democracy: it is completely absurd."

It is imperative that we rediscover the possibilities that we all have of influencing social and public life. Often we don't realize what we can do or achieve, we are not mindful of the duty we have of christianizing first our own professional and social environment, and then of christianizing – each one according to his or her own possibilities – the whole of society from within by participating in public life. But in 1932 the founder of *Opus Dei* wrote that we must be present in the forum where legislation of the greatest importance is being debated and promulgated, such as the laws concerning matrimony, the family, education, the minimum of private property which is necessary for each individual or family, the dignity – rights and duties – of the human person. All these topics and some others are of the utmost interest to religion and we cannot remain indifferent to them.

We have to carry around with us our own atmosphere, the atmosphere proper to a Christian, even though this could mean clashing with types of behaviour that may be currently fashionable. The world, and everything that goes to make up the world, should be in accordance with God's plan of creation, and with the lofty and high destiny to which the person, every person, is called (...). Do not be afraid of being consistent with your faith. Such courage, such witness, is what this world of ours need. This is what we read in the Epistle of St. Paul to the Ephesians where he says that "It was God's loving design, centred in Christ, to give history its fulfillment, by resuming everything to Him, all that is in heaven, all that is on each summed up in Him..." (1:10). And to the Colossians he says that it was God's plan to "win back, to reconcile all things, whether on earth or in heaven, into union with himself" (1:20).

A few days ago, on June 13th, the Holy Father told a group of 350 members of the Harvard Law School Alumni Association, an institution of higher learning of worldwide reputation, that legal structures must respect the universal moral law. He was speaking to them in Rome, "this city so closely associated with the development of Western law, both civil and canonical." The Holy Father pointed out that "the century now drawing to its close has been marked by unprecedented crimes against humanity, often carried out under the guise of legality. But we are also seeing a rebirth of hope in the power of law and legal institutions to protect human dignity, to foster peace and to promote justice between peoples."

"The fulfillment of this hope," he continued, "will require not only the establishment of more effective structures of law, but also, more importantly, the renewal of a juridical culture of respect for the objective requirements of the universal moral law as the basis and ultimate criterion of positive legal enactments." John Paul II concluded: "What is needed, in effect, is a rediscovery of those essential and innate human and moral values which flow from the very nature and truth of the person, and which express and safeguard the dignity of the person."

The Pope was only insisting on what was already stated more than thirty years ago by the Vatican Council: "It is in full conformity with human nature that there should be legal and political structures providing all citizens (...) with the practical possibility of freely and actively taking part in the establishing of the juridical foundations of the political community and in the direction of public affairs (...)." We have the "duty of rendering the political community such material and personal services as are required by the common good." It would be the height of irresponsibility to abstain from having a decisive influence in the machinery that makes policy for the entire nation, and from having a strong hand in the legislative process that determines the life of all citizens, sometimes down to issues touching on basic principles of natural and moral law and the dignity and ultimate end of the human person. Tell me, of what use would it be to labour hard to establish and run educational and health services at the grassroots level, if the policies and directives that determine the way such services are to be rendered nationwide are drawn up by unbelievers and atheists? If instead you help in promulgating just laws that respect the dignity and eternal destiny of man you will have rendered us all and the entire Nigerian society a much greater service.

Be mindful, therefore, of the great responsibility that falls on the shoulders of the laity. Don't simply shelter in the shadows of the parish compound. Go out, into the heart of society and make Christ present there, actually put him at the summit and peak of all human activities. Have you ever stopped to think how absurd it is to leave one's Catholicism aside on entering a university, a professional association, a cultural society, or Parliament – like a man leaving his hat at the door? There is a need for a crusade of manliness and purity to counteract and undo the savage work of those who think that man is a beast. And that crusade is a matter for you.

May the intercession of Blessed Josemaria and of Mary, Our Mother in heaven, help us to take in our hands this beautiful challenge and contribute to leave the Christian imprint in the whole of society. To do otherwise would be to put the light of Christ under a bed.

Archbishop Onayekan sees our most recent past this way: "We have been living witnesses to this drama. Tensions have been piling up over the last two years – piling up because of lack of freedom; because of misuse of power, arbitrary detentions and denial of the freedom of Nigerians to express themselves. In place of freedom and expression of the truth, the air was saturated with lies and deceit and these lies and deceit have piled up like a pack of cards giving way eventually under its own weight. Society cannot support misrule indefinitely. There are laws which guide human relations based on the need to have order, harmony, peace and progress. When those basic laws are neglected, the result is total disruption in the social life of the people. Unfortunately, in such circumstances, avoidable sufferings and misery are unleashed on the people who have to pay the greatest price for misrule. This is why it is important to go down to the basic norms of ethics and morality in the act of governance."

As a result of these shortcomings of an ethical and moral nature, we have been in decline as far as national development is concerned. This 'new morality' more than the lack of morality has produced instability. Few indigenes, much less foreigners, like to invest in such times. The result is that we have faced stagnation. As I say frequently, we can measure the decline in terms of the indices of economic groups. In times before when morality was better paid attention to and values were more inclined towards fairness and the common good, the economy grew at the rate of 3.2 percent per annum between 1956 and 1966. Since 1973 we have basically stagnated. In spite of oil prices quadrupling in 1973 we have 'grown' by 0.017 percent per annum between 1973 and 1996.

You can therefore draw correlation between growth and values.

A recent article by Chery W. Gary and Daniel Kaufnan in the journal *Finance and Development* notes that the costs of corruption are enormous. Drawing on empirical evidence and results of efforts of task forces at the IMF and World Bank, they assess that "corruption and lack of economic and public sector reform go hand in hand, with causality running in both directions." The outcome is perilous underdevelopment and low quality of life for the citizens. Surely we deserve differently.

When our values - those things we care about - reflect universal concepts of the common good and public choice comes from value focussed thinking, then we can only make those decisions that move our country forward. This is the reason that I argue so forcefully for shared values that orient us towards the better society that the resources, human and material, in this country makes our birthright.

23

Faith, Values and Principles in Nation-Building*

Landmarks are important to me because they provide an opportunity for reflection. As we reflect with Father George Ehuisani on the occasion of the 40th anniversary of his earthly sojourn, it is noteworthy that Nigeria's 40th anniversary as an independent nation is less than three years away. The fact that Nigeria is nowhere near the man that Father George has become suggests something is amiss. This means that it will be in order to reflect on Nigeria's quest for maturity. When a grown man crawls, normal people must ask why. It is as such that nation-building will be the subject of our attention this evening.

The challenge of nation-building has to be considered with hope about the possibilities of the new millennium. This century, the twentieth, has not been our century. Charles De Gaulle already made the point decades ago when he said this was not Africa's century. Many are asking if the next century will not be another lost century. As you evaluate the seriousness with which African leaders have reacted to the scourge of poverty among their people, the savaging of the tribes by disease and deprivation and the devastation wrought on the clans by illiteracy and ignorance make the pessimists believe that nation-building remains illusory. This illusion of nation-building, they say, will make the next century just as sorry for most Africans as this century.

History does provide rays of hope in the face of apparent self-doubt on how today's people can affect tomorrows prospects. A typical example of how we can misread the possibilities of recreating the social order is this view of Japan expressed in 1950 by one of the leading Japan experts in the United States. The author of the views we refer to is Edwin O. Reischaller who was an eminent authority at Harvard in those days. The words in question? "The economic situation in Japan may be fundamentally so unsound that no policies, no matter how wise, can save her from slow economic starvation."

---

* Speech on the occasion of Fr. George Ehuisani's birthday.

Seen in the light of Japan's economic success in the years following this statement, it sounds almost ridiculous. The satisfactory outcome Japan experienced can come only from the force of effort at nation-building in Japan which went into a reconstructive phase following the Meeji restoration and then after the ruins of World War II. How can Nigeria learn from the experiences of nations like Japan as we seek to rebuild? It is my experience that the values that matter when shared abroad in the land can jumpstart a pattern of doing things right.

Experience leads me to conclude that values are a veritable anchor for effectiveness either at the level of the individual or at the level of the nation-state. To show how values can drive nation-building, therefore, we should make effort to understand what we mean by values.

What are Values?

Very often we assume everybody understands what we mean when we use some words. My experience suggests many a misunderstanding has its roots in such confusion. Value is that which is desirable and worthy of esteem for its own sake, which when it is internalized becomes the road map to a future desirable end. Indeed values are the building blocks of a strategic orientation and can affect our personal lives as well as it does our corporate and societal life.

Winning Values in Personal Life

How can values help us achieve victories in the challenges of personal life? A discussion of this will certainly be incomplete if it fails to mention Stephen R. Covey whose book, *The Seven Habits of Highly Effective People,* was a long-standing No. 1 national bestseller in the United States. We shall therefore give Covey his due by opening with his ideas. Covey identified fundamental values that are of a permanent and enduring nature that are part of the human condition, ingrained in the consciousness and conscience of all men, across societies. These fundamental values he calls principles. He cites among these principles, the principle of fairness out of which flow universal concepts of equity and justice; the principle of integrity and honesty which are the foundation of trust; the principle of human dignity; the principle of service; the principle of potential and growth.

Do people who live by these principles triumph and those who do not, fail? If you look around you at the conduct of most of the men who have apparent success in Nigeria today, you may actually laugh these kinds of principles to scorn. If you take a longer time perspective, however, you find that those who neglect these principles are unable to sustain success.

Trust-based relationships elude these people. Cowards awed by their power, sycophants attracted by benefits they could derive from the relationship pay obeisance to the dubiously accomplished, but once they are unable to bring gain to those who flock around, their loneliness is brought into sharp relief. If you ask some of my bank MD friends after they were removed how many Christmas cards they got a few weeks later, you will learn something interesting. I have in my repertoire stories of evening shared with friends who had been military governors, in the weeks immediately following their redeployment. It is truly a testament to the values response.

What is important here is that trust which is so critical for success is dependent on attributes of both character and knowledge. Where one is lacking, the capacity to lead is deprecated. The situation of soldiers in a trench with an officer highly decorated from Sandhurst for skills in trench warfare should illustrate the point. If he is a scoundrel who can sell his mother, no matter his decorations, his men will not trust him enough to act on his command. How can they be sure he has never done a deal with their lives? Ditto for when he is a fair person, but is ignorant on trench war; leadership as trust assessments flow from two dimensions of behaviour and knowledge.

Trust-based relationships and orientations are important for nation-building for several reasons. They facilitate communication, for one. Effective communication will no doubt make the implementation of public policy easier. If we recognize that the essence of public policy is to effect attitude change in people it should be less difficult to achieve that goal if the meaning intended in a policy arrives as conceived in the consciousness of the target group. The fidelity of communication is enhanced by the presence of the two dimensions that result in trust-building.

Effective communication also makes it easy to develop shared values as goals and the commitment of the leaders to societal or national objectives cascade down more easily. With shared values comes national stability which is often a necessary condition for rapid economic development and the confidence of foreign as well as local investors.

How can we effect this? Again Covey is instructive when he talks about beginning with the end in mind. The illustration of the funeral parlour is appropriate. Think of a funeral. Imagine the man in the coffin to be yourself. What would you like those filing past to think of you? Live in a way that will achieve those feelings. Beginning with the end in mind is about faith and how it keeps hope alive and allows men to move mountains. If we turn to the gospels we see the example of Simeon and how faith in the promise that his eyes will behold the Messiah kept him going. For Christians the promise of a hundredfold reward and eternal life keeps these faithful striving and struggling with overcoming their defects.

Beginning with the end in mind should lead us to question the grave abuses in our system, for personal gain. A good view of the expected end of all men should be a signal that perhaps the wrong effort was being made in pursuing what may be called 'ill-gain' as against what I have described elsewhere as spiritual and material immortality.

Since reference is made often by newspaper reporters to these 'two immortalities' I referred to in a 1992 *Mr.* magazine interview, I should refresh your memories on what I said then. I had, in response to an interview question, suggested the essence of life to be the pursuit of immortality which at the spiritual level is the will to be a friend of God so that one can have his company for all eternity. At the material or temporal level the ultimate good seemed to me to be the preservation of one's name from generation to generation. It seemed to me then that the most proficient way of attaining that was by way of the printed word, especially in the authorship of books that remain relevant to many generations, as with Shakespeare, Socrates etc.

This view still remains valid to me with the express notation of the fact that one does not have to be a writer to attain material immortality. Any man who can pursue a career diligently and ethically with the public good served by that career deserves a place in the chronicles of his age and those chronicles are his path to material immortality.

Beginning with the end in mind and working towards that end is not only about hope, it is about faith in the possibilities of such attainment.

It is this which busies the mind with the positive even where all seems lost as with Job in the Old Testament. The fruit of the loss of faith by a generation is seen in the rise of cults in universities and crimes bordering on social vendetta by young people. The rampant nature of advance fee fraud (419), and other economic crimes which are devastating our country can be traced to a loss of faith in the possibilities of individual effort pursued in the right way. My fear is that few of the powerful and privileged in Nigeria begin with the end in mind. A painful manifestation is the mushrooming of churches in Nigeria. In spite of all these churches preaching Christ, who is light, darkness continues to envelope the land. It stands like replaying Mahatma Ghandi and his view on Christians. "I love your Christ," he said. "The problem is most Christians I know are not like the Christ they profess." If most Christians were truly like Christ, the great Ghandi had said he would have been attracted to Christianity.

Values in Family Life

The building block of the nation is the family. How do values which mould the man emerge from this primary sociological unit? These days it is often referred to as being in crisis. One of the institutions badly weakened by the ascendance of a materialist culture is the family. As both husband and wife rush off striving for a little more, either just to ensure a decent existence or to have more Mercedes Benz than their neighbour, the socialization of the offspring has been much affected in the negative. That core duty of educating the children and sowing the seed of the platform that carries values is today often abdicated to domestic staff inappropriately prepared for such a role. The effect can already be seen in the society. Children do not, as we say, "resemble their parents" anymore because the role of parents as primary educators of their children has suffered from changes in social patterns. This is frightening because there is no better place to learn the values of fairness, tolerance, respect for the difference and the space of others than in the 'crowded' space of family life with sibling rivalry being properly managed. Surely parents can do more even with the pressures to earn more income.

Winning Corporate Values

Values make the firm. This axiomatic expression is given experiential basis in one of the better books of 1994, Collins and Porras *Built to Last*. In the study that looked at long surviving successful American companies, the bottom line indicates that long term success is value driven. Perhaps few examples are as clear in illustrating the issue as the Tylenol poisoning in Chicago in October/November 1982. Global winners like 3M have largely been sustained by shared values at the epicenter of their being.

Seeing the retrenching corporate landscape, it is easy to conclude that their lack of overarching values leads to unimaginative responses to environmental challenges. The hemorrhaging banking industry is a good example of what can happen when values are ignored. As someone who teaches venturing and entrepreneurship, I could probably sustain a five-hour discussion on how values can enable a firm continue to renew itself in the direction of opening up new sustainable opportunities for capturing value. But that is not our objective here today. Let me point out, however, that Ralph Keeney in his book on value-focussed thinking shows how much more effective decision-making can be when it is driven by closer values of the firm. A good reading of the book is encouraged.

Social Level Values that Win

Leadership effectiveness is at the centre of winning at the societal or national level. Embedded in the idea of leadership effectiveness is followership cooperation and satisfaction with extant social order. It is therefore an imperative of successful societal intercourse and economic progress that trust be built between those who lead and those who follow. Your guess on how our reality is reflected in these matters is as good as mine. The level of cynicism about leadership and almost all forms of social action tells of how much trust exists. It is no wonder we keep stumbling from one disaster to another.

Critical for winning at societal level is a sense of service and a conscience that is not polluted and seared by what is clearly a pervasive narcissism driving most people who hold public office today. This self-love has taken away from a sense of service necessary to attract followers to a leadership.

Service, another fundamental value or principle of Covey's, is very much lacking. Service as the desire to make a contribution is motivated by what I have referred to as material immortality. It may be driven by the desire to light up the sky like a flame as in the film, *Fame*, or by the sheer fulfillment of being a benchmark of good for generations. Whatever drives service, the sense of it is so fundamental to social success.

Service does not come from political leadership alone. Most times the activities of a concerned and articulate elite, you and I in this room, counts for more than the actions of those in public service. Perhaps, I should leave that to your consciences. Talking about conscience, it is increasingly clear to me that even though I continue to insist that many Nigerian leaders do the damage they do to this country because of their ignorance, whether they admit ignorance or not, the quality of conscience is so important.

Conclusion

We have looked at faith, values and principles and their place in nation-building. If we look to South East Asia we will see how fundamental a role these played in the most rapid economic growths rates known to human history. The trust among entrepreneurial Chinese communities that dominate enterprise in that region, the traditions of filial piety, those of work ethic, enterprise for order, and the faith the people have in what is possible, are traits we could profitably imitate.

In concluding I must remark that this exercise is useful only because it is possible for human beings to become self-conscious and, as a result of this self-consciousness, to change. Of all created beings man alone has this capability. Unfortunately we can continue to reinforce a deficient pattern because man tends to operate within the comfort zone of a dominant paradigm, a phenomenon literally explored by C. Write Mills in *The Sociological Imagination*.

Marking a paradigm shift does not come easy. Stephen R. Covey in another book worth reading, *Principle-Centred Leadership*, points out that the lack of a common vision blocks change. We know that we have to be grossly deficient in the matters of a common vision. This is what I believe the Vision 2010 project set out to correct. The field we have covered today suggests that hope remains.

It is pertinent to recognize here that the Vision 2010 project is about developing values and negotiating an end which all could have in mind and begin with. It is not surprising that the objectives of the vision include, as recently published, a programme for instilling some core values in Nigerians. The taste of the pudding reflects these values in all their private and public conduct. Unless they do, successful implementation of the goals of Vision 2010 will peter away into history.

24

Creating Wealth Through Performance Evaluation

For many managers, the year end is fraught with a lot of anxiety. One major source of anxiety is performance appraisal. In the Nigerian cultural milieu, performance appraisal is often a testy chore during which telling people the truth about their performance can bring a lot of animosity. The truth however is that 'objective' performance appraisal that does not create any bad blood is quite possible in our cultural setting and can, in fact, be utilized to motivate and to create new wealth. This technical paper seeks therefore to present techniques of performance management that remove anxiety and uses parameters that detect whether real wealth is being created by managers or whether 'profits' have been going up due to inflation, 'Chinese accounting' or disregard of the real cost of capital by managers and executives.

The Anxiety of Appraising

In many companies the level of anxiety raised by appraisal is dysfunctionally high. Having to look at someone who spends more of his non-sleeping time in your company than with his wife and children and tell him that he is not worth the salary he is in fact complaining is too low literally brings out the goose to be seen as less than a nice fellow; this is compounded in our business environment by nepotism and the ease with which people retreat into ethnicity to explain away their inadequacies.

In the face of these unpleasant possible outcomes of the appraisal process, many supervisors, and managers turn to defense mechanism such as blaming their appraisal on "management" which has decreed a distribution that must follow a bell-shaped curve. Others, especially in the public sector, turn to closed appraisal systems where they comment too freely, sometimes making comments they cannot provide objective information to substantiate.

All of the foregoing creates a poison environment which damages the synergy possibilities in a team and prevents improved performance, the primary reason for introducing the appraisal system. In such situations where appraisal anxiety is so dysfunctional it is better not to have an appraisal system at all. The good news, fortunately, is that you can easily eliminate the anxiety and convert the appraisal system into a powerful tool for adding value. But before the tools we must ask ourselves what the objectives of performance appraisal are.

Objectives of Performance Appraisal

The subject of performance appraisal is in its simple form an aspect of performance management which involves gathering and evaluating information about the performance of employees in line with organizational goals with a view to using the information to improve performance by reinforcing appropriate behaviour either through monetary or other rewards. The objectives of the appraisal system can be seen from both the point of view of management and that of those being appraised.

From management's point of view the key objectives of performance appraisal are:

1. Improving performance
2. Renewing the focus of individuals on the vision and mission of the organization
3. Assessing potential
4. Making compensation decisions
5. Developing training plans

while from point of view of the appraisee the appraisal is:

1. A point of reference on where he is from the expectation of superiors
2. A compass to where the organization is going and how he fits in
3. An opportunity to review his career map to see where his opportunities lie and perhaps why his ambition is unrealistic or should be raised
4. A window into how he can obtain the salary increase he desires
5. An opportunity to let his superior know of the behaviour that gets in the way of optimum output from the subordinate.

Essentially, management expects to use the process to see how more returns can come from its most valuable asset, its human capital. The process is more effective therefore if management is able to use it to renew the focus on the vision of the leadership of the company and to communicate what it takes to attain this vision. This is a key function of leading an enterprise and as we can see in the section on the process which follows, the appraisal process provides a key opportunity for communicating meaning and developing shared values. Warren Bennies in his seminar discussion of "Some Truths About Leadership" [from his book: *Why Leaders Can't Lead*] does remind us that a major leadership competency is the management of meaning imperative if leaders are to make dreams apparent to others and to align people with these dreams. This competency is achieved in communicating the vision by reducing it to concrete metaphors that people can relate to their own real experiences.

It should also be a distinct objective of the appraisal process to marry the available potential in those being assessed to what is required if the organization is to pursue a strategy that will give it sustainable competitive edge and the capacity for long term superior performance. In effect therefore, our view is that beyond using appraisal to achieve the assessment of the potential of the individuals, use of the appraisal process to give meaning to the vision of organization leaders should put it in good stead to evaluate whether there is a fit between available human capabilities and the strategic intent of the enterprise. This strategic objective of appraisal is an imperative if creating wealth into the future and enhancing shareholder value is of concern to leaders of business.

Naturally, when appraisal is done right, it shows forth the difference between what is and what is desired, prescribing in itself the nature of the training intervention required for higher effectiveness or for capacity to cope with future assignment. But none of these tremendously important objectives surpasses in value the fact that employees can see a relationship between a fair evaluation of their performance and their income. The link between employee compensation and the appraisal of their performance is critical for the system to remain valuable.

These values of performance appraisal for management are matched in importance by how well the process tells those being assessed how well they are doing on the job and what their future is likely to be at their **current level of contribution toward organizational goals.**

The Appraisal Process

The appraisal causes anxiety because many feel that objectivity is hard to achieve. Indeed pure objectivity does not exist in human judgement. All of us see life through prisms tinted by our experiences. Clearly defined bases for judgement do, however, reduce the scope for variance. Where the mission, objectives of the firm and expectations from the individual are very clearly and measurably spelt out, it is hard for our biases to be so significantly damaging in an open appraisal system. We shall however address techniques that can make it clear that fairness, if not objectivity, is attained.

Effective appraisal process will of necessity involve:

1. General education on the objectives of the appraisal exercise
2. Creating common meaning for measures used in appraisal
3. Communicating expectations
4. Continuous reinforcement of specific behaviours
5. Review of the specific experiences
6. Assigning value to these experiences from both points of view
7. Assessing the gap between values from both points of view
8. Using assessed value to redefine goals and clarify objectives for the future.

The process should begin by the use of appropriate organs of internal communication to remind all of the reasons for appraisal and some company specific objectives the process was concerned with. After communicating the objectives a glossary of key terms including levels and types of acceptable and unacceptable ways of doing things should be developed and communicated as part of building a body of shared values that drive the enterprise. Concrete examples of what would constitute good performance on a job should be given.

Next, each individual should get a clear statement of what their job entails and specifics, hopefully measurable expectations from them for the period to be covered by the appraisal. It is against these clear sets of expectations that actual behaviour will be stacked up for comparison and deductions about performance.

To reduce anxiety from assessment, and show that fairness or objectivity is built into the process, it is best not to leave evaluation until the appraisal interview. Each time appropriate behaviour takes place it should be reinforced by acknowledgement and commendation. A note on the particular behaviour carried out, when and how it was done, should then be made and filed away. The same should be done with inappropriate behaviour, beginning with a gentle admonition or pointing out of what the appropriate should have been. Preparing for an appraisal interview should then involve a careful study of the rates on appropriate and inappropriate behaviour.

The appraisal meeting would then be the process of the appraisee and appraiser exchanging views on the values they place on these clearly documented behaviours. Where expectations were clearly set out in line with the mission and goals of the organization, it should not take long to get closer together on the values placed on these behaviours.

Some Universal Criteria of Expectations

The key to effective measurement of performance is the expectation effectively communicated to the individual. Against the criteria of these expectations a fit with actual performance is assessed in appraisal. Some of these criteria are applicable across most organizations. One is the use of the idea of economic value added in assessing private sector managers. The EVA concept, which is currently a hot financial tool feeding famous US management consultancies like Mckensey, was made popular by Stern Steward and Co. of New York. It is essentially an approach that measures profitability through subtracting the total annual cost of capital from after tax profit.

In my view this concept is extremely important and a powerful tool because it is my experience that the only form of capital that gets true value in the thinking of many Nigerian managers is debt capital. Because many Nigerian managers treat equity capital as 'gift' capital or cheap capital most Nigerian companies are sitting around with huge inventories of idle capital. If managers are appraised on true return on capital, not an accounting return on capital, wealth creation will be dramatically enhanced.

Reality is that equity is higher risk for its owner than debt sold by a bank. Economic logic suggests therefore that equity should attract a higher return than debt. A look at shareholder value of quoted companies on the NSE does not suggest so – a reflection of the usual view of equity as cheap capital by the Nigerian managers. A proper costing of equity will show that many Nigerian companies currently maligned by public officials as making 'outrageous' profits are actually not adding economic value, thereby losing shareholder wealth. (For further reading on EPA see *Fortune Magazine* editions of September and December 1993; *The Definitive Guide to MA and EPA* by Stern Stewart Management Services, New York).

In applying EPA to performance management, the objective is to get Nigerian managers to think creatively of the total and real cost of the capital they are employing, especially considering the alternate use or opportunity cost of that capital. Only in so doing can many of our companies move from declining into extinction like dinosaurs to becoming champions of wealth creation.

Conclusion

Our objective was to show that you can, not only purge performance appraisal of the anxiety it seems to generate in managers, but also use it as an objective method that motivates managers to create wealth. In using the process to establish a clear link between performance and reward, and between performance and the strategic intent of the firm, you can make the appraisal an invaluable tool for delivering sustainable superior performance building on the value chain. One measure of performance which is clearly objective and relates directly to sustainable superior performance is the EPA concept. Certainly a formula that takes operating profit, subtract taxes and then subtracts from the outcome a multiplication of the capital employed with a market determined weighted average cost of capital, will clearly be objective. This can be calculated for strategic business units as it is done for the whole enterprise and even further down. Every manager whose EPA is going up knows how he is performing. Reward should follow accordingly.

25

The Place of Industrial Relations in a Learning Organization*

First let me express my regrets at not being physically present with you. After one or two shifts of date because of clashes in the travel schedules of some of the principals of the event, it became likely that I would be away at the time of this presentation. I would have very much preferred to be physically present because I am happier speaking outside of a written script which can sometimes be very constraining of my approach to self expression. Unfortunately, a long scheduled trip to continue research I have been working on in Asia has come in the way. I am, however, most confident that the person who is standing in for me will discharge the responsibility of responding to questions quite creditably.

I have been asked to address the issues of Industrial Relations and the Learning Organization. Perhaps we should begin by stating what both of these value-laden concerps mean to me as they do sometimes mean different things to different people. Let us begin with the Learning Organization.

Introduction to the Idea of Organisation Learning

Organizational learning and the idea of a learning organization are the new frontiers of management fashion. The less charitable may describe the learning organization idea as the latest management fad. If it were a fad it would blow away quickly but I will bet that the ideas at the heart of the learning organization will be around for a very long time.

In its bare essence, the learning organization is one that has created a culture which facilitates extracting a return from experience by encouraging an emotional climate that leads its members to share knowledge derived from experience such that learning helps the organization adapt itself to its changing environment at a pace that ensures

---

*Address to the Institute of Personnel Management on 14/7/98

optimal performance outcome. In other words, an orientation that allows an enterprise to have all its members learning continuously and using the outcome from such learning to proactively face developments in its environment, makes it a learning organization. This broad view of organizational learning is the platform from which different emphasis is developed by scholars and practitioners.

Some of the work on organizational learning that has been done at the Organization Learning Centre at the Massachusetts Institute of Technology (MIT) has focussed on the challenge of breaking subsystems barriers which prevent knowledge or values from being transferred to all crannies of the organization. The work of Peter Senge, author of *The Fifth Discipline* and director of the centre, and others at the centre identify the march of management philosophy and science in western thought as reifying subsystems and/or fragmentary thinking. The challenge of learning organizations is to break those barriers and make members of the organization think in total organization terms. This identification of subcultures within the organization and the sharing of values across the whole system in a way that erodes suboptimization are considered the essential thrust of a learning organization by some writers in this tradition.

Yet another set of thinkers in the learning organization tradition see the essence of the idea as developing people to make the transition from specialists (functional specialists) to generalists who have a 'helicopter view.' The emphasis on director development in this tradition is mainly associated with the works of Bob Garratt, the British consultant.

However, we express our application of the idea of organizational learning. It is clear that it is not synonymous with training. Bob Garratt quotes two practitioners, Nick Georgiadis of British Airways and Paul Marsh of Jaguar, who make this point in *Learning to Lead*. Georgiadis begins:

"Training is a liability in situations where you have to flex quickly – what price the training you had yesterday because today I want you to do something different?! But you will not do it because you are so wedded to what we trained you to do yesterday." Paul Marsh of Jaguar expands the point on learning organizations: "The first thought is that it's about a company, as a priority objective, developing all its human resources, enhancing all their skills ... but not being content with that ... learning from those people how the company can be improved ... so that it becomes a cycle of learning."

I have myself made the point of the difference between training, training the total organization, and organizational learning in the 1998 book, *Managing Uncertainty: Competition and Strategy in Emerging Economies* (Utomi, 1998). The learning organization has more to do with culture and a strategic orientation which allows the leadership of an organization to recognize that its primary task, when a vision of the future has been established, is to create what Garrat calls "the emotional climate" within the firm that allows the firm to develop knowledge from experience of its members and to facilitate the knowledge being shared consistently. The absence of this climate in the organizations often leads to knowledge being bottled up in a department or subsystem until a crisis leads to a probe which often discovers that the information to avoid the disaster was already available in the organization but was not communicated to all parts of the firm. The key is that the rate of learning to which this climate is conducive should be greater than or equal to the pace of change in the environment. The alternative is for the organization to become more and more out of sync or in disequilibrium with its environment, becoming less and less relevant until it becomes extinct.

We shall return to the concept of a learning organization but first let us introduce the subject of Industrial Relations on which the learning organization is expected to have measurable impact.

The Basics of Industrial Relations

The nature of how work is organized has evolved considerably since James Watt redesigned the steam engine and made the industrial revolution possible. In the power imbalance that ensued between the man who offered his labour for wages and his employer there was tension that was debilitative of optimal output in the work place. A body of practices to help manage this relationship for the mutual benefit of all has come to be known as industrial relations. T. M. Yesufu lists the activities that the field of industrial relations is normally concerned with:

-   employment problems and employment security
-   conditions of work: hours of work, shifts, holidays etc.
-   remuneration: level, frequency, methods of wage payments and wage fixing

-   labour and employer grievances and disputes
-   levels of production and efficiency
-   safety, health and welfare at work
-   social security: sickness and old age benefits, maternity leave, injury compensation
-   employment development: training, upgrading and promotions (Yesufu, 1984, p.6)

In its modern form industrial relations is essentially concerned with good faith collective bargaining and developing grievance procedures such that organizational harmony is ensured to enable employees cooperate in a way that leads to a higher level of efficiency of production and focus on the things that are dear to the organization, its values.

The practice of industrial relations is predicated on a view of the process as managing conflict. Institutions such as trade unions, trade union federations, federation of employers and departments of government charged with regulating the practice of industrial relations have emerged essentially to set boundaries of acceptable conduct.

New views of the modern enterprise have emphasized the link between shared values and organizational effectiveness. If industrial relations is about conflict then, surely, it will be difficult if not impossible to build an enterprise in which the vision of the firm and its core values are internalized by all its members in a way that leads to effective response to situations that arise for the customer facing staff. Indeed there is ample evidence that the tradition of disputes in the work place as celebrated conflicts is on the wane. Sander Meredeen tells us, for example, that "In recent years the number of officially reported industrial disputes in Britain has fallen dramatically – from an average of around 3,500 separate disputes in the mid-1960s to an all-time low of 900 in 1987" (Meredeen, 1988, p.3).

There is no doubt that industrial relations has advanced beyond table-pounding unionists hollering about the oppressors. Yet it would be a grave error to suggest that the interests of the employers and the employees have become a perfect fit. The sets of interest of these two, of the many stakeholders of the firm, overlap much more in the modern organization. The overlapping is more complete where there is a closer fit between the strategy of the firm and its human resource function strategy such that the kind of people hired fit into the demands of the strategic intent of the organization. If orientation-induction socialize the newly hired people more quickly and properly into the culture of the enterprise and a deliberate practice of managed inclusion helps them get accepted, and training and development policies help keep them in line with performance expectations, then the probabilities of disputes and heightened conflict is reduced to a minimal level. Ensuring that these alignments to strategy take place is at the heart of the learning organization.

Industrial Relations and the Learning Organisations

We have already seen a little of what is involved in a learning organization to have a feeling for how learning organization ideas affect employee-employer relations. A further elaboration on a few learning organization ideas will help show how Industrial Relations practice will be fundamentally altered by the embrace of learning organization ideas by firms.

As we have already indicated the Learning Organization is about regeneration and renewal within the enterprise based on learning. For this learning to take place fast enough to adapt the enterprise as fast, if not faster than the rate of change in the environment, that organization needs to create a climate that encourages the sharing of ideas and the ease of information flow. This means that trust should be a premium in the organization. It also means that excessive hierarchical layering will be counterproductive. Regarding the value of information flow Bob Garratt makes the point that "True Management Information Systems," i.e. those that give the directors and managers of an organization the ability to ask discriminating questions of data produced from MIS and get valid information from it, "are central to the Learning Organization" (Garrat 1990, p.106).

In addition to the climate for information flow, other attributes of learning organizations include the ability to value people as the key asset of the organization; the recognition of the existence of sub-cultures which draw their essence from different frames of reference in most bureaucratic organizations; and the resistance to change that derives from function-based tunnel vision preventing managers from developing a helicopter view of the organization. The organization learning approach also recognizes that if the knowledge of an organization, be it explicit or tacit, is embedded in the culture and the alignment of its sub-cultures, then it follows that transformation is tantamount to a change in the culture itself, that is a change in the organization's sense of identity, its goals, core values and primary ways of working (Schein, 1985, 1992, 1996).

If cohesion helps deliver efficiency, then the fact that some sub-cultures have their reference frame outside the organization, perhaps in the values of professional groups such as the society of engineers or the Institute of Chartered Accountants, is a source of difficulties. We have to find a way of making people in one firm see a problem from a similar prism. If they all see things from different reference frames then decision-making in the interest of a specific firm-defined goal becomes difficult. This inevitably affects performance outcomes. This is the empowerment of people to see beyond the natural frames of reference set by their antecedents to one of shared values of the organizational learning.

The net effect of all these factors that make a learning organization work helps attune people in the organization to some of the workplace dynamics that generate conflict in non-learning organizations, creating work in those areas for industrial relations practitioners. So, does a learning organization mean the end of industrial relations practice? Not really. What it entails is a shift in emphasis. Let us take some industrial relations activities and assess the implications of organizational learning for them.

Recruitment

In the past companies tried to recruit people based on specific skills that prepared them to fit into certain functional roles. The location, recruitment and deployment of human resources into an organization was traditionally a matter of identifying institutions that prepared people to have such skills, ensuring the capacity to attract the highest performers coming from these institutions and deploying them to that part of the organization that their skills fit the most. In my days as an undergraduate it meant that the annual calendar included the recruitment tours of the leading employers who went for the fellows with the highest grade point averages in particular disciplines.

Psychometric testing and quasi-objective methods of establishing the suitability of new hirings for the functions they were designated entered the path of the advance of the personnel function. Experience around the world suggests mixed results on the efficacy of these products. In the learning organization scenario, however, the key is more of strategy of the firm, the core values of the organization and the potential staff's ability to learn continuously from experience and through formal individual development programmes. In that sense orientation-induction and inclusion become more important parts of the recruitment function than used to be the case. The imperative of sync between HR and Firm strategy in a learning organization is clear, as when the Bankers Trust Company went from commercial banking to an investment banking niche driven by derivatives; and then when it was moving to relationship transfer corporate finance in the 1990s as derivatives began to plateau; the kind of human resources it had and the underpinning culture of the enterprise needed radical transformation. If the recruitment function is not quickly responsive to such a need the enterprise will be unable to adapt to competing in its new terrain and slow death can ensue.

Employment Security

Part of the concordat of the modern work place, until very recently, was that the employer made good faith effort to provide job security to the employee. With the wave of corporate restructuring in Europe and North America it is clear that the idea of job security, which reached its climax in life-time employment in Japan, is not what it used to be. In a learning organization, however, the orientation towards being ever adaptable through learning means that both the individuals and the organization never lose their value and relevance even in a rapidly changing world in which obsolescence is programmed in. A learning organization therefore provides job security which reduces the tensions of work place conflict based on anxiety about security. This does not mean that anxiety about job security is eliminated completely. What happens is that this anxiety is harnessed to ensure that learning continues. As Ed Schein puts it, "Normal resistance to change involves at the individual level two kinds of anxiety: survival anxiety, i.e. the anxiety that if I do not change I will no longer be able to get along, or keep my job, or maintain my sense of identity and competence; and learning anxiety, or anxiety that if I do attempt to learn or change I will lose my identity and sense of competence. The challenge of the leader as a change agent is either to escalate survival anxiety with its attendant costs, lower learning anxiety, or do both" (Schein, 1996).

Part of the challenge of Industrial Relations in this brave new future is, therefore, to help employees climb what C.K. Prahalad and Gary Hamel have called the forgetting curve, that is, to unlearn that which they invested so much to learn yesterday but which is irrelevant to tomorrow's effectiveness of the firm, even though it made the firm successful earlier today. This brave new world is already about as far as George F. Will has said so profoundly: "The future has a way of arriving unannounced." The learning organization makes us part of that future by what life helps us labour to forget lest we become victims of that great barrier to change, getting caught up in yesterday's successes whose only real value is in the history books. To win the future we have to learn to unlearn.

Conditions of Work

In the learning organization driven by the need to create value for the customer, conditions of work are determined by how the vision and values of the enterprise define how to deliver customer value. Since those values, where they draw from a universal reference-point of fairness, will always include a balanced sense for the interest of a learning stakeholder group, the employees, the conditions of work that emerge would tend to generate less conflict. Or at least the conflict would lend itself better to resolution within the context of these core values than in the complex dynamics that characterize negotiation in a non-learning organization.

Grievance Procedure

One of the biggest sources of grievance which create conflict in the work place results from sanctions on staff who have made mistakes in the course of their work. In most non-learning organizations, mistakes are visited with heavy sanctions. In the learning organization the mistakes is seen as a source of learning, a return on experience, rather than a matter for sanctions. The American multinational 3M is particularly famous for this orientation towards mistakes. It is no wonder that 3M is considered one of the most innovative companies in the world. Its rate of learning from such a culture has kept it consistent for so long that it was a prominent feature in the bestseller *Built to Last* which surveyed long-surviving top-performing companies for reasons to which their consistent success could be attributed.

Lessons from Review

We can go on and on taking such other Industrial Relations activities as remuneration, health and safety at work, etc. But this is not necessary to prove our point. There is already enough to suggest that the learning organization, because of its emphasis on the strategic dimension and the sharing of values flowing from that strategic intent or vision within the firm, will make Industrial Relations easier. This is primarily because most work place conflict flows from lack of information and distrust of motives of the partners. In a situation of an emotional climate created for information sharing, as in Learning Organizations, the likelihood of conflict is much reduced.

It is clear that such Industrial Relations tools as the Joint Consultant Committee will be more welcome in a learning organization than in a non-learning organization where distrust of management motives sometimes leads the Unions to oppose the idea of a JCC. In a learning organization where the essence of the culture is to share information, a JCC will simply be seen as a viable tool for ensuring that information can travel from subsystems across the organization.

In these days in which organizations are becoming boundaryless – in terms of the level of cooperation needed with suppliers, distributors, etc., to ensure that value is delivered to the customer – the firm cannot afford internal barricades created by turf battles and fragmented subsystems thinking. Surely, therefore, any platforms that help break internal walls will add value that will affect firm performance, which is what the JCC is available to do.

Conclusion

In the foregoing we have tried to show that a learning organization is one that recognizes the ecological fact that, for an organization to survive and have a chance of growing, the rate of learning by which it can adapt must at least equal the rate of change in the environment. We also said that the primary role of its directors, its executives, is to create the emotional climate for making that happen (Garratt, 1994). Today's firm is therefore recognizing that the Henry Ford model of breaking the organization down into functional chunks may have worked for most of the stable period of this century but is in crisis as the pace of change accelerates, propelled by technological changes such as convergence of telecommunications, computing and broadcasting, changing structure of the global economy, political and ideological shifts and trends in workplace organization. The organization is turning into learning systems (Utomi, 1996).

Systemic learning capacity in itself is severely affecting the nature of employee-employer relations and the kind of conflict in the workplace. It would seem that the more of a learning organization we are, the less the Industrial Relations type conflicts of old get in the way of pursuing organizational goals. In the main, we can conclude that organizational effectiveness tends to be enhanced in these conditions.

It is my humble submission that the Learning Organization concept is one that is priced enough in improving the climate of the work place that IR practitioners should seek to build learning systems of their organizations.

References

Garratt, Bob. *Learning Organization* (London, Harper Collins, 1994)

Garratt, Bob. *Learning To Lead* (London, Harper Collins, 1990)

Meredeen, Sander. *Managing Industrial Conflict* (London, Hetchitson Education Books, 1988)

Utomi, Pat. *Managing Uncertainty: Competition and Strategy in Emerging Economies* (Ibadan, Spectrum Books, 1998)

Utomi, Pat. "Thriving in Nigeria's Chaos" in *LBS Management Review* (Vol. 1, No. 1, 1996)

Yesufu, T.M. *The Dynamic of Industrial Relations: The Nigerian Experience* (Ibadan, Oxford University Press, 1984)

26

The Idea of a University: The Nigerian Situation*

It is perharps fitting even if somewhat paradoxical that this homecoming to the community in which I was first cast into the deep end and left to discover manhood in those uncertain days following the end of the Nigerian civil war should be another survival drill.

With a few other speaking commitments, I had but a few days to reflect on so important a subject as the idea of a university which has drawn epic discourses through the centuries. For such a subject, spending so little time to prepare is bad enough. It should make one vulnerable. To contemplate the idea of a university under the shadow of the profundity of the discourses of John Henry Cardinal Newsman, without prolonged reflection, is truly like pushing a novice into the deep end of the pool. Indeed, the challenge of setting a mission for the Nigerian university today is as daunting as it was for the Catholic University in Dublin when that educator and prince of the Church tried to articulate the essence of the corporate setting for moving forward the frontiers of knowledge. I can only hope that the modest thoughts I share will today stimulate an exchange of ideas that proves useful as we evaluate the future.

As I prepare to raise issues which should profit our efforts to come to a better understanding of the role of the university in the context of extant Nigerian experience, I am indeed mindful of the favourite pastime of university bashing. My sensitivity is indeed heightened by the fact that I graduated from here many years ago and my recognition of a tendency of alumni of institutions to believe the institutions went into decline the day after they graduated. I am actually quite entertained each time I go to old boys meetings of the secondary schools I attended. The fellows from the 1930s always seem to think nothing good has happened to secondary education since they took their London set examinations while the late 1960s graduates worry about these 'unfortunate' latter-day 'products' who did not get the treatment that allowed them 100

---

*Address to the UNN men university students at Hillpoint Study Centre, Enugu.

percent performance in the West African School Certificate Examinations. Few remember that the schools now have computers, a thing not even imagined in their time; nor do they recall that many of the teachers now have second degrees while their own teachers had London Matriculation at best. My being conscious of this tendency should advise a perspective that does not cheaply degrade the march of history past graduation.

As for the idea of university bashing it is an age-long preoccupation which is not without its useful endowments for the essential purpose of a university. Evidence of university bashing is as available in the pages of Nigerian tabloid newspapers as they are in books by people of some standing. Jaroslav Pelikan, in the book *The Idea of a University, A Reexamination*, writes thus on the subject:

"University bashing seems to have become a favourite indoor sport, the modern academic equivalent of the anticlericalism of the eighteenth century. It has also become a cottage industry, with books bearing such titles as *Professors and the Demise of Higher Education, Tenured Radicalism: How Politics has Corrupted our Higher Education, Killing the Spirit, Illiberal Education,* and *The Moral Collapse of the University* appearing one after the another" (Pelikan, 1992).

I recognize all of the foregoing in this caveat preceding my exploration of the subject this afternoon. My analysis certainly bears these tendencies in mind and strives to check their effect. With this, we can turn to the subject proper.

In the views expressed hereunder, I try to identify what constitutes a university, its essential characteristics origin, voyage through time, and its modern form following its democratization, or opening up to all peoples. University democratization is particularly a point of note in discussing the American ascendancy and in later years the emergence of the colonies at the sunset of Pax Britannia after Winston Churchill signed into law a bill to take university education to the colonies. From these essentials which recognise the university as existing for the advancement of knowledge, I pose a question regarding the purpose of this knowledge. This allows us to explore the idea of the common good and how the universities in Nigeria live out the idea of the university as somehow related to the Common Good. A periscope is raised therefore to peep at the Nigerian condition and how the nature of the pursuit of knowledge has affected the way the universities have intervened in promoting ideals universities supposedly exist to inspire. The discussion will also take us through a review of a utilitarian view of knowledge, its outcomes elsewhere in the world like Singapore and its less edifying manifestation in what I call a mercantilist view of education that seems to have become a major disturbing aspect of the Nigerian condition. To round up the reflection, I try to focus a little more on the nature and effects of the intervention of the state in the university system and the peculiar situation of the Nigerian university in the challenge to restore the dignity of Man.

What is a University?

In defining a matter that is both of general or broad interest and also of particular interest to some holding deeper insights, I have usually found it of benefit to begin with a general understanding and proceed to fuller and more wholesome unravelling of the subject. I think it appropriate therefore to begin this excursion into the idea of a university with a general, more commonplace explication of what a university is. For that I have turned to the ever-handy International Encyclopedia of the Social Science. It tells us that:

"Universities are organizations engaged in the advancement of knowledge; they teach, train and examine students in a variety of scholarly, scientific, and professional fields. Intellectual pursuits define the highest prevailing levels of competence in these fields. The universities confer degrees and provide opportunities both for members of their teaching staff and for some of their students to do original research." (Ben-David, 1968)

Yet another definition tells us that universities are:

"Institutions of higher education, usually comprising a liberal arts and sciences college and graduate and professional schools and having the authority to confer degrees in various fields of study. The modern university evolved from the medieval schools known as studia generalis;...The earliest studia arose out of efforts to educate Clerks and Monks beyond the level of Cathedral and Monastic Schools ... were institutions in which the essences or universals were studied." (Encyclopedia Britannica, 1968)

These essences or universals set the course of higher education at this ultimate level along a path that was deliberately comprehensive in scope. This point is in fact more richly summarised in the 1952 preface to John Henry Cardinal Newman's *The Idea Of A University*. He takes the view here that the university is a place of teaching universal knowledge. This implies that its objective is, on the one hand, intellectual, not moral; and on the other, the diffusion of knowledge rather than the advancement of it. The diffusion need brings the students but they will lack the osmotic capability of absorbing fully the existing base of knowledge unless the universal knowledge includes values that give context, meaning and relevance to the knowledge gained in the university. This is why this university confers its degrees on people who have been found worthy in 'character and in learning.'

There are many who wonder if the character part of this qualification is still a serious consideration given the values of graduates in the workplace, the incidents of cult violence, examination malpractices etc., that have come to become pronounced aspects of the public view of the contemporary Nigerian university.

The idea of a university from the foregoing is of a place that diffuses ideas to people of character so the ideas can be properly utilised. But utilised for whose benefit? Since man is a gregarious animal and has always lived in communities which provide the non-appropriability goods he requires, it should seem reasonable that knowledge should be utilised both for his individual benefit and the benefit of the university community, and the progress of the society in which the university is located. A one-time chancellor of the University of Navarra in Spain, the Spanish priest Josemaria Escriva, states this most richly when he points out that:

"A university must play a primary role in contribution to human progress. Since the problems facing mankind are multiple and complex (spiritual, cultural, social, financial etc.), university education must cover all these aspects." (Escriva, 1974)

To contribute to human progress, the university has necessarily to advance knowledge to new frontiers that make living more comfortable than has hitherto been the case.

Bearing all these in mind, we can say of the university that it is a place of enlightenment for exploring the frontiers of knowledge and socializing people into the application of discovered things, ideas and values; the knowledge of the natural order; for pursuit of the common good and individual well-being. The university is an enterprise in which freedom is a critical variable if the frontiers of knowledge are to be challenged because the status quo often resists new ideas for, as Machiavelli reminds us, those who benefit from extant order usually try to frustrate a new way of thinking.

The university which we have just defined does not differ in Africa from the traditions of Europe even though the academy of learning was a feature of medieval African civilizations such as Timbuktu. Those early civilizations became fully extinct so that when colonial experience led colonials anxious to staff the bureaucracy with locals decided on universities for the colonies, they were recreating the western university with hardly any influence from the traditions of the academies of earlier African civilizations. The challenge of the modern academy drawing from ancient African traditions is part of the considerations for today's universities. But few even have a sense for the early African academies. Ali Mazrui richly articulates the progeny of the African university:

"The African university was born as a subsidiary therefore of precisely that Westernizing transnational corporation to which I referred – Western academic establishment (Ashby, 1964, pp. 1-2). Colleges like Makerere, Ibadan and Legon in Ghana, and colleges in the Francophone African part of our continent, were literally cultural subsidiaries of British and French academic traditions.

"The African university was conceived primarily as a transmission belt of high Western culture, rather than as a workshop for the transfer of high Western skills (Ibid.,96). African universities became nurseries for nurturing a westernized black intellectual aristocracy. Graduates of Ibadan, Dakar and Makerere acquired Western social tastes more readily than Western organisational skills.

"They joined my generation of Africans – the lost generation of the colonial period. They embraced the new gospel of respecting

Westernism, and the new gospel was not only born but expanded. The one change which did not take place was a transformation in the role of the university. The university became a place for perpetuating and expanding the Westernized elite, creating new members for it. The ghost of intellectual dependency continued to haunt the whole gamut of African academia. The semi-secular gospel of Westernism continues to hold African mental freedom hostage."

The imprisonment of the Africa academic in Western tradition leads us to the question of the place of freedom in the advancement of knowledge.

Freedom and the Advancement of Knowledge

The advancement of knowledge which is important for improving the quality of life of the citizenry and social progress in general is best cultivated in an atmosphere of freedom. That freedom is necessary, as we have suggested, to prevent the current dominant paradigm from blocking out a potentially better social order. Machiavelli presents the context of this blockage to advancement:

"It must be considered that there is nothing more difficult to carry out, nor more doubtful of success, nor more dangerous to handle, than to initiate a new order of things. For the reformer has enemies in all those who profit by the old order, and only lukewarm defenders in all those who could profit by the new order. This lukewarmness arises partly from fear of their adversaries, who have the laws in their favour, and partly form the incredulity of mankind, who do not truly believe in anything new until they have had an actual experience of it." (Niccolo Machiavelli)

To be unhindered by extant order to advance knowledge seems of its own to be a good idea but the question is freedom for what. A colleague of mine often refers to a metaphor of the university faculty as a collection of anarchists linked together by a common car park. Surely freedom is not for disruption and destruction except where such destruction is a schumpeter type creative destruction, entrepreneurial effort that is the source of economic advance. This is a fact first captured in economic sciences view of progress by Joseph Schumpeter.

The search for freedom in academics is not only a path of conflict with political order, it is often a battle against the institutions designed to advance knowledge and sometimes against the self. The seminal work of Reinhardt Bendix, *Embattled Reason*, is for the most part a critique of how the dominant paradigm of the Social Sciences Research Council in the United States affected research funding set in the early years following the end of colonial rule.

Just as freedom is limited by the funding traditions in the discipline, the idiosyncrasies of academics can become a block to freedom. My experience in the evolution of ideas about the Nigerian political situation will suffice to make this point. In the days of the last elected federal government under Alhaji Shehu Shagari, there were academics who for personal, ethnic or other idiosyncratic motives besides regime performance waged a war of attrition against the regime in newspapers. Ostensibly, their objective was to inveigh against the corruption and poor performance of the regime. When the military intervened, many were so blinded by this prism through which they viewed the regime that they warmly welcomed the military and were unable to think through the putative damage to the social order of military rule. I recall a series of views I expressed in interviews on the subject of military overthrow of the Shagari regime which appeared in *The New York Times* beginning on January 8, 1984. I had predicted that the people would find ultimately that the baby had been thrown out with the bath water. Fifteen years later, many of those same academics who used up much prose welcoming the military are wondering why they have not found the truth of the Nigerian problem. Not considered still by many of them is that the judgment of yesterday in which the military was a legitimate option against a 'corrupt' elected government can be logical in rebutting an election annulment on the grounds that the potential for corruption existed in the coming order. Those of us who criticized the military answer of 1983 and 1993, staying consistent with a principle, have had to find a kind way of letting our colleagues recognize that their problem is rooted in loss of freedom brought about by their idiosyncratic dispositions to the subject matter. The cultivation of values which can crystallize into externally visible principles that indiscriminatingly guide our conduct will more likely give us true freedom to act or think without the inhibition of our momentary likes and dislikes.

The point I am trying to make here is that the pursuit of knowledge, which is the pursuit of truth, requires general principles by which if we adhere we are more likely to be consistent and eventually come to the truth. Academics who departed from this found themselves not only in error when the situation of the 1990s came along but found they had a moral problem. Having dressed military intervention in messianic robes earlier, it was harder to impugn its consequences for the common good as fundamentally negative. Another problem in this matter has to do with humility. Not having the humility to recognise that they may not have full comprehension of the dynamics of the 1983 intervention, it was hard for many of them to have a logical rather than emotional appeal for a rejection of military rule.

The freedom that can help advance an edifying pattern of inquiry, discovery and dissemination of what is discovered is freedom of one bound, chained or 'restricted' by the desire for the common good and the pursuit of happiness which can only be attained by a clear sense for the essence of disorder, it is a freedom of order and conduct. We have raised the question of freedom for what. It should help to illustrate a little. A benchmark should be the view of the former Chancellor of the University of Navarra we mentioned earlier. Blessed Josemaria, the priest who has been beatified by the Catholic Church, teaches in one of his homilies, *Freedom, a Gift from God,* that Freedom is used properly when it is directed towards the good; and is misused when men are forgetful and turn away from the Love of Loves. "Personal freedom which I defend and will always defend with all my strength, leads me to ask with deep conviction, though I am well aware of my own weakness: 'What do you want from me, Lord, so that I may freely do it?'" (Friends of God, 1977).

In this sense, freedom is the ability to choose between options within the context of clear principles that lead to the ultimate good of the individual. Blessed Josemaria in this instant uses the story of the rich young man in the 19th chapter of the Gospel of St. Matthew. The rich young man chose to say No to the call to perfection even though he was basically a good and generous person. He was recorded as having gone away "forlorn." It is freedom to learn to dance or not to dance. But what kind of freedom is it to choose to dance naked in the market place? In the metaphor of our time, our minister makes the choice "to dance naked in the market place." It is no wonder the state of the nation is tense and in shackles.

The University and the Common Good

The freedom of the academic to pursue activities that advance and disseminate knowledge does not come free. It comes often at a cost to society. Take the example of tenure. The tenured professor is free from the threat of loss of his position after his early work has given his evaluators cause to believe that he will be able to perform. Becoming tenured means a loss of flexibility to deploy faculty by the community that sustains the university. Most universities indeed depend in large or small measure on taxpayers for funding and have an obligation to build Town-Gown partnerships that benefit the community. The cost to the community of the academic being free is a trade off in favour of the right freedom leading the scholar to ultimately produce for the common good for social progress. There remains the possibility that a tenured professor can choose not to advance knowledge for the common good without any effective threat to his position. It is a cost but the value of freedom makes this cost worth while.

It is also important that the university which grooms the bureaucrats who man the institutions of society have a sense for what is the common good that these students will have to deploy. The common good, which to a large extent is a universal attribute, is something which universities are honour-bound in their tradition to protect. The values of their essence may, however, lead them away from it. As Mazrui has shown in the earlier quote, university values may be as disconnected from society as the past in colonial Africa.

The Promise of Knowledge and the Structure of Universities

The ability of universities to contribute to the progress of man is affected by the way meaning is derived from the structure of disciplines and of the university itself. The desire to specialize so that we can have deeper insights in a narrow area often prevents the whole truth of reality from dawning on many a student. So many are buried into the study of psychology trying to explain man's conduct without reference to his environment. That is a hard task, for as C. Wright Mills cogently argues, in

The Sociological Imagination, "Neither the life of an individual nor the history of a society can be understood without understanding both" (Mills, 1959).

Man's sense of meaning flowing from his sociological imagination shifts as the journey of discovery and the march of science break new ground. It proceeds incrementally within the context of discipline othordoxies until, as Thomas Kuhn puts it, "there is a paradigm shift." In the context of a new dominant paradigm, the essence of meaning is transformed. The value of recognizing this salient point about the sociology of knowledge and the progress of history is, humility and moderating the arrogance that often goes with our asserting that our intellect has value. Let us take the march of the Nigerian political economy for example. At the close of the 1970s when oil prices peaked and began a decline that was inevitable for a commodity, the relationship between our exchange rate and Nigeria's purchasing power parity was such that Dutch disease and severe distortions set in.

Surely Nigeria could not attain fiscal viability and begin new growth unless an adjustment programme was implemented. The common tradition of adjusting at the time was through securing an IMF adjustment facility. This was not a matter that the paradigm that dominated the social science community at the time would allow them to even begin to discuss. What we got was austerity without adjustment under the Buhari regime. Frozen lines of credit from correspondent banks meant that 'essential community' queues were soon upon us.

After a debate that raised more dust than light, a clever way to begin adjustment started. Years later, communism collapsed and with the USSR giving way to a democratic free enterprise, pursuing Russia, paradigms shifted. Meaning is today found in the prescription of privatization, an IMF type policy by the same people who vehemently proposed such a few years earlier. Perhaps humility in recognizing that the ancient perspective was not God's final word may have reduced the damage to the country's policy choice process during the mid-1980's. In this regard, the Nigerian university system with its very vocal marxists and political left wingers arrogantly played itself out of relevance in shaping the future to be dominated by market forces in an age of corporate globalisation.

What we have found and raised here for review is that a normal discipline focus can lead to tunnel vision and ultimately to irrelevance. This tendency to narrow the scope of learning has also produced an utilitarian view of the university that in my opinion has added to its degradation in the present day Nigeria.

The Utilitarian View of the University

Knowledge has its rewards. A job for which one's training is appropriately suited, prestige of the profession etc, are reasons many seek university education. This leads some men and women to seek university education not necessarily to be complete men and women in the fashion of the scope advocated in yet another book by John Cardinal Newman, but to just get the meal ticket: the certificate of having completed the course of study leading to the award of a degree. An overemphasis on this utility of the degree has in my own opinion created a 'mercantilist' view of the university. In this mercantilist perception, a certain desperation to obtain the certificate has crept in. With the society such as today's, charlatans can get by for a long time through nepotism and cronyism of different types, the employee could go on for a long time without being exposed as incompetent. Some people do not seem to care much about the quality of education they really have. If they can get the certificate without attending any classes, there are unfortunately quite a few people in classrooms who will celebrate it. The desperation this has introduced has also come, it seems, to affect teachers who, being unreasonably under-remunerated, sell notes to students and use the purchase of such materials as the basis for judging students. I recognise the challenge that poor remuneration, frequent intimidation by government regarding accommodation etc. have brought on university faculty and tend to incline them to take advantage of the mercantilist approach to education by students, abusing the trust in the relationship, as they sell handouts to students. This use of handouts as primary basis of evaluating the students has an additional disadvantage in its extinguishing of independent study and the development of a consciousness of inquiry in students. This inquisitive nature once denied the student is an inhibitor to future scholarship. The general mercantilism results in a corrupted environment in which a professor is murdered in cold blood at the University of Ilorin for fishing out students not qualified for places in the institution. It is indeed hard to see how character can be formed in this mercantilist wasteland the universities are degenerating into.

In my days here at UNN, we used to talk about not just passing through the university, but the university passing through us. Mercantilism will not be conducive for the university to pass through today's venture. This tendency towards a utilitarian view of knowledge is not peculiar to Nigeria. Mazrui does indeed make the point that "the trends towards greater practical utilitarianism included the great land grant universities and the elevation of agriculture into a university discipline long before most Europeans caught up" (Mazrui, p.9). The American university in its rebellion from European tradition shaped the new utilitarianism. It also fired development in the US. In post oil boom Nigeria, this American influence has been Nigerianised to the point that it has become a threat to social progress especially in the post-Babangida era when the corruption of the psyche of the Nigerian and the pervasiveness of rent seeking behaviour reached unprecedented levels. In a place like Singapore, a utilitarian view of knowledge has meant the predetermination of the number of people to train in a particularly skill area in a year. Even though Singapore has emerged as one of the most efficient states in history, its limitation for individual initiative remains.

Peculiar Challenges of the Nigerian University

The Nigerian university is of heritage the same tradition from medieval Europe when groups of students and masters agglomerated to form corporations for universal sharing of knowledge in places like Bologna, yet it has peculiar challenges established by the condition of its environment. Nigeria received the tradition of European universities because the university idea first came to Nigeria by Act of the colonial regime which was of European origin. Universities came here because in 1943, Winston Churchill set up the Elliot and Asquith Commissions which recommended setting up universities in the colonies of West Africa.

By 1948, Ghana and the Nigerian city of Ibadan were hosts to University Colleges. C. O. Taiwo, in his recollections on the administration of Nigerian Universities, points out that the Ibadan College of the University of London had attracted criticism because of "its low annual intake conditioned by the residential nature of the college, its continual dependence on the University of London, limited range of disciplines and absence of disciplines and professions crucial to development." The consequence of these criticisms was the appointment of the Ashby Commission whose recommendation led to the founding of the University of Nigeria and those of Zaria and Ife.

The peculiar nature of University of Nigeria both as a land grant University and one which emphasised a broader base of knowledge through the general studies programme was quick to become more relevant to the economic and political development challenges of the time. At first, it would seem that these peculiar characteristics of the University of Nigeria attracted denigrating comments from rivals. It is indeed a tribute to the riches of the idea of broad academic exposure for undergraduates that the earliest Universities which lacked the scope of general studies activities have since seen the light and adopted the idea of compulsory general studies for undergraduates no matter their discipline. The legend of how University of Nigeria graduates far outperformed their Ibadan colleagues in civil service examinations no doubt takes some credit for these changes.

Even with the buy-in into the idea of General Studies and the implication of a Land Grant University, the origins of which are American institutions supporting and supported by exploitation of agricultural and other wealth of their community, we must ask how well our university has supported the march of progress in its vicinity. If academics in the universities so frequently tell the people that peace and stability is of value in society's forward march, we expect that the same should apply to the universities. Since universities are centers of excellence in which knowledge about how to create those conditions is domiciled, one would expect the universities to be models of orderly progress. Unfortunately, our experience has been somewhat the opposite. This stumbling from crisis to crisis in the universities could be understandable if it flowed from the situation of the metaphor of anarchists united by a common car park. The truth is that the persistent crisis of the universities is not about competing ideas about the best approach to the common good. Oftentimes, it seems at least to the outsider as a pursuit of petty selfish interest devoid of any ideals and just about as much care for society's good as in the squabble of the proceeds of a never executed contract by a group of soldiers.

With crisis visitation panels like the Okara Visitation to the University of Nigeria and the Aguda Panel to the University of Ilorin exposing those who occupy the ivory tower as men with feet of clay, the university finds itself handicapped in its primary calling of advancing knowledge.

As the universities fail to show the light, a people so generously endowed in land, labour, mineral wealth and a reasonable core of educated manpower lies prostrate, its people among the poorest of the world, dying of malnutrition and other diseases, and lacking shelter. This really is the challenge of the university in Nigeria today. In spite of all I have said about how universities have not delivered, I am assured that a restoration of the condition of being, for many in the university community, will reinvigorate the commitment to this higher-order goal of the common good.

It would seem to me that a scandalous and unreasonable reward for the effort of the university teacher is a contributory factor which is complicated further by absence of resources to pursue self actualization in research. The consequence is that more energy than necessary is channelled into competing for administrative appointments like the position of Vice Chancellor.

In many ways, the diversion of energy from the daunting of our time, crippling poverty in the midst of plenty, in academia is a betrayal. We may understand the constraints but we recognise a certain missionary calling in being an academic. It used to be that the debates on matters of political economy were fractured and impassioned. Now there is silence. Marx is dead but many do not know how to depart the funeral grounds. Those who have recovered have followed the trail of the dollar into university chairs in foreign lands. The hapless poor in Nigeria are left with no buffer between them and a capricious dictatorial military establishment. Still the consciousness of these poor people, their personal troubles, is disconnected from their place in the march of history. Their sociological imagination is frozen by the deep slumber of an intellectual class overwhelmed by bread and butter issues. This is as much a catastrophe for Nigeria as the founding of the State of Israel 50 years ago was for the Palestinian people and is therefore remembered by them as "the great catastrophe."

The failure of university as a source of ideas that builds up civil society and provides anchors around which the public domain is contested is the shame of Nigeria's Political Science faculties. With the demise of Billy J. Dudley and lately Claude Ake, Nigerian Political Science seemed orphaned. Those who have not been incorporated into the corrupt establishment have either "fled" to foreign universities or preoccupied themselves with activities other than those which illuminate the mysteries of the power game and the educating of society on how to challenge the existing order with the agenda of change and a more just and democratic political order. One would expect that as those of their kind who have served in repressive regimes return to the campus or leave office, they would be engaged in civil debates about the reason we have what has often been referred to as a failed State. Instead what we see is a quiet, almost detached, tradition in political science.

One would expect that as people like Paulo Freire responded to their environment by proposing the need for a Pedagogy of the oppressed, the Nigeria Social Scientist should be building a Lexicon that would help the poor capture the injustice of the terror that official abuse uses to rape them. This stimulation of Nigerian underclass, this reconstruction of their sociological imagination, is perhaps the biggest bulwark against oppression and the path to escape from poverty for the majority of the · Nigerian people. Ideally suited for this lexicography is the Nigerian Social Scientist currently searching for relevance in his internal exile on the university campus.

Government Interference in the Universities

Civil society lies comatose. Most Non-Governmental Organisations are penetrated and fractured by military regimes lacking in legitimacy and much afraid of questions that institutions of civil society will raise that could trigger the process of power erosion. If NGOs are trouble to these regimes, the universities are a nightmare.

This vested interest of military governments in the state of restiveness of university campuses has caused the robustness of expressions of ideas on campus to be retrenched. Like in the army where the Officers Mess has been abandoned in the atmosphere of suspicions and finger pointing at coup plotters, the universities seem to have lost their soul in the swamp of security agents and lecturers who know the way to Abuja because they want to be Vice Chancellors and enjoy some booties of office. This has damaged scholarship. The whole idea of a university, as it has been considered by some of the people we have referred to so far, is wasted and worsted by perdition of government action fuelled by fear that the easiest way its legitimacy can suffer atrophy is student protest. In fact, as we speak, there are rumours that under the guise of PTF renovations, most, if not all universities, will be closed down so the political agenda of the next few weeks can proceed with minimal resistance.

The paradox buried here is that the surrender of our collective will to an agent called government is ostensibly so that our well-being can be advanced and our dignity enhanced.

The University, Scholarship and the Dignity of Man

The wisdom of the founding fathers of the University of Nigeria is clearly evident in the choice of its motto: To restore man to the dignity which it has since lost through advancing and spreading of the truth regarding the nature of man and his environment. For the university to lead to restoration of the dignity of man, it has to pursue inquiry in a way that does not demean the human being but instead elevates man such that man is served by new ways of doing things. As we find in decaying values in Nigeria which make man serve material things and become enslaved by money, it is easy for this dignity to be brutalized unless the discovery of the new ways of doing things recognizes in its process the need to get progress to serve man and not man 'progress.'

How can we pursue the advancement of knowledge in a way that upholds the dignity of man? Let us fall back on three great 'philosophers of knowledge' of this century: Karl Popper, Thomas Kuhn and Paulo Freire. For Kuhn the history of science moves forward within a dominant paradigm. Patterns of research funding reinforce this view of reality until anomalies in efforts at explanation generate crises which get resolved by the emergence of a new paradigm which is dominant. This Kuhnian conception of the structure of scientific revolution refutes the traditional notion that science progresses by accumulation of true facts and refutation of errors. Kuhn's insight has consequences for choices we make in the university. If there exists a dominant paradigm that depreciates the dignity of man, do we not have a moral obligation to discourage a generation of scientists from pursuing that course?

When I was an undergraduate at Nsukka, the Marxian paradigm was very fashionable. My colleagues thought it hip to call each other Comrades. For some reason, I cannot quite understand why I was unattracted to Marxist ideology even at this impressionable age and was willing to continue to criticise this ideology in which man's freedom is abandoned to the bureaucratic machine. I think my reputation as opponent struck long enough that my now liberated friends, particularly ABU Professor of Economics, Mike Kwanashi, often exclaims on sighting me these days; "You won!" The point here is that many people who could have done good work as academics lost good time in a paradigm which ,because of the way it reacted to the restoration of the dignity of man, was doomed to failure.

Karl Popper who is perhaps the Philosopher of Science of this century indeed recognised this weakness of Marxism and was a most productive critic of that worldview. To criticise Marxism is of course not to criticise the need to challenge social inequity or to identify the tools of oppression. Indeed Paulo Freire established himself as one of the great Educators of this century with identifying these instruments and how teaching models and learning can deliberate the oppressed.

Unless academics, particularly those in the social sciences, can pursue excellence in how man can live better instead of escaping into number crunching which Frederick August von Hayek called pretense to knowledge in his 11th December, 1974 Noble Acceptance Lecture, it will be relevance lost. I can tell because in my last year as a Ph.D. candidate in Political Science at Indiana University in the United States, the qualitative people began to take control of the department. I have had occasion of meeting people who went there afterwards lament how they spent two years studying mathematics and felt lost in analyzing relationships between phenomena in political life.

I have tried to explore the idea of a University. In the main, what I have found, you need not have travelled such distance to discover because you see it everyday. The idea of a university is essentially about furthering the frontiers of knowledge and spreading them in a way that makes people worthy in character and learning to solve the problems of men and society. Simply put, the idea of a university is about restoring the dignity of man. That is the motto of this university: To restore the dignity of man.

References

Ashby, Eric 1966. Universities: British, Indian, Arican. London: Weidenfeld & Nicolson.

Ben-David Joseph and Sloczower A. 1964. Universities and Academic Systems in Modern Societies, in European Journal of Sociology.

Bendix, R. 1970. Embattled Reason. New York: Oxford University Press.

Mills, C. Wright 1959. The Sociological Imagination. New York: Oxford University Press.

27

A Tribute to the Flickering Lamp: Nigeria's Knowledge Enterprise

On a day like this one can be so humbled by the generosity of so many which has come abroad so palpably that a strong risk exists of not knowing where to start a response. It could actually be in order to collapse under the enormous weight of gratitude to God and to so many people I am indebted to for the small legacies I have been privileged to leave here and there, and just say thank you and then take my seat. It would, however, be unfortunate if I did that. I would be passing up a chance to make a statement crying out to be put on record about the state of the knowledge enterprise in Nigeria. That line of endeavor is without doubt a flickering lamp threatened to be consumed by the darkness of visionless leadership, a society unsure of its sources of true strength and a domination of national agenda setting for too long by people who could be better served by an education that guides away from and obsession with self love and power, to a focus on purpose and a hunt for immortality. I will therefore be taking a bit of your time to make my comments. I pray that you be patient with me and I hope that you draw from it for a deep think on the state of education, academic research, publishing of academic works and the Nigerian condition, especially as my thoughts are deeply rooted in the belief that knowledge is the key to the improvement to the quality of life of the ordinary Nigerian.

Information

Before I proceed with tracking this course that I have mapped out for myself permit me say me thank you and to introduce some coming attractions consequent upon my effort at expressing myself through writing, the part outcome of which has caused us to assemble today.

---

* Speech given on the occasion of the 1999 Abiola Award

Beyond God to whom all the glory is due for all my undeserved accomplishments, the primary source of my debt can be tracked down without employing the services of Sherlock Holmes. It is usually made public in the dedication and acknowledgments. *Managing Uncertainty* is dedicated to my wife Ifeoma. I need not say more. The only thing I should probably say is that I have ample evidence of her love in the wholehearted way she supports me in everything I set my heart to. The only thing I am not sure of is if I were to set my mind to seeking public office tomorrow, whether she would be as supportive. I say this because each time speculations about a possible cabinet appointment for me start she goes into serious prayers for it not to come to pass. Given the tremendous evidence that God answers her prayers you can imagine how important it is to me that, if I ever decide that it is time to be directly active in the authoritative and binding allocation of values in society, I would have to secure her prior consent.

On display today as a prelaunch teaser is a book titled *To Serve is to Live: An Autobiographical Reflection on the Nigerian Condition.* It is a testament to the ideas, values and experiences that have fueled my passion for a Nigerian Renaissance and my struggle, so far, to bring about what I have often referred to as *the Nigerian Restoration.* That book is dedicated to my mother. Also due out in the next month is another book, *Critical Perspective On Nigerian Political Economy and Management.* It is a book of readings and cases in the Social and Political Economy Environment of Business (SPEB). Having pioneered the teaching of SPEB (the interface of government policy and business policy) at the Lagos Business School I have generated a series of technical notes, public speeches on subjects related to the environment of business and public speeches about the policy environment of business. These have been collected in this forthcoming volume. That volume is dedicated to the memory of my father who left his children a legacy of hard work and a profound sense of commitment to duty.

In the 22 years since I began commenting on Nigerian affairs as a young youth corper writing for *Newbreed* in 1977, I have written more than a thousand columns and OPED pieces and made several hundred speeches. My friends are often shocked that I do not keep good record of these contributions that seem to have affected a whole generation. Since Pini Jason, Kola Animashaun and others put out collections of their columns many have asked if I would not make available a collection of some of mine. I have taken liberty to authorize that a small selection of those articles appear in a volume. That book titled *Conscience: Opinions on the Challenge of Nation Building* has been dedicated to the Unsung Journalist, that breed of young men and women often taken for granted but sometimes courted by publicity seekers who are in the main underpaid and inadequately recognized but who set the agenda that defines the course of social action.

My gratitude for the support that made *Managing Uncertainty* and these other writing enterprises possible also extends to my colleagues at the Lagos Business School, Professor Pankaj and others who gave me shelter at the Harvard Business School to write the book, to companies like Coca Cola, Nigeria, Zenith International Bank and friends like Umar Abba Gana, Faysal El-Khalil and Tunde Amosu of the Flour Mills of Nigeria who have supported my research effort. There are many others I do not have the time to salute but they know how my heart beats for them. A little later in this presentation I will stop to pay a special tribute to someone whose memory sustains this award. His reaction when I told him I would leave Industry for Academia is worth recalling.

Let me now turn to the main comments I have. In the comments that follow I first reflect on the mixed reactions to my persistently expressed views in the 1980s about my wish to return to academia and how fortune structured the transition; the phenomenon of knowledge and the common good, the sociology of knowledge and the challenge it poses for scholarship in Nigeria, my struggle to build theory and yet be readable by the practitioner, the demise of the Nigerian academic, the imperative of knowledge speaking truth to power; and a brief review of consequences of the ideas in *Managing Uncertainty* for extant public choice.

Journey to the Classroom

It is a fitting paradox that Professor (Mrs) Abayode should be on the panel that adjudged *Managing Uncertainty* the best academic book published in Nigeria in 1998. Her husband of blessed memory was chairman of the board at Volkswagen when as Deputy Managing Director I first indicated that I would return to academia after a few years on the job. He found the indication curious but praiseworthy when I told him I most desired that the cream of whatever legacy I would like to bequeath should flow from work I do as an academic. As a scholar he found it pleasantly fascinating. To see that a book that marks notice of my return to the classroom would be so honoured by a panel that includes his wife would have made Professor Abayode somewhat misty-eyed were he around. May God bless his soul.

The other Volkswagen connection to get a preview of my pursuit of an academic dream was reported in an early teaser. In 1991 Volkswagen AG had decided on selling their interest in VWN. I was to lead a buyout. For reasons too numerous to go into today, I arranged to turn the deal over to Bashorun M.K.O. Abiola. During the period of the negotiations he called me aside one day to cross-check the veracity of the rumour that I planned to leave the firm once the deal was done. I replied in the affirmative suggesting that the idea was driven by a desire to teach and to research more than a wish to abandon him. He was quite charmed by my candour and commitment to academic work. In that experience and in my close association with his struggle to actualize the mandate of the 12th of June 1993 Presidential elections I got to know some sides of this enigmatic historical figure that is yet to attract the tribute he truly deserves. It is my feeling that a proper historical evaluation of Bashorun M.K.O Abiola, if we research and write it, stands the chance of being the academic book of the decade because of the richness of the material to be worked from. I am flattered to be the first to win this award since it was named for him after his passing. I salute today what he stood for.

The Teacher and Nigeria's Future

Let me state publicly that I am deeply saddened by the handling of what has led to the current ASUU crises by the Obasanjo government. I am not as concerned about the merits and demerits of the case of the teachers as I am disappointed that the new regime did not seize the opportunity to signal that the administration values the university teacher.

The challenge of national competitiveness and the leapfrogging necessary to improve the quality of life of the Nigerian in this age of the knowledge worker depend much on increasing the quality of human capital. The university teacher is at the epicentre of that enterprise. The time is now to recognize what we must do: better fund for the universities, reassert the prestige of the university teacher and remunerate him at rates that are internationally competitive and release Nigeria's energy to reclaim its potential. If we were to be concerned with just the welfare of the academic our horizon should be seen as limited. What I want to call for is a rethink of the concept of higher education.

The Knowledge and Specialized Tertiary Institutions

Since the convergence of three streams of technology – computing, telecommunications and broadcasting – the vision of the information age has materialized and the possibilities for the future remain infinite. These infinite possibilities have redefined the competitive advantage of nations. To compete today countries not only need knowledge workers, they also need centres of excellence in academic research.

Ever since the Japanese showed that you could build successful technology companies without investing in basic science research and the Americans followed suit with companies like the Bell companies getting rid of Bell labs, tertiary institutions have had to play a more critical role in the research that moves society forward. How do our universities measure up in research?

Books of worth cannot be published unless the best of academics are attracted to the university and have the resources to engage in research. Yesterday the best graduating students stayed back as junior fellows when the average like myself were thrown into the world. Unfortunately today what Nigerian society has done to the dignity of the academic led many of them to seek greener pastures outside the academia. This phenomenon has been made worse by the new idolatry of our time, the elevation of money to the level of God worshipped by society.

Those who stayed behind found themselves unable to find basic journals, not to talk of travel grants or funding for serious research. The need of the moment is therefore finding the best formula for ensuring that the best people stay behind and that the books, journals, travel grants and research funding are available. In my opinion one of the best ways to achieve that would be to have more specialized institutions in tertiary education and to encourage the other universities to become particularly known in some fields. In that way they can have closer cooperation with industry in the areas they add value and industry can better support them.

In my opinion we need to redesign many masters degree programmes as finishing schools where people who have developed decent skills that are inadequate or obsolete can realign their knowledge base to new realities. Take as an example the issue of engineering skills. Our professors are diligently striving to impart engineering know-how to their students. But the reality of our times is that micro-processing skills drive innovation and productivity gains.

We cannot expect business-as-usual professors in such areas. The challenge is to have a centre of excellence that brings the best minds with engineering degrees and provides them both micro-processing skills and entrepreneurship training. To deliver the kind of value we hope to see in such a situation the institutions cannot afford to be all things to all people, so they have to focus.

In suggesting specialized tertiary institutions I am in no way consigning the traditional university with a broad spectrum of disciplines to the dustbin of history. Far from that. There is a place for universities that serve to provide raw materials for the finishing schools that many graduate programmes will have to become. The very specialized institutions complementing work done as undergraduates could be the anchor for the specialized skills needed to stay competitive.

The idea is to have a complementary network of knowledge providers, some of which train the average to maintain systems while others function as centres of excellence that shape the best for the challenges of moving society forward. At a time when we must leapfrog to close the development gap that has opened up between Europe and us in this century we cannot afford to ignore the ideas of centres of excellence that will light the torch for society to follow. It has by now become familiar refrain for me that the challenge of development is to restore in 2000 the relationship of the lowest decile of the population in Europe and Africa in 1900. In 1900 the difference between the quality of life of these groups was marginal. Today the difference is as with day and night. Technology driven productivity increases, which have given mankind more productivity growth in that last 100 years than in the 10,000 years of recorded history before the redesign of the stream engine by James Watt, have separated us from the industrialized West. To bridge this yawning chasm we need to reinvent education and create special centres of excellence that will provide the leadership for circumnavigating stages of development; competitiveness in knowledge is a function of the quality of human capital.

In the network of complementary institutions we also need to encourage diversity. There should be private and public institutions unrestricted by bureaucratic requirements that serve no purpose beyond the restriction of imagination and the satisfaction of the bureaucrats' desire for control. Whereas the university should be a place for ideals and idealism where faculty are, as a colleague jokes frequently, a collection of anarchists united by a common car park, we should have competing concepts. There should be tertiary institutions with a niche in the locus of praxis where making things happen is treasured above the idealization of reality.

Values and Academic Excellence

To close it is important to note here that no matter the quality of the educational institutions we build in terms of research and teaching, unless people are fit in character and living their knowledge is limited value. The values we internalize and the principles that guide our conduct in society give meaning to education. Given what has happened to the Nigerian value system during years of military rule the search for values in university education remains the real anchor of the reinventing of the university. Ethics and morality have a place in shaping the future for modern man.

SECTION VI

CASE STUDY

28

Nigeria: The Dilemma of a Private Sector*

The big chief entered the imposing reception area of the recital hall of the MUSON Centre with much apprehension. He had been to a few of these pre-budget seminars in his life. Two years before, he had decided it was a waste of his time to gather businessmen and managers of all shades together at these pre-budget and post-budget sessions. To exhaust them in terms of suggestions on how to better fashion the budget and get the economy on track, and end up with such disaster of an annual budget every year, was in his opinion a theater of the absurd on instant replay. He had voted not to attend budget workshops anymore. In September of 1994, however, a good friend had told him that the Harvard Business School Association of Nigeria's (HBSAN) joint budget seminar would take a new approach.

At the urging of his friend, the chief decided to come to the workshop if only to confirm to himself that no approach would make the regimes that govern Nigeria initiate and faithfully implement a budget that could keep the economy on a sensible course.

He walked briskly to the registration desk. The formalities over, he was directed to the next table. Here, there was a list of subjects that would be themes of group discussions after the plenary. One list of breakout session subjects quickly caught his eyes. That was unusual at these events. It should be interesting to see how that would go, he thought as he signed up, before going up the stairs to join the workshop which had just started.

He listened with rapt attention as Dotun Sulaiman of Arthur Andersen introduced the subject of a change in approach for the budget sessions. A paradigm shift was taking place in the sense of moving away from a sector by sector analysis of economic performance followed by prescription of what the budget should include to stimulate economic activity in those sectors. That approach had clearly been a failure as government either ignored the recommendations, took some it was comfortable with and declared the budget a dictate of the organized private sector; or announced aspirations in tandem with the recommendations of private sector workshops, but proceeded to do the exact opposite during the year. This obvious failing of the attempt to positively influence budget policy, Mr Sulaiman declared, had led to a re-evaluation of the approach of engaging policy makers by the alumni groups interested in an enhanced environment for private sector-led development.

Perhaps there was a problem of lack of understanding of the basic logic behind the recommendations by government officials. Perhaps it would help to approach the 1995 budget with reviews of basic ideas about the kind of economy we should have, general discussions of macro-economic frameworks and the policy imperatives that flow from such frameworks, Mr Sulaiman added. These issues would be trashed out by several of the breakout groups. Fitting neatly into this new approach was a breakout session to discuss business and politics. Should the private sector with enormous stakes participate in influencing who governs and how Nigeria is governed?

This last breakout group was the one the chief had signed up for. To his surprise he saw that many other chief executives had signed up for the same group. It was unusual for so many executives to show interest in dealing with politics. Could it be, the chief thought, that these other executives were as concerned as he was about the seeming impotence of the private sector as soldiers and politicians went about making a thorough mess of governing Nigeria?

The chief was a member of the council of the Lagos Chamber of Commerce and Industry, and the national council of the Manufacturers' Association of Nigeria (MAN). It was clear in his mind, uncertainty about what the private sector should do and how to do it had bogged down these business associations during the preceding year. He remembered pointing out the difference between MAN and its British equivalent, the Confederation of British Industry (CBI), when CBI, incensed by the then Chancellor of Exchequer, insisted that Norman Lamont must go and indeed Mr Lamont departed from the government of Prime Minister John Major. He was frustrated at the apparent powerlessness of Nigerian business groups in the political arena.

As he walked from the Agip Recital Hall to the Shell Hall at the MUSON Complex where the breakout rooms were located, the chief recalled the last meeting of the council of the Lagos Chamber of Commerce and Industry he had attended. At the meeting a council member had requested to know what the council was doing in the face of near total collapse of normalcy and economic activities following the political impasse that arose when Chief Moshood Abiola renewed his claim to the presidency for which he was a candidate on June 12, 1993 when he was believed to have won but the verdict was never really known. The military president Ibrahim Babangida had announced an annulment of the elections.

When he raised the issue at a Chamber of Commerce Council meeting, the president of the Chamber had referred him to a publication of the Chamber in a newspaper advertisement. That advertisement had been the product of two very contentious and rowdy sessions. The carefully worded advertisement had been a compromise that did not really satisfy any one of the two sides of the divide on whether the Chamber should lend its voice to protestations against the injustice of annulling elections widely believed to be free and fair. There was clearly a strong feeling among some that businessmen should keep clear of politics. A small group was, however, emboldened to insist that unless businessmen took active interest in what politicians and soldiers did the environment of business would continue to suffer.

The breakout session proved quite lively and most interesting. It would seem that the main thrust of discussion was how the private sector could seek to be more active in the policy arena. The breakout group chairman and rapporteur, Pat Utomi of the Lagos Business School and Mohammed Hayatu-Deen of FSB International Bank, had the charge of synthesizing so many ideas on how the private sector could better influence the budgets and policy process to ensure an environment conducive to private sector growth.

Background on Nigerian Political Economy

Nigeria is perhaps best approached with some analytic distance. It is a country where many myths dominate attempts to explain reality whereas many of these myths are fallacies reified over a long period of regurgitation. Modern Nigeria found political expression when in 1914 the British colonial governor, Sir Frederick Lugard, amalgamated the British Protectorates of Nigerian and Southern Nigeria and the Colony of Lagos. During the preceding century the hundreds of ethnic nationalities in the forest savannah and sahel belt on the west coast of Africa from latitude 4° to 14°N had been gradually subdued or induced to come under British protection.

It was not long after amalgamation that the nationalist movement began, spurred largely by an active Lagos Press. It is a fascinating irony that the language used to described the Lagos Press by some Nigerian leaders during the 1993-94 political crisis was remarkably similar to the language of Lord Lugard in a letter to his biographer, Dame Margery Perham, when he complained about the abusiveness of the Southern press boys in Lagos.

The Nigerian Youth Movement soon emerged as a political force. A few years later political parties such as the NCNC, the Action Group and the NPC were active. Each major political party was to be dominant in one of the three regions that existed at independence. The leaders of parties were from the more populous ethnic groups making up the majority group in each of the regions.

One of the great myths of Nigerian politics is that ethnicity or the more pejorative usage, tribalism, is the common denominator of politics. That the three major parties at independence were each apparently anchored on one of the tripods of ethnic nationalities is often cited as an example of the primordial basis of Nigerian political activism. A more discerning eye identifies the more ideological base of those parties. As is clearly evident, the Northern People Congress (NPC) encompassed many ethnic groups. Its philosophy, to gradually shift a feudal culture to modernity within bounds of traditional commonalties between the groups was challenged with significant success by the Northern Elements Progressive Union (NEPU) led by Alhaji Aminu Kano. This perspective is not shared by a typical myth of a monolithic North.[1]

In the same vein the Action Group was clearly an attempt by people who for the most part came from a linguistic stock to found a socialist basis of association. But the Action Group also had support in many other minority areas in the East, and in the Western elections other Yorubas chose differently and joined up with Dr Nnamdi Azikiwe in the

---

[1] Sklar, Richard L. *Nigerian Political Parties: Power in an Emergent African National.* (NOK Publishers International, 1963).

NCNC and won the elections into the Western House of Assembly before independence. The idea of competitive communalism which defines the relationship between the regions' states essentially that when elites compete, in search of differentiating factors to give them the edge, they turn to the fear of the unknown by telling those they wish to win over that this fellow from a distant community is not as known and may not be worthy of trust. As is the case with approaching all change situations, this worry about the unknown, once excited at the right time, can sway decisions back to the tried and tested.

In the East, the NCNC won under the leadership of a minority person, Professor Eyo Ita who became the first Premier of Eastern region. When Dr Azikiwe saw NCNC candidates switch to Action Group in the Western House and Chief Awolowo form the government, he moved East where his ethnic group was the dominant group. This forced Eyo Ita off the premiership. Nigeria became independent on October 1, 1960. By 1965 the political process had suffered a few traumas with inconclusive elections, shifting alliances and a bit of violence all of which are not unusual in other nascent plural democracies such as in India which has remained, without break, the world's most populous democracy.

In January 1966 the military entered the Nigerian political arena following a military coup. Within one and a half years of the coup a major pogrom had left thousands of Ibos dead in Northern Nigeria. The Eastern region leadership declared secession, renamed the area Biafra, and a civil war was under way. The war ended in January 1970 and in 1979 the first civilian to rule Nigeria since January 1966 was sworn in. In December 1993 the military returned, making military rule the single most dominant factor in Nigeria's political culture.

Under military rule the process of governance went through extensive centralization. Even though General Aguiyi Ironsi, Nigeria's first military leader, was ostensibly killed for trying to impose unitary government on Nigeria, the command structure of the armed forces inevitably produced unitary government. Part of its effect on Nigerian political culture is a tendency for the states to turn to the center for handouts to survive. A scramble to get a piece of the national cake becomes the character of the political economy. This phenomenon came to be described by American political scientist Richard Joseph as bureaucratic prebendalism.

Related to, but not necessarily caused by, bureaucratic prebendalism was the development of patron-client networks which had all along been the basis of political association since before independence. Leaders were patrons who attracted clients to whom they dispensed favours and these clients in turn served as satellite patrons all the way down through the network. Patron-clientilism is said by many to have reached its peak during the leadership of Ibrahim Babangida when jargons like 'settlement,' meaning to be taken care of, entered the lexicon of Nigerian politics. During this period, rent-seeking economic behaviour became part of national life. The spectrum of graft went from exchange rate arbitraging to brokering the facilitation of government payment of contractors' fees. Access to opportunity for rent extraction, such as banking licenses, was a part of the patronage system that might, in part, explain the longevity of the regime (eight years).

This patron-client networking also better explains why a man like Chief Moshood Abiola, who for nearly 20 years had invested his enormous personal resources in procuring goodwill, making clients of emirs and chiefs across the country, could win a national landslide in the aborted 1993 elections. This logic it would seem is superior to the ethnicity based search for meaning in Nigerian national politics.

The Nigerian Private Sector

Until the 1950s there was practically no industrial activity in Nigeria. The 1946-55, Ten-Year Development Plan of the colonial administration did not envisage any industrialization beyond rural arts and craft.[2] Industrial development began to be given serious consideration only with the emergence of self-government in 1950. It began with soap making, oil seed milling, cigarette manufacturing and confectioneries.

As import substitution industrialization became increasingly popular, flowing primarily from the intellectual output of liberal-socialist economist Arthur Lewis and the philosophy that dominated the Economic Commission for Latin America (ECLA) under Raul Prebisch, some luxuries and light consumer goods like electronic equipment began to be assembled locally. By 1970 Nigeria had a flourishing private sector, by African standards. This sector experienced fairly rapid growth

---

[2] Okigbo Pius. *Essay in the Public Philosophy of Development. Vol. 1* (Enugu: Fourth Dimension Publishers, 1987) Chapter 16.

sustained by a long tradition of support institutions.

The Lagos Chamber of Commerce, the oldest of the support institutions, had been in existence since the 1880s. An umbrella Chamber of Commerce Organization (NACCIMA) as well as a Manufacturers' Association were established after independence. The third leg of the Nigerian private sector apex organizations, the Nigerian Employers' Consultative Association (NECA), was also set up to provide a forum for cooperation in the management of labour and for industry sector joint collective bargaining with Labour Unions. These institutions have acted as pressure groups to get government to provide an enabling environment for private sector development.

One of the ways of putting pressure on government to create an enabling environment has been for these organizations to send pre-budget memoranda to government for consideration before an annual budget. The chambers of these organizations are stuffed with tales of frustration at getting the government to take appropriate decisions.

Economic Perspective

In the macro-economic sphere, Nigeria became independent as a largely agricultural country producing such cash crops as groundnut, palm produce, cocoa and cotton for export. The management of these commodities was in the hands of produce marketing boards which became the plums of the politicians. The marketing boards were remarkable in their capacity for exporting the surplus of rural areas to urban areas where the politicians lived and canvassed for support. Understandably monuments like Cocoa House in Ibadan, once the highest building structure in Nigeria, and Western House in Lagos, became symbols of the marketing boards. Very little reinvesting was taking place in the production of these crops.

In the desire to industrialize after independence, the charm of the logic of import substitution was bought into by the politicians and the earlier military governments. In the wake of the oil boom following the Yom Kippur war and the quadrupling of oil prices in 1973, the government talked of taking over the commanding heights of the economy as they invested in numerous industrial activities. By the time the oil prices crisis came in the 1980s privatization had to be an imperative of reform.

The commanding heights logic provided the opportunity to dispense patronage to those appointed to the boards of many of the government enterprises. The patronage angle also meant that as leadership changed, which was frequent, these boards changed. Sometimes they could change several times within one regime, as in the Babangida days, to broaden the base of beneficiaries. This meant that clear, steady policy could not be pursued, increasing the ineffectiveness of these institutions and their cost to a rapidly depleting national treasury.

One of the remarkable commanding height investments is a huge steel complex in the middle of nowhere around which a whole new town is being built. The Ajaokuta Steel Complex, started with Russian technology at a time when there was a steel glut in the world market, was unreasonable when it was conceived. It is even more unreasonable and uncompleted more than 20 years after but continues to suck in significant national resources even though it will be obsolete technology on the very day it is commissioned. For several years more than 20 million Naira a month was used to pay the salaries of people who have never produced anything and are unlikely to produce anything of value for the Nigerian economy.

Structural Adjustment Programme (SAP)

The most significant effect of the oil price increases of the 1970s was the overvaluation of the Nigerian currency and its effect on Nigerian consumption patterns. Nigeria was inundated with consumer electronics and consumer goods of all types in the years following the 1973/74 quadrupling of oil prices. By 1979 Nigeria's buying binge which had produced a globally notorious port congestion, with ships waiting several months for a chance to berth, had generated such a taste for electronics that Nigeria had one of the highest per capita ownership of video cassette players in the world. Only in two other countries were there more video sets.

While Nigeria was buying video recorders, encouraged by a very strong Naira the country's non-oil export base, once the country's mainstay, was gradually destroyed. Farmers unable to maintain their farms on the Naira value of international commodity prices abandoned the farms and came to the cities, taking up jobs as messengers in government agencies that were multiplying by the day. The myriad of government agencies with a battery of new programmes had the effect of ballooning the government budget and creating system control problems in the machinery of public accountability. Poor corporate governance resulted in high levels of goal displacement by managers of public agencies, creating a culture of corruption and rent seeking behaviour.

When the almost predictable drop in oil prices came, the managers of the Nigerian economy had difficulty containing *Dutch disease,* the economic ailment that is associated with managing an economy which has experienced rapid growth based on mineral commodities with a burgeoning of the government budget followed by a decline in market value of the mineral. As Nigeria's earnings and purchasing power declined the managers failed to adjust the value of the managed exchange rate, encouraging old habits to continue.

By 1984 Nigeria's short term trade debts had built up into a mountain as the Central Bank of Nigeria could not meet its obligations as they came due. Correspondence banks began to freeze lines of credit open to Nigeria and queues began to build for consumer items which Nigerians came to call 'essential commodities' (essenco). Austerity measures were introduced in 1984 by the new military regime that overthrew the civilian government. But the austerity measures were not accompanied by adjustment to the structure of the economy and proved to be too much pain with no benefits. In 1985 another military regime opened to public debate the question of how to adjust the economy. This debate, tagged 'the IMF debate' produced the best in national pride and miseducation of the citizenry on the meaning of economic adjustment. The regime, perceiving an IMF loan as politically difficult in the face of emotion against IMF conditionalities during the debate, introduced what is called a home-grown Structural Adjustment Programme (SAP).

The key instruments of policy in the Structural Adjustment package introduced in 1992 were exchange rate deregulation, dissolution of the marketing boards, abandonment of import licensing and removal of price controls which had created a vast black market. The World Bank reports that during the period from 1986 when SAP was introduced to 1992, Nigeria's Gross Domestic Product (GDP) grew at an average of 5 percent per annum compared to 2 to 3 percentage decline (-3 percent) prior to SAP. This growth came from export of cocoa, cotton and a new growth came from manufactured goods in the textile industry.

The budget process had as objective checking the decline, stabilizing the economy, ensuring fiscal viability, and stimulating growth.

Budget Analysis

Following the announcement of each annual budget during the 1980s and 1990s, policy analysts lined up before television cameras to laud the budget provisions and strategy. Workshops and symposia by business associations and interest groups held to evaluate the budget. Oftentimes they attracted very positive comments on the quality of the budget.

In December many of the same analysts would gather and blame poor implementation for failure to meet targets. This would be followed by prescriptions on what should be done with tariffs in various sectors, broad fiscal and monetary policy initiatives and implementation strategies. Often the following year's budget reflects some aspects of the prescriptions, attracting grateful approval of private sector operators only for implementation to bear little resemblance to what was proposed.

The gathering of September 1994, a year in which the budget swung from slow movement towards a market economy back to controls and by mid year was shifting to 'guided deregulation', needed to review more than individual policies.

The Business and Politics Breakout Session

The group Chairman set the tone with examples of models of business/politics interface around the world. From examples of the role of Japanese businessmen (the house of Mitsuie) in financing the overthrow of the extant order before the Meiji restoration that then opened up Japan and privatized towards the end of the 19th century to traditions of lobbying in the United States.

In the end the consensus was that business should:

– encourage transparency in government by rewarding honest public servants with board appointments
– speak up more forcefully on abuse of policy process
– quietly support political candidates that favoured an enabling business environment
– educate government functionaries that if they baked a bigger pie there would be more to 'steal from' if they must do so. The

practice of rent-seeking was leaving too little to scramble over
– build institutional frameworks for continuing public-private sector
dialogue.

Conclusion

The unease with partisanship and policy-makers using the power of the
state to damage companies they feel antagonize them ran deep at the
breakout group but many participants thought advocacy and activism
were the only options left because the price of the old way had become
too high for business. The uncertainty created by the old way had very
high transaction cost consequences.

29

Organizational Transformation in Berger Paints Plc*

It was March 1993, and he had hardly settled down to his job, when the bombshell came. Clement Olowokande, Managing Director/Chief Executive of Berger Paints Plc, could not have anticipated what had just hit him but managed to conceal the shock he felt. What could have gone wrong? he repeatedly asked. The foreign technical partners, U.B. International of India, who had acquired 40 percent stake in Berger Paints had on this day given notice of their willingness to divest their interest in the Nigerian company.

To Olowokande, this decision seemed a serious error of judgement on the part of the foreign partners. In his words, *"We have consistently returned good operating results. An investment they got for less than $485,000 had yielded ten times that amount."* The foreign partners were however not swayed by such arguments as the economic horizon in Nigeria appeared to be getting darker compared to opportunities in South East Asia which continually beckoned on them.

What would the loss of a foreign technical partner do to the competitive strength of Berger Paints which had a structure that was a cost disadvantage compared to the mushrooming small players? Its quality advantage which derived from its multinational status could be perceived to have been eroded under the new dispensation.

History

Berger Paints was incorporated in 1959 as British Paints (W.A.) Limited and commenced business in 1961 importing paints from its foreign partners in the United Kingdom. The company's original authorized share capital on incorporation was ₦500,000 with British Paints having the majority shares. British Paints was also responsible for the technical

---

*·This case was written by Research Associate Emeka Iwelunmor under the supervision of the author

know-how supplied to the company. Its factory, the first of its kind in the country, was commissioned at Ikeja in March 1962. In 1972, the company purchased the Port Harcourt factory and other assets of Berger Jenson and Nicolson Paints (Nigeria) Limited and its issued and fully paid up capital was increased to ₦531, 514.

Berger Paints was the first paints company to be quoted on the stock exchange and in 1978 was among the companies that won the Nigeria Stock Exchange President's Merit Award. This accomplishment was again repeated in 1995 and 1996 at the 18th and 19th President's Merit Award respectively. It was engaged in the manufacturing of decorative and industrial paints, marine and protective coatings, automotive vehicle refinishing, general chemicals and ancillary products. Supported by a distribution network of 19 depots and numerous appointed agents, the company had become a leader in the industry. As at 1997, the called up and fully paid up capital of ₦54.9 million was held by thousands of Nigerian citizens, institutional and overseas investors. The shareholding structure was as follows:

Nigerians	80.62 percent
CAB (Overseas Holdings) Limited, London	14.62 percent
PZ PLC Manchester	4.76 percent

The Competitive Environment

"The Paint Industry has been in distress for the past three to four years and most of the companies continue to make losses" – Margaret Taiwo (President, Paint Manufacturers Association of Nigeria, speaking in 1999). When Berger Paints made its entry into the Nigerian market, the indigenous paint industry was largely undeveloped and so it was the dominant market leader. With the quadrupling of oil prices following the 1973 Arab- Israeli war, Nigeria embarked on a number of development projects. Construction exploded as a result of the programmes and invariably the paint industry witnessed a boom. As a result of the perceived opportunities from growing demand, there were many new entrants into the industry and a number of indigenous paint firms were established. African Paints led the pack. Other major players included CAPL, a diversified chemical group that was previously a division of the multinational giant ICI. This resulted in a situation where there were

over 40 registered members and twice as many operating illegally because of high entry barriers as at 1997.

However in the 1980s owing to declining economic fortunes of Nigerians, the dominant position of Berger Paints appeared to have been threatened with the declining purchasing power of most Nigerians. The tendency was for customers to patronise the products of some smaller low-cost and low-quality producers, some of whom were in the informal sector as their prices were low. In response, Berger Paints also tended to cut down on the quantity of their high-grade products and only produced them on request. This resulted in declining profit margins and loss of market share.

The industry was also adversely affected by the extant regime of tariffs where duty on imported paint was fixed at only 45 percent whereas duty for most of the import dependent raw materials ranged between 20 to 45 percent. The industry had therefore remained largely unattractive to people who would rather not invest in a high fixed cost structure like the paint industry. Many of the competitors to Berger Paints preferred to operate illegally from the sides, taking advantage of an unlevel playing field as government failed to yield to calls to protect the local paint industry. As Mrs Taiwo lamented, *"All appeals to government to raise the duty payable on finished imported paints did not elicit any favourable response."* If Berger Paints suffered from the low end of the market going to fringe producers, it experienced double jeopardy with the huge construction firms relying more on imported finished paint stocks.

However, where Berger had been able to build strong loyalty in the decorative sector, especially in the premium quality market, new entrants found it difficult to penetrate. In the low quality market segment Berger Paints was in a state of surrender and in the premium segment rivalry intensified with very active companies like IPWA, African Paints, CAPL and Peggy Chemical Industries (PCI). Over time these companies carved niches for themselves with PCI in the automotive paint market and IPWA in the marine and maintenance coatings market. Reminiscent of the relative complacency of the so-called big banks before the distress syndrome in the banking sector, Berger continued to lose market share while its big size and the fact that it was growing volumes continued to give it a false sense of security. It was to be rudely awakened when the foreign partners decided to divest.

The Decision to Divest

The crash of oil prices after it had peaked during the Iranian revolution resulted in the introduction of austerity measures and regulations such as import licensing and price controls. Policy makers also tried to coerce manufacturers into backward integration to save foreign exchange flowing out to pay for raw material imports. A Structural Adjustment Programme (SAP) was eventually introduced in 1986 resulting in significant devaluation of the Naira. Once that massive devaluation took place, some companies like Berger Paints which had earlier brought new investments on an overvalued Naira suddenly found their investments worth very little in terms of returns as purchasing power and markets were declining.

This condition naturally created more anxiety and increased competition with the already narrowing margins being competed away in promotional considerations. The inclination of most foreign partners like U.B International at this time was towards divesting from the Nigerian market. It would also appear that the discipline of adjustment policies did not seem to have been sustained as huge deficits returned by 1990, triggering a surge of inflation. At the same time as companies were challenged to turn to replacement cost pricing to lose grounds to inflation, purchasing power began to collapse as a process of de-industrialization and downsizing in many businesses ensued.

The political situation in the country following the annulment of the June 12, 1993 presidential election worsened an already bad economic situation resulting in capital flight. Besides, the Nigerian market as a ratio of the world paint market was getting smaller and less attractive in a business where scale economies were very critical even as new investment outlets in South East Asia were beginning to attract serious attention with their relatively stable political and economic climates. With consolidation in the industry proceeding on a global level, it became necessary to rationalize marginal markets.

Some in the industry argued that the foreign partners seemed more interested in maximizing short-term profitability. It would appear however that Profit after Tax increased from ₦23,483million in 1993 to ₦43,136million in 1994, the inflationary trend in the country meant that these profits translated to modest gains for the company. For the foreign partners, the money did not amount to much when denominated in hard currency. The decision to sell their Nigerian interest seemed rational enough. They decided to sell. Faced with this challenge, the Olowokande-led management considered several options, most of which were passionately discussed. These include:

1. A management buy-out
2. Sourcing for another foreign partner
3. Selling the divested shares to members of the public

The first option did not elicit as much enthusiasm from the management, who felt that it would not be wise at this stage to go it all alone, considering the not too strong financial base of the company and the need for it to continue to improve on standards and quality. This strength lay with foreign partnership with its technology advantage. The second and third options were considered feasible and pursued with vigour. More disturbing for the Berger management however was how to communicate the news of the divestment to the numerous shareholders without a negative backlash of loss of confidence.

A decision was therefore taken to invite all the shareholders for a meeting and it was agreed that the options chosen by the management be executed to the letter as they passed a vote of confidence on the Olowokande-led management. An aggressive campaign was initiated abroad to convince prospective investors of the need to come on board. The company promoted their 'impressive' performance records over the years, a major selling point in wooing new investors. The Chairman of Berger Paints, Allison Ayida, a one-time Secretary to the Government of Nigeria, deployed his goodwill and connections with some foreign companies abroad to tilt the balance of opinion in favour of investment in the company.

The Divestment

In 1996 a new foreign investor, CAB (Overseas Holdings) Limited, United Kingdom, desirous of a new investment outlet and convinced of the viability of the Nigerian market, entered into discussions and negotiations with Berger Paints. At the end, they decided to acquire 14.62 percent of the shares. Under the terms of the agreement, the foreign partners would not be involved in direct management but would offer the following services, namely:

- Complementary services in the purchase of raw materials
- Marketing assistance through its wide network of investments in other African countries
- A whole new set of technology to enable Berger continually improve on standards

New Management

"The competition for power is characteristic of all political structures and whatever else they may be, business organizations are political structures in that they provide both a base for the development of executive careers and platform for the expression of individual interests and motives." Having succeeded Mr Adelakun variously described as being weak and ineffective to the position of Managing Director in 1992, Olowokande had carefully and strategically bided his time, waiting for an opportuned time to assert himself, and when the foreign partners made good their intention to divest from the company the tone was set for fundamental changes. Part of the problems he had to grapple with on assumption of office was large scale fraud in the Purchasing and Sales departments, low staff morale and poor organizational effectiveness. In his words *"There was a strategic drift and therefore an overwhelming need for a paradigm shift and total organizational transformation."*

Andersen Consulting got the brief for a strategy review. The observations resulting from the review include:

- Berger Paints was not well positioned
- There was a sustained attack on the market share of the company by younger players
- Rising costs and declining margins
- The absence of clear business ethics
- Increasing globalization of the industry and associated need for a much higher capital base to be a global player
- The importance of developing market niches

Proceeding from this diagnostic examination, the Olowokande-led management decided to make a clean break from the past and reposition the company. Management decided to write off a fraud of over ₦6 million in the purchasing department to enable him to start on a clean state. To forestall future frauds that were rife in the environment and were getting worse as many workers in manufacturing feared for the future, new ethical standards were put in place. To give direction to the company, a Mission Statement was crafted: *"To manufacture and market Nigeria's leading quality paints, other surface coatings, allied products and services which meet the needs and expectations of discerning customers, ...employ creative and highly motivated people supported by modern technology to spearhead product and process innovations, achieve market dominance and maximise shareholder value, while contributing to Nigeria's economic and social development."* This was supported by a VISION to be *"Nigeria's dominant manufacturer and marketer of paints, coatings, and allied products and services."*

Strategy

Given the low staff morale, key motivational factors to secure commitment and loyalty had to be addressed. They included:

–   Review of reward system to drive performance, effectiveness and efficiency. Here salaries and other emoluments of staff were increased by 50 percent across board while a contributory pension scheme was reviewed to accommodate the inflationary trend in the country.

–   Promotion of deserving workers, which had been slow in coming over the years, was revived and witnessed the elevation of about 20 management staff as well as 40 factory operatives and other intermediate staff.

–   Continuing Training Programme for staff in the area of Corporate Direction Focus as contained in the company's vision and mission statements. Olowokande having attended the Chief Executive Programme (CEP3) of the Lagos Business School benefitted from such exposure which further affirmed his faith in deepening the value of his human capital. As a result, both management and lower staff were made to attend courses both at home and abroad to enhance overall organizational effectiveness.

–   Enhance increased profitability by avoiding wastes, and judicious management of resources. The purchasing and sales departments identified as corruption-prone were overhauled and controls strengthened to block all avenues for leakage. Staff in the two departments were transferred to other sections of the company. An open and transparent system of purchases which involved the companies submitting their price list and other requirements in an open tender was initiated. A committee comprised of members drawn from all departments of the organization usually made purchasing decisions after exhaustively analyzing all bids.

– Use continuous innovation to rattle competitors. Here, in spite of adulteration of its products by unscrupulous paint manufacturers intending to cut costs, it was decided to continue to provide customers with high quality products while at the same time making the prices affordable to most Nigerians in order to choke competitors and drive them away from the market. The apparent loss of the low paste segment of the market led the company into another partnership with Rubielac of Portugal to produce and market Rubielac paints. This would be an exclusive franchise controlled by Berger Paints Nigeria Plc. This bold attempt at re-entering the low-quality segment was a strategic move to regain lost market share.

Challenges Ahead

The Olowokande-led management would appear to have shaken off the anxiety that followed divestiture by the foreign technical partners. It however remained to be seen how well they could cope with the competition in the industry. The declining economic fortunes in Nigeria and the attendant weakening of purchasing power of most Nigerians had predisposed them to patronising the low-quality market in paints, leading to a fall in the patronage of the premium quality brand where Berger had established itself as a market leader.

Also smaller niche players like PCI, backed by the renowned Dupont in the United States, in seeking to continually innovate for competitive advantage would soon commence the local production of resin, an important ingredient for paint manufacturing. The plant believed to be the first of its kind in Africa could spell doom for competitors expected to queue up for its products. How could a supposed industry leader like Berger Paints cope in this situation?

30

Leaders And Company: *This Day Newspapers**

This Day newspaper is arguably one of the leading newspapers published in Nigeria. When newspaper cover prices went up, some businesses chose to reduce the number of newspapers they subscribed to. Quite a few chose *This Day* as the paper that best covered business and politics. But many experts 'worry' about the unconventional style of the newspaper's management. Still they marvel at the success of a periodical to which they gave little chance of surviving six months when it debuted in 1995.Their doomsday expectations were rooted in the perceptions of the antecedents of *This Day*, especially its precursor, *This Week* magazine.

Introduction

On the day it all began, he was in an upbeat mood. Here was a lifelong opportunity. He vowed not to let it slip through his fingers. The occasion was the formal inauguration of the board of *This Week* magazine in June, 1986. Nduka Obaigbena, having had stints with the influential *Time* magazine where he became the African representative in charge of English-speaking countries, wanted to have his own magazine. He was determined that the magazine would be just as influential as *Time*. This board being inaugurated would help him to do it. There was much reason for such great expectations.

The gathering was like a shortlist from Who is Who in Nigeria. The range ran from Gamaliel Onosode, Arthur Mbanefo and Hope Harriman to late Professor Kwaku Adadevoh. They had all consented to provide corporate governance to this new venture as directors. The strategic intent was very clear: "*To get a crop of reputable, credible and influential gentlemen with enough financial clout to invest significantly in the beginning of a new mission to re-define journalism practice in Nigeria.*" The authorized share capital was to be ₦8 million and Nduka was quite

---

*This case was written by Research Associate Emeka Iwelunmor under the supervision of the author.

confident that with the calibre of people on the board, it was a mission accomplished. He shifted uncomfortably in his chair when the board members collectively came up with only ₦90,000 on this day. This was a far cry from the projected amount.

The response of one of the directors to Nduka's facial display of disappointment was pointed: *"Let us try you with this amount; depending on how well you are able to manage this and come up with something credible, we will make further commitments."* Though disappointed, the new publisher accepted the challenge and added a personal sum of ₦20,000 to the first call on equity. *This Week* thus commenced business with a capitalization of ₦110,000 in 1986 when the dollar exchanged for about ₦1 to $1 officially. At the launching of the maiden edition of the magazine in July 1986, it was obvious that the venture was grossly undercapitalized. More money would be needed if production were to be sustained. To ensure high quality printing the strategy was to print the magazine abroad. *Newbreed*, which dominated the magazine business the decade before, was printed in England. But with the exchange rate of ₦3 to the dollar at that time, the capital outlay for this project which would involve frequent commuting to the printers in Europe and payments in hard currency for colour separation and printing, the capital base was obviously inadequate.

At this time the exchange rate was ₦3 to the dollar. A series of devaluation which would affect what could be a reasonable cover price were about to begin. How much would people who were witnessing rapid erosion of their incomes be willing to spend on magazines? This would be a haunting question especially for a start-up that would need to be around for a while before advertisers had enough confidence to commit.

A resolution to inject an additional ₦500,000 to shore up the capital base was not matched with action. The second call for equity had responses that came in trickles and was often delayed. In Nduka's words, *"They resorted to giving me money piecemeal: ₦5,000 today and ₦10,000 the other week; apparently these people have big names and not money."* Planning became difficult and this was to adversely affect the fortunes of the magazine. Besides, the high cost of printing abroad which translated into a higher cover price made the magazine less competitive against other magazines whose cover prices were not as high. Obaigbena's displeasure with his shareholders was mutual. Several of them complained about lack of transparency in management and the absence of orderly management. One even said the experience was so traumatic he would never invest in a very young man again. Nduka was 26 at the time.

After a series of complaints and pleas without any response from the shareholders, Nduka's resolve to keep the magazine going became increasingly weakened. He managed to maintain an epileptic performance for five years. According to him, *"Once I stopped looking forward to the arrival of my magazine on the newsstand every Monday with great expectation, I knew it was time to quit."* In 1991, the magazine was rested. Out of job and having invested all his resources in the failed project, he was distraught and full of anxiety about the future.

Obaigbena was determined that a fall was not going to stop him from dreaming big. In the tradition of the entrepreneur as a man who falls seven times and gets up eight times, he returned four years later to the more perilous terrain of daily newspaper publishing.

Nduka's quest throws up the whole issue of persistence in entrepreneurial ventures and the value of prominent names as shareholders and directors in the success or otherwise of a business. The other question raised here is: must the entrepreneur own and have all the resources before venturing? What kind of commitment an entrepreneur should expect of others sharing in the venture initiative at the initial stages of the enterprise also comes out of this experience. The *This Day* challenge provides perspectives on the effects of the personal characteristics of the entrepreneur and how it does contribute to the success or failure of the business. Finally, the *This Day* challenge raises issues on business competition in a depressed economy. Can a venture remain competitive charging higher prices for its products and at the same time return consistent superior performance over rivals in an economy experiencing decline in purchasing power?

The Company

Leaders and Company, publishers of *This Day*, was incorporated in 1995 with a share capital of ₦1million as an integrated communications company. In the same year, it successfully organized and hosted a symposium on the Nigerian situation in conjunction with a South African-based communications company. The theme of the symposium was "The

Pen is Mightier than the Sword." The symposium attracted a lot of eminent participants. From this platform the newspaper venture lurched forward. This Day Newspapers was subsequently started, in Nduka's words, *"to give a new direction to economic journalism as well as make reading pleasurable without losing its seriousness."* Office accommodation was secured in a rented apartment on Norman Williams, Ikoyi from where Nduka and the initial staff of four plotted strategy and carried on their daily chores.

The acceptance of the newspaper and its rising profile meant increased tempo of activities. Additional staff had to be employed. This made the Ikoyi office too small, prompting relocation to Ikeja. From a staff of five at inception, there were by 1998 more than three hundred employees with offices in 34 different locations in Nigeria and abroad. The advent of *This Day International* led to the opening of four additional offices in London, New York, Washington D.C. and Johannesburg. More titles were added with *Weekend This Day* and *Sunday This Day* which established themselves in the market.

Nduka Obaigbena: The Man, His Passion

Obaigbena can be different things to different people. His influence and interests traversed many spheres of human endeavour from politics, journalism, creative arts to public relations. This enigmatic venturer provoked passion in people. To some he was the quintessential entrepreneur while to others he was a slippery and shrewd political operator. What is sure is that it is hard to ignore him. A product of the Edo College, Benin where he earned an indefinite suspension in 1976 for spearheading a food riot, he was also at Government College, Ughelli for his Higher School Certificate (HSC) between 1978 and 1979. There he formed the Black Cultural Movement – an organization whose essential activity was the campaign against the apartheid policy in South Africa. He was to organize one of the first 'rag days' in secondary schools and a variety of activities to raise money for the anti-apartheid struggle.

He cut his teeth in journalism when he started writing feature articles for the *Nigerian Observer* newspaper. At the same time he ran a regular cartoon column known as 'leke-leke.' He secured admission to the University of Benin in 1979 to study for a combined honours degree in Creative Arts and English. His combative style and journalism instincts became fully alive at Uniben. His emerging personality first played itself out with Nduka's brief foray into students' union politics. Pitched against a less endowed opponent for the post of Public Relations Officer of the Students' Union, Nduka was dismissive and apparently condescending on his opponent when students gathered on the manifesto night to listen to the contenders. The student population took offence at his tone and voted against what they considered arrogance. Whether Nduka's later affable and more humble mien took roots from such experiences has remained a matter of conjecture.

In any case, he later teamed up with the former editor of the *Nigerian Observer* newspaper at that time to start a magazine called *The Dawn* which, as it were, never saw the dawn of another year and was soon rested. After the compulsory one year of Youth Service in 1982, he travelled out to London and started work with the Nigeria Advertising Limited. He also had a part-time contract job with Michael Jarvis and Partners there in London. His work entailed doing exclusive media relations and advertising work for some Nigerian and foreign companies. It was at this point that *Newsweek* magazine presented him an opportunity to do some special advertising features sections on Nigeria.

In 1985, *Time* magazine made him an offer and he switched. Operating out of New York, Nduka was exposed to the global media. The high point of his career came in 1985 when he got *Time* magazine to host a special on Nigeria on the occasion of the country's 25th independence anniversary. It was an occasion to celebrate the Nigerian nation and it was marked by the gathering of eminent persons. Satisfied with his performance, Nduka felt it was time to move ahead. The disappointing outcome of *This Week* temporarily halted his passion for journalism as he turned to politics for succour.

He contested for a senatorial seat in 1987 under the Babangida transition programme and lost. Not new to losses he took it in his stride. He soon bounced back as Political Adviser, first to Tom Ikimi, Chairman of one of the political parties and then later, Hamed Kusamotu. Both men were chairmen of the defunct National Republican Convention (NRC) at different times. The dismantling of the political structure in 1995 and the emergence of a new political dispensation led to his election into the Constitutional Conference to represent Ika North in the Abacha transition programme. There he was elected to serve in the Law, Order and National Security and the Transition Committees, which afforded him the opportunity of touring all parts of the country and making friends across the political divide. He was to find these experiences very enriching.

Nduka also served as a member of the TCPC (now Bureau of Public Enterprises, BPE) subcommittee on the commercialization of FRCN as well as the privatization of Nigerian National Shipping Line (NNSL). In his words, "*Having garnered these illuminating experiences, I thought I should bring them all back to journalism.*"

Political Economy Environment

It was a rough economic terrain that *This Day* landed on. The Abacha regime had gone from controls in 1994 to 'guided deregulation' in 1995 because controls had frozen economic growth. Inflation was raging and the Nigerian leadership was getting about in a way that would soon earn the country pariah status and economic sanctions. Full warehouses of manufacturers because of low purchasing power were affecting commitment of resources to advertising spending, a life support line for newspapers.

On the political level the iron grip of the dictatorship was closing in. The media were a clear target. There was ample opportunity for getting into issues that could be explosive as a national constitutional conference had been convened by the Abacha government.

Early Constraints and Solution

Like many entrepreneurial start-up ventures, *This Day* faced the problem of adequate start-up capital. The dip in the economic fortunes of Nigeria and the depreciating value of the Naira meant that the capital outlay needed to establish a newspaper would be massive. In 1985 when he ventured into publishing with *This Week* magazine, the exchange rate was ₦3 to the dollar but by 1995 it had risen to ₦80. Having had his fingers burnt trying to invite people he considered rich, he thought it best to go alone. He pooled his resources, convinced that a good product would pay its way through. This new venture would be a sole proprietorship.

Staffing was another problem encountered at the initial stages. In his earlier experience, Nduka went for big names in journalism. He says he came out disappointed. This time around there was the challenge for him to prove that he could succeed without the big names in journalism. Besides, most of the staff who were employed in the defunct magazine became very skeptical about the success of this new project and did not want to associate with Nduka. He decided to go for young men and women who were relatively unknown but who had a burning desire tò excel. This would seem to have paid off, given the rising demand for the paper.

There was also the problem of infrastructural facilities like good accommodation to support the efficient take-off of the newspaper. In most cases makeshift arrangements were put in place to keep the organization going. They moved from Ikoyi to a bigger space in Ikeja to enable the paper take advantage of the presence of other publishing outfits like the Concord Press, Punch and Daily Times, all of which were concentrated in that area. Besides, premises were cheaper there than in Ikoyi, the old location.

Corporate Culture

Nduka wanted the culture to recognize that customer satisfaction was a critical success factor. A culture that would sustain such service performance in all departments of the organization was therefore desired and pursued. Quality human resources with limited past baggage was key to the desired culture. In view of the disappointing performance of some so-called big names who had a tendency to be laid back and arrogant, he wanted some core values of responsiveness to the customer in his people. He speaks often of coming to the conclusion that among the baggage of problems people carry about, past success was one of them. In going for people not contaminated by previous and corrupting influences, it was his aim that they learn on the job while they would be subsequently groomed to take up higher responsibilities. This learning process became institutionalized in the sociological foundations of the company. Observers think he seems to have judged well. Hardly known founding editors like Eziuche Ubani, Editor of *This Day on Sunday*, Victor Ifijeh, Editor of *This Day Daily,* and Eniola Bello, Editor of *This Day on Saturday*, became instant successes in their own right. According to Nduka, *"All these people were basically minnows before I employed them."*

Integrity in all aspects of their relationship with the public was one virtue highly venerated as frequent admonitions that anybody caught in any shady deal would be made to face the music continually assailed the ears of staff. Nduka was quick to recall an incident in 1996. In his words, *"The chief photographer and his assistant attended a function for journalists organized by the British High Commission and at the end of the show, a gift and some amount of money was given to the journalists to share, but instead the man decided to split everything with his assistant."* As soon as this information got to the management, they were both summarily dismissed. There are however staff who wonder if these ethical codes are universally applied.

Hard work was another virtue vigorously pursued and rewarded. Nduka led by example as a journalist. He was always out sniffing around for breaking news and, at other times, using his connections to smoothen the path for his men to reach personalities that were rather too difficult to track. When the paper succeeded in breaking down the wall of defence that had been built around people like Aliko Dangote, Hakeem Bello Osagie etc whose largely withdrawn nature most news hounds found difficult to penetrate, the paper was hailed as a good thing to happen to journalism. In this regime of hard work, Nduka found willing allies in people like Okagbue Aduba, Ide Eguabor, Eziuche Ubani etc who cultivated this habit and passed it down the corporate ladder. The culture of workaholics had due reward that came in the form of several awards which the newspaper won in the industry.

Quality Management

The complexities of management in a fast changing economic environment led Nduka to attend the Advanced Management Programme (AMP) of the Universities of Wits and Johannesburg in 1996, in South Africa, to acquaint himself with the latest management practices. The exposure not only deepened his knowledge but also affirmed his faith in the value of equally deepening human capital. He therefore took practical steps in training and retraining of his staff. In keeping with the current of events in technology and modern tools of work, the Modern Business Machine Computer School was retained to train staff in computer appreciation. This, apart from adding value to the staff, also resulted in timely and efficient quality of service. At other times, resource persons were invited from outside to conduct in-house management development courses, one of which was conducted by officials of the World Bank on Economic Management.

Nduka's management style is described by staff as participative. Towards this end, a proper and clearly defined line of authority structured to delegate duties appropriately and motivate employees was put in place. The emphasis here was on team work rather than individual collection of tasks and they were empowered to take decisions and, in the event of mistakes, learn from such wrong decisions. All the four divisions that made up the organization were to remain largely autonomous.

A compensation strategy that sought to motivate employees was also put in place. After a survey of what obtained in the industry, Nduka decided to pay above the industry standards. This resolve though well intentioned seemed to have been rubbished by frequent delays in payment. Sometimes salary arrears of three to four months would build up. All departmental heads were assigned motor vehicles with drivers as part of the compensation. What was particularly remarkable was that morale did not seem to wane even with a three-month delay in salaries. The boys still produced one of the best newspapers in town. They took real pride in the paper.

Operations and Strategy

Operationally the organization consisted of four divisions which were autonomous and managed independently, namely Editorial, Newspaper Operations, Advertising, Sales and Management Services. Nduka by so doing hoped to eliminate the administrative bottleneck and unwieldy nature of most businesses Headed by Nduka himself and three other General Managers, each was a profit centre on its own, thus engendering competition. The result was a smooth operating system which allowed for neat, tidy and timely delivery of services to the public. In its one year of operation in 1996, profit after tax stood at ₦20million.

Again having noted the paucity of materials, especially on economic journalism as it concerned Nigeria and other parts of the world, *This Day* moved in to fill the lacunae. An agreement with the influential *Financial Times* of London enabled the paper to carry authoritative and latest financial information as it concerned businesses round the globe. Each edition carried the day's FT supplement. This, apart from offering readers the benefit of getting facts without buying the *Financial Times* which was quite expensive, added value by offering more for less price in a single paper. The emphasis on economic journalism would appear to have become a niche market for *This Day* newspaper. The section on Management adapted from series of articles by academics from Harvard Business School and other renowned management institutions made the paper a must-read for most people, a pocket MBA programme.

The focus on celebrities and people who had distinguished themselves in every field of human endeavour by *This Day on Sunday* helped in creating role models for the youths and, in the process, reinforced the positive value of hard work in the country in the view of some readers. In focusing on their problems and triumph, the message became clear that perhaps all hopes to steer the country away from self-destruction had not been lost.

The paper also pioneered the printing of newspapers in colours, with *This Day* positioned as a premium brand attracting a higher newsstand price than other newspapers. In identifying the paper with its glossy and beautiful prints, people kept buying at the price of ₦50 which remains the highest price for any daily tabloid with patronage increasing as the days go by. Strategically, it placed itself in good stead for competition by opening up offices in 34 locations in the country, thus widening the reach of the paper. An international edition was soon to join the stable.

Future Challenges

Within three years of its appearance in the newsstands, the paper had established a leading position in the industry. But as the young men and women in the organization strive to continually improve on this performance, their morale appears to be at its lowest ebb. Some complain that while salary arrears of up to four months are owed them, Nduka is busy shuttling between Lagos and London. His staff do not trust him and have confessed this openly. The morale issue that seemed so distant became real with so many decamping to join *The Comet* newspaper when it was founded in 1999.

Index

318 *Index*

320 *Index*

www.ingramcontent.com/pod-product-compliance
Lightning Source LLC
Chambersburg PA
CBHW072059040426
42334CB00041B/1455